Sacred Attunement

for Mary Ann Mertz –
Miryam Hannah
one of the weavers of the 'garment' –
Blessings,

Sacred Attunement

A Jewish Theology

MICHAEL FISHBANE

The University of Chicago Press ❋ *Chicago and London*

MICHAEL FISHBANE is the Nathan Cummings Professor of Jewish Studies at the University of Chicago. Among his many publications is, most recently, *Biblical Myth and Rabbinic Mythmaking* (2003).

The University of Chicago Press, Chicago 60637
The University of Chicago Press, Ltd., London
© 2008 by The University of Chicago
All rights reserved. Published 2008
Printed in the United States of America
17 16 15 14 13 12 11 10 09 08   1 2 3 4 5
ISBN-13: 978-0-226-25171-4 (cloth)
ISBN-10: 0-226-25171-3 (cloth)

Library of Congress Cataloging-in-Publication Data
Fishbane, Michael A.
    Sacred attunement : a Jewish theology / Michael Fishbane.
        p.   cm.
    Includes bibliographical references and index.
    ISBN-13 : 978-0-226-25171-4 (hardcover : alk. paper)
    ISBN-10: 0-226-25171-3 (hardcover : alk. paper)
        1. Judaism—Doctrines.   2. Spiritual life—Judaism.
    3. Hermeneutics—Religious aspects—Judaism.   I. Title.
    BM602.F57 2008
    296.3—dc22
                                                    2007048321

for Mona

תורת־חסד על־לשונה.

(PROV. 31:26)

Contents

Preface

This work is an attempt to "do" theology in a dark and disorienting time—a time sunk in the mire of modernity. Naïveté is out of the question. The mirror of the world reflects back to us our willful epistemologies, our suspicion of values, and the rank perversities of the human heart. Like Kafka, we prowl aimlessly around the debris of old Sinais, in a wasteland of thought. The tablets of despair are strewn everywhere. Old beginnings do not work; they are a dead end. Is theology even possible in such circumstances? And if possible, can it be done without denying the undeniable?

Rosenzweig found a breakthrough. For him, the stark consciousness of mortality broke the iron claw of impersonal reason and philosophy, and opened up a theology of existence marked by the temporal rhythms of speech and liturgy. But now, nearly a century later, we are beset by other enclosures of thought; strangled by subjectivity; and also told that language can never mean what it says or even quite reach its object. Meaning is endlessly deferred. Hölderlin has even turned the obligation to wait into a virtue, musing that the gods have wandered off through the rifts of language. But not only the gods. And thus another breakthrough is needed. I would call it the consciousness of natality, the spring of beginnings that comes with a reborn mindfulness. Perhaps this may loosen the grip of indecision and attune us to the shapes of worldly existence, with their diverse obligations and challenges. Natality is the route to transcendence—to the many forms of otherness, ever present and ever beckoning, all around. The path to theology undertaken here is grounded in the *forms of experience* found in the natural world. In the course of time, these forms and their linguistic expressions weave a web of habitude; the raw and the real are stifled by routine. There is much to do, one thinks, and it is good to work in a settled sphere with established patterns. But the fissures happen in any case, and in unexpected ways; and then the human being is awakened, if only for the time being, to vaster dimensions of experience and the contingencies of existence. These breakthroughs of consciousness may even transform one's life; but they are not inherently theological. Their power is to remind the self that the "merely other" of everydayness is grounded in an Other of more exceeding depths and heights. But forgetting is the norm. And thus it is one of the chief virtues of artistic creativity to reformulate the sounds and sights of existence, and thereby create new openings in one's ordinary perceptions. Hereby, the daily routine of life is more intentionally ruptured, and the shapes of perception are experienced as subtended by infinite possibilities—such that our everyday consciousness is experienced as shot through with traces of transcendence. Aesthetic experience gives us these moments of reborn mindfulness on occasion; whereas artists may live more continuously in these spaces of awareness, often disconnected from ordinary perceptions.

Theology does something more: it receives these perceptions of transcendence and tries to sustain (and even revive) them in the normal course of life. It does so not solely in terms of the experiences per se, but especially in terms of the duties these perceptions impose. The special sense of *le transcendance immanente* (in Jean Wahl's phrase) thus sets the standards of spiritual truth and value, as distinct from *l'immanence transcendente* of ordinary perception. The result is a bimodal consciousness, whose reality and imperatives are variously formulated by different theological traditions. The lines of these perceptions of transcendence, shining through the forms of worldly immanence, which so variously impress themselves on the human spirit, run outward infinitely. They gather nowhere and everywhere. Theology calls this unsayable ground God. It is a word that focuses the mind and heart. But it is only a cipher for something more radically Other. This is the transcendence of transcendence. For if the first saves the phenomena, grounding them in something "More" (than mere human perceptions), the second saves God (both the word and the reality) from being delimited by human language and consciousness. These matters are central to this work.

Jewish theology is of a particular sort. It is grounded in these natural and supernatural realities, but speaks its own language. This language is the result of its own interpretations of these matters, both the experiences and the duties, and the interpretation of these interpretations. These *forms of interpretation* constitute the shapes and content of Jewish hermeneutical theology— as well as its possibilities. I have tried to give a new dimension to this feature of Jewish thought, and in this way save the study of scripture from being a merely historical retrieval of information, and the history of interpretation from becoming an archive of achievements. With respect to the first case, this is done by reading specific events in this corpus as theological expressions of primordial truth. The narratives of scripture thus become paradigms of perennial matters bearing on divine presence (both transcendence and immanence), as well as the human response to them. The second case (the history of interpretation) takes us further, building on the fact that the study of scripture is a venerable spiritual discipline in Judaism that has produced (during more than two millennia) a multifaceted system of Bible interpretation. The results are now not simply received as so many solutions to the plain sense of the text, or to its legal, allegorical, or even mystical character. Rather, these types of interpretation are understood to foster diverse modes of attention to textual details, which in turn cultivate correlative forms of attention to the world and to divine reality. In this way, a network of correlations is proposed between forms of reading texts, by attunement to their nuances and meanings, and forms of reading external reality, by attunement to its manifold details and their significance; and between (both) these various forms and modalities of divine perception, by cultivating types of theological consciousness and attunement. Textual study thus becomes a discipline of ethical and spiritual self-cultivation; and scripture is transformed thereby from an authoritative corpus of received laws, beliefs, and memories into an authorizing matrix for ongoing meditative reflection and reflective action. The result of such processes is that ethical and theological matters are bound to scriptural language and its interpretation, leading to different experiences of time and judgment. Such considerations take Rosenzweig's notion of "speech-thinking" a step further. For if his great insight (stimulated by Rosenstock-Huessy) is that the grammatical forms of language structure thought, and that thinking is also bound to the grammar of temporal existence, we would now add the dimension of "exegetical-thinking," whereby the speaking of texts in the process of interpretation puts one into diverse temporal and grammatical rhythms; these latter prepare the reader for life and for theology. The Jewish theology that results is multiple and pluralistic. It is alive as a living practice, but is not life itself; it is rather a preparation for it: an attunement for attunement. Interpretation requires one to stop prowling, and to take a stand before the teachings of texts and experience. This may reorient the self to the world and to meaning. Torah is thus a pointing of direction (and an indication of possibilities) along the way; it is no quick fix.

Through the process of reading, the world is disclosed as a great variety of *forms of life* that are variously interpreted and attended to. This is the double-faced nature of attunement: it involves both perception and performance. Accordingly, theology is not merely a type of thinking but also a type of living. For it is in just this way that it is tested and put to the proof (Buber's notion of Bewährung). Otherwise, theology is a mere bundle of words—dead letters without soul. Scripture and the vast enterprise of legal exegesis in Judaism establish normative structures for such a rich enactment: structures that are initially disclosed through interpretation, and then discovered and applied in the course of life. These must also be attended to. On the one hand, the world provides *forms of attention* for theology that must be carefully discerned and enacted. All this constitutes the vast realm of *halakha* (normative action). On the other hand, the world is experienced in terms of fullness or lack; these positive or negative valences variously impose themselves on our attention. Theology gives expression to this through forms of prayer and blessing, which also attune us to modalities of divine immanence in all its numinous depth and height. Finally, there are those forms of attention cultivated by sacred study, both alone and in partnership. Such practices further prepare the self to engage in the world, through the reflective consideration of textual scenarios and topics; and they cultivate both an inner and an outer discourse, through the ways one speaks about things to oneself and with another person. The partner-in-study may thus be related to as a modality (or actualization) of divine presence, even as the forms of law and prayer may train one to see traces of this reality in more impersonal things and events. Alertness is all. The call of God (through all expressions of reality) may everywhere break the veil of our daily stupor, and then natality overcomes mortality. This is an ecstatic transcendence of mortality in a (specific) fullness of time, without denying the finality of death and dying. In the eros of attunement, "love is strong as death."

But this eros in the theology to be presented here is fraught with risk. One must take with the utmost seriousness the great difficulty of establishing and sustaining a theological position of vigilant attentiveness—given the constraints of our cognition and the nature of the knowable; given the lethargy of our moral will and the urge to flight; and given the reality of evil and the dissonances which rupture our sense of significance. All these exude the vapors of futility, and constitute a kind of *kelipah* or "shell" mentality, whereby things are encrusted by a sense of despair and only disjunctions are felt or seen. The present theology attempts to stare all this down and, without denials, promote the virtues of spiritual resolve and self-overcoming. A vital means toward this end is the rabbinic tradition and its reinterpretation. In various ways, these serve as aides-de-camp in the ongoing struggle for intellectual integrity and the natality of renewal.

The following passage provides a clue. Regarding the performance of religious duties, scripture repeatedly exhorts: "you shall do them" (*va-asitem otam*) (cf. Lev. 26:3), and in this way underscores the need to enact one's theological commitments. The tasks of life are always already there, outside the self, for one to do and fulfill them as the commandments of God. They thereby exemplify the conditions of heteronomy. But the theological imagination often resists reducing the law (any law) to something "other" or exterior to the self, and reconceives it in terms both more personal and more interior to selfhood. For this reason, an ancient commentator took up our biblical text and wrought an exegetical revision of exceptional significance—reading the object pronoun *otam* (them) as *atem* (you), and thereby transforming the exhortation decisively. For it is now made to say, "*va-asitem atem*," namely, that in the doing (of the commandments) "you will make (or refashion) yourselves"! Here is the essence of hermeneutical theology in a nutshell. The old words of scripture are spaces for ever-new moments of spiritual consciousness and self-transformation. But this new reading is no mere assertion of autonomy, to counterpoint the original heteronomous emphasis. It is rather a complex blend of the two. Interiority and exteriority are intertwined and interdependent. And lest we fail to notice, this blend is itself effected by the exegetical act. At such moments, Sinai is reborn in the mind, and one must humble oneself to oneself—all ears.

1

Toward Theology

Rethinking Theology: Some Preliminary Considerations

Theology is a sacred enterprise, to be enacted with awe and probity; for it is the ever-new attempt to speak of the reality of God and direct the self toward this truth. So considered, theology is a *spiritual exercise* of the highest order. Its work is conditioned by time and place and tradition, and by the differential impact of these factors. Whether theology strives for eternal and abstract formulations—or for expressions that are more temporal and concrete—depends on the particular practitioner of these thought-forms as well as diverse cultural factors. Styles of theological practice vary greatly. Some center on brief images, born in intuitive flashes and connected by a spiritual logic; others derive from more discursive acts of reason, and adhere to more formal standards of coherence. In addition, these different versions may evoke authoritative sources in explicit or covert ways—or not at all. The phenomenon of theology is thus multiple in nature and protean in form. Each generation produces the expressions appropriate to its conventions and needs. The impact of life and the search for meaning and integrity crowd one's consciousness continuously. A living theology tries to meet this challenge again and again.

Thus, despite the natural desire for enduring explanations, new times will repeatedly impeach inherited consolidations and induce their constant reformulation. Disingenuousness or fear may seduce one into self-deception and disregard; but authenticity is their moral counterforce, and demands repeated stocktaking and reassessment. It requires one to step out of the shadows of tradition and routine and say: "Here I am; this is life as I know it." Such a confession clears a space for honest theology. Too often is our sense of the world affected by habit and familiar ideas. We have eyes to see, but our minds are filled with idols. The result is a living death. Almost unknowingly we become caretakers of our moribund sensibilities. Only through self-examination may one hope to begin anew.

THEOLOGICAL INTEGRITY

The call for integrity demands an assessment of what we take to be real and true in our religious lives. Traditions mask our thoughts, and glib pieties provide the hiding places where we crouch against the thunderous question: Where are you—just now in your life? We must therefore have the courage to examine our beliefs (both received and constructed) and determine what is intellectually or spiritually viable. No evasions should be permitted as we each ask, in what sense is God a living reality in our lives, or merely some abstraction of thought; and in what respect is religious life a matter of true engagement, or simply an expression of inherited behaviors? And insofar as we are also heirs to religious formulations from the past, sometimes centuries and millennia removed from our present circumstances, with their often vastly different intellectual ideals and challenges, it is also necessary to ask, in what way is the language of scripture real or true or compelling for us, given its personalized portrayals of God and divine dominion, or its particular picture of the world order and its spiritual entities? How do they jibe with our contemporary sense of language and spirituality and cosmos? And by the same token, we must also ask, now as Jews with a particular history and culture, in what respect (if at all) is the language of the ancient rabbis a living truth or instruction for us today, saturated as it is with age-specific personifications of God and the divine universe as a whole? To be sure, such questions need not always arise or come to roost in the same nest; and one may even find ways of filtering these matters in the course of encountering them—as may be the case, for example, in the process of study, when one may integrate some topics and terms while casting others aside. But such intellectual sifting is less easy to do in the course of statutory prayer, when biblical and rabbinic images fill one's mouth and mind in steady succession; or while performing certain ritual acts that have prescribed formulations, though these latter might not ring true to our natural or metaphysical sense of things. It would be easy to resolve these matters by shutting down one's mind or simply going through the verbal motions—out of loyalty at best. But such practices smack of compartmentalization and retreat from the difficulties at hand. Alternatively, one might say that (traditional) religious language is different from ordinary speech, and should therefore be tolerated as some linguistic hint of the archaic or primordial beyond normal experience. But such a resolution would split religious language off from everyday reality and usage, and could even dichotomize these two spheres.

A living theology cannot take such paths. It must rather be direct and forthright as it seeks to create integrations between the various domains of one's life (the everyday and the religious), and between one's intentions and behaviors, verbal and otherwise. This has always been the conscious ideal and unconscious impulse of genuine theology; and for its part, authentic Jewish theology has always been marked by strategies of accommodation between the earlier and foundational strata of theological tradition (such as scripture) and the challenge of quite different moral attitudes or truth claims (from the broader intellectual environment). Thus the concern for integrity is not merely a modern dilemma, faced with cognitive gaps between the past and the present, but a historical phenomenon, evincing ongoing attempts, from antiquity on, to adapt the worldview and values of ancient scripture to new considerations—be these the ethical virtues and cosmological ideas of Greco-Roman times; the moral and metaphysical topics of medieval thought; or the scientific and epistemological revolutions of the modern period, with its ever-more awesome vision of an unfathomable universe filled by infinite particles and subuniverses, and by biological achievements that transform the very sense of being human and evaluating it. In earlier times, when only some particular moral or intellectual issue was deemed out of joint with scripture, specific reinterpretations and textual transformations effected local remedies, and the dissonance was dissolved. But when broader conceptual issues were at stake, such as the structure of the universe—be it three-tiered or more complex; or the very notion of God's being—be it deemed person- or mindlike, dynamic or abstract, and so on, more massive intellectual transfigurations were required.

For the most part, such changes were accomplished with a deliberate self-consciousness, and a concern for the integration of the revision into the total fabric of tradition. This often created the semblance of a seamless or at least harmonious tapestry, with the result that older spiritual universes passed into the minds of later students as integral conglomerates of authoritative teachings—carried forward from generation to generation by the canonical sources themselves and the teachers who embodied them. Thus, to the unsuspecting eye, focused on the great body of traditions to be mastered, this complex content had the aura of a sacred and integrated whole. But the traces of revision are nevertheless always discernible in the sources, even when older materials are simply cited or spliced into new anthologies; and this ongoing process of adaptation or clarification attests to the vitality of living theology. Whenever that pulse no longer beats—due to a failure of nerve or felt irrelevance—theology dies with it and its achievements become a mere specter or irrelevant chatter; unless (as may also happen) the theological tradition becomes an object of veneration in its own right, the imposing surrogate for an absent god or a suspended search for meaning. But both developments are signs of death, not life.

Two exemplary types of cultural transformation will provide some concrete character to these abstract statements, and further specify the dynamics involved.

I shall consider first the case of philosophical rationalism as expressed in the voluminous works of Philo and Moses Maimonides—two quite distinct though related instances, from the ancient and medieval periods respectively. On the one hand, both thinkers produced bold edifices of speculative thought, ranging hierarchically from the heights of heaven and its most spiritual or godly realms, down to the material earth below and its most inanimate clod. These great ventures of ideas were the product of natural reason and its relentless attempts to grasp something of the totality of Being, and even to dare think the unthinkable about Divinity itself, so utterly beyond human thought and conception. But these two philosophical systems were not altogether isolated or independent acts of thought, for all their very distinctive qualities. Quite the contrary; both thinkers were thoroughly grounded in older and contemporary philosophical traditions. For Philo it was middle Stoicism especially, whereas for Maimonides it was Plato and Aristotle in their later Islamic recrudescences. What is more, both Philo and Maimonides were committed to and convinced of the ideals of truth that were part of this Greek intellectual heritage. All this is quite significant for present purposes—precisely because of the vast difference between the worldviews and values of the philosophical corpus and those found in scripture. In the first case (that of philosophy), the standard of authority was human reason, whereas in the second (that of scripture) it was divine revelation. Moreover, philosophy yearns for the abstract and universal, and its God is formed in this image; whereas, in starkest contrast, we have the phenomenon of scripture, which is the historical account of a particular people, and its God appears in an all-too-human image. Such differences are fundamental, the abyss between them immense.

But there is another side to Philo's and Maimonides' achievement. These men were not merely philosophers, thinking the thoughts of reason; they were also exegetes of the highest order, and their philosophical works are marked by this feature. Deftly and dynamically, both claimed that the surface of scripture is but the narrative expression of a deeper wisdom, which may be penetrated through the hermeneutical devices of allegory. By its means, the terms of scripture are variously shown to be anything but popular and naive figures; rather, these latter are markers of philosophical notions, both intellectual and profound, and the inner intent of the text is to provide a guide to philosophical enlightenment and thus be in the intellectual service of an utterly incognizable God. Hence, for those in the know, there was no gap between scripture and philosophy. *Au fond*, the two were one truth—different dimensions of the same reality. To understand this matter through an initiation into the secrets of allegory was thus to overcome one's perplexity before the seeming limitations of the native religious tradition, and to reground philosophy in the truths of scripture and its language. Wondrously, the alembic of hermeneutics transformed Moses into a philosopher who spoke foreign ideas in a native idiom.

To sharpen and summarize the foregoing observations, let it be stated that utterly nonbiblical ideas and perspectives (from worldview to moral values), understood as true and provable, were acknowledged by both Philo and Maimonides on the basis of an independent intellectual tradition, and that the real and manifold gaps between these formulations and scriptural tradition were closed through bold interpretation. The results are remarkable hybrids of truth-saying. Vital to this whole enterprise was the incorporation of all wisdom in the matrix of sacred scripture. Indeed, through the dynamics of philosophical exegesis, external modes of thought were naturalized and given acceptable religious authority. There was now no abyss between the surface of life, language, and scripture on the one hand and philosophical truth on the other. A bridge of interpretation joined them together.

Comparable dynamics exist in various strains of Jewish mysticism over the ages, as we may readily confirm from the repository of ideas embedded in the medieval Book of Zohar and from their diverse reinterpretation in the teachings of R. Ḥayyim Vital or Hasidic masters of more recent centuries. On the one hand, these quite diverse corpora evince complex speculative universes and posit great chains of Being that interlink all imaginable worlds and conceivable entities—from the most concrete earthly matter to absolute and pure spirit, and that even propose divine dimensions beyond all this in the most supernal realms of reality. Like their rational counterparts, we have in these cases bold attempts to comprehend the entirety of existence and more, though in these instances vision and contemplation (rather than speculative reason) were deemed the surer guides to the cosmic hierarchies. Withal, even the briefest glance at this most remarkable output reveals enormous differences between it and the overt sense of scripture—whether in speculations posited about the emanation of world-being out of the undifferentiated depths of Divinity, and its various configurations and dynamics; or the notions of the emergence of evil through successive divine purgations, resulting in demonic structures and realms of anti-value; or even the expressions of a feminine modality of Divinity (called Shekhinah), sometimes displaced from its cosmic conjunctions and wandering the world in sorrowful exile. Plainly, such matters have more in common with Neoplatonic (philosophical) thought and Gnostic (mythic) dramas than anything one might readily perceive in scripture. Once again there appears to be a formidable gap with substantive differences between such notions and the native Jewish religious heritage.

It is therefore once more remarkable to note that this abyss was also crossed through the most deft and dynamic exegesis of scripture—of such a magnitude, in fact, that the biblical text was not simply regarded as the mere historical account of a nation, and its travails or victories, as would appear to common sense. It was rather, and most remarkably, shown to be the outer garment of ever-deeper layers of divine spirit and soul—so that the language of scripture was deemed a virtual ladder of (symbolic) ascent into God, for those in the know. Exegesis was thus (here too) the means of a thorough transformation of scripture, revealing the true reality of God. As a result, the process of interpretation was nothing less than a spiritual initiation into greater and more profound levels of this cognition. Indeed, scripture was even transformed into the template of all reality, into nothing less than the ultimate code of Divinity itself. Accordingly, there was no gap between the values of scripture and any truth whatever. Once again, complex hybrids of the foreign and the indigenous are produced through the arts of interpretation; and once again the conjuror's trick takes place within the orbit of scripture—the sacred matrix of all possible and acceptable truth.

CHALLENGES AND COMPLICATIONS

The foregoing instances (and many others, such as Hermann Cohen's more contemporary attempt to correlate neo-Kantian forms of reason with scriptural sources) would seem to provide precedence for our present situation. Based on these historical examples of exegetical synthesis and transformation, one might suppose that our present theological task should correspondingly involve, first, the recognition of the most dominant modes of thought in modernity, such as structure our experiences and sense of reality, and then finding ways of accommodating them to scripture and its theological teachings. Following older paradigms, such a procedure would take truth on its own terms, as we find it through natural and philosophical inquiry, and then conjoin it with the formulations of scripture (and tradition), whose terms have become authoritative over the ages. In this process, the mediating link would again be interpretation, shuttling back and forth between the two systems.

But such a time-tested procedure fails at several points, due to complications of a distinctly modern sort. Three typical issues may be noted in this setting; for we must first be aware of the factors impeding a traditional solution before we can chart a new path toward the same end.

The first complicating consideration to be adduced is the felt absence in our times of one coherent or compelling worldview. A dizzying swirl of methods populate the landscape of modernity, and variously claim to be the most suitable cognitive matrix for perceiving or assessing reality. In some cases these assorted claims run parallel to one another, but others are contradictory or intersect at different points. For example, a great variety of psychological structures are proposed which purport to reveal fundamental features of the mind and its processes, and these variously coexist with other epistemological claims deriving from new and old philosophical positions, or even mentalities said to originate in deep social or economic structures. But these multiple analyses (as wholes or parts) hardly add up to a comprehensive or fully cogent worldview. One is left with piecemeal mentalities, subject to personal preference or group pressure. Even subscribing to an overarching scientific mode of thought—imbued, say, with the values of material empiricism and generalization—would not be sufficient to address the modern mind, since there are altogether different scientific mentalities, with varying degrees of positivistic or intuitive intensity, and with different ways of dealing with subjectivity and value. Indeed, it is a commonplace that these diverse mindsets do not provide inherent standards by which to assess or resolve such matters; and metalogical moral positions are either lacking or subject to contention. As a result, Protagoras's dictum that "man is the measure" has been trivialized into the canard that the human is the mere "measurer" of all things. Without a standard of judgment, we cannot evaluate our actions in terms of what would constitute a just or humane way of existing on earth; and in the process, measurement serves the most narrow or self-serving ends.

The humanities provide little guidance in these matters. All kinds of skepticism and methods of suspicion dog the path. These attitudes are often turned into ideologies as well, with the result that every standpoint is deemed a relative one or the expression of some will to power; and also that every determination of values is considered a type of enslavement to conscious or unconscious authorities. The upshot is that forms of inquiry that might provide some critical value turn against the very resources which might serve as some basis for thoughtfulness or judgment. For example, the narrative texture of canonical works is analytically unraveled to such a degree, and by the most diverse methods, that the models of selfhood they represent become threadbare. In the process of this analytical pursuit we forget that the life positions these texts articulate are not just "events of language," whose cultural and unconscious forces must be duly exposed, but types of life-worlds which may help us reflect on our human condition. In the end, such deconstructive acts adversely affect our personhood. Our moral character is stripped away and we become congeries of ideologies among other similar human types, whom we may join for certain utilitarian benefits or ideological ends; or else we simply live (and let others live) with different matrices of thought for different purposes. But surely none of this is conducive to grounding our lives and universes of thought in some coherent setting, or integrating these patterns into a larger theological perspective—let alone aligning such matters with textual matrices from the past, such as scripture.

This leads to a second consideration that complicates our contemporary theological situation. If we are beset by competing forms of cognition, with no clear standard of adjudication or sense of correlation, we are also affected by diverse sources of cultural value and memory. Moderns read the sacred texts and classics from different cultures (for pleasure, in translation, and without any moral prerequisites), and are influenced by them in varying degrees—so much so that our values are strange hybrids of all these canonical sources. Few persons are formed by one or another foundational text (such as scripture) to the exclusion of other influences, and these diverse materials may even challenge or complicate the foundational text and infuse our lives with a bevy of multicultural matrices of unequal value. Even where one can still speak of the role and impact of core narratives among specific groups, recited or celebrated in ritual settings, one's knowledge—or mis-knowledge—of the "other" cultural sources conditions the values found in these "native" sources. The result is that one's own cultural matrix or sacred text is far from an unalloyed arbiter of incoming values, but is affected by an array of dimensions deriving from many other areas of education or media exposure. How then could one even think of turning to scripture (or some other textual canon) as a self-sufficient matrix to be correlated with our knowledge of the world? And even if we did consider this matter, the fact is that most moderns have lost a strong sense of texts and language, such as might bear the weight of interpretations seeking support for life's tasks. Hardly do people feel the value of accommodating their new thinking to the challenge of older scriptural (or other textual) sources, but rather easily and more readily assimilate the latter to their own standpoint or psychological matrix; and hardly do most moderns wish to center their lives around an ancient source, when there seem to be so many other texts of a secular or purely literary character that more evidently claim their moral and intellectual attention. Such conditions surely complicate the theological enterprise, and would seem to put it beyond the pale of past attempts to accommodate new thoughts to ancient texts. But without some grounding in scripture, of whatever sort, would a Jewish theology even be "Jewish"?

This brings me to a final consideration bearing on the renewal of theology. It goes to the very heart of the task and even seems to put the whole project in jeopardy. For the issue to be reckoned with is whether theology is even possible in our time. Whatever be the complications of diverse mentalities and scriptures for modern thought, theology is a precarious enterprise in its own right. Ever since Kant produced his great "Copernican revolution" in philosophy, the metaphysical ceiling has lowered considerably, shadowing the ground of human experience. So much is this the case that whether one looks up or down, the only thing that can be reliably perceived or known is the world and its things—and even this is shaped by our minds in endless circuits of interpretation. We are altogether encased in the phenomenal realm that we experience through our senses and process through the structures (and schemata) of our reason. Indeed, everything is tangibly here "below," and there is no invisible realm "above" to which the mind (or spirit) might turn, as to an independent domain of pure truth and value. Old Plato and his heaven-soaring chariot of ideas have taken a nosedive, and the ideal essences we have projected heavenward by abstract thought have crashed into the earth of murky experiences, where we muddle along as best and as thoughtfully as possible. Accordingly, when Schopenhauer chided Kant for his metaphysics, he did so not because he assumed there to be anything other than our earthly, phenomenal realm, but principally because Kant dealt with it exclusively through the prism of abstract thought, and not via the more primary factors of human experience and emotion. But just this latter sphere is where we find ourselves—inherently and necessarily; and it is our ineluctable challenge to act with integrity in this mortal sphere of life and death. So much is this so, that many contemporary thinkers would even limit philosophy to the forms of human consciousness and will, and focus on the intentional acts of meaning related to our living and dying and deciding.

But if there is no other knowable realm of reality than this one, and we are trapped under the ceiling of interpreted phenomena, are we not forced to ask, is there any place here for theology as an attempt to speak about the reality of God, so irreducible to the phenomena we apprehend, and to orient the self to this truth? Indeed, from within the murkiness of human knowledge and experience, we rightly wonder, is there any room for theology as such—or has it gone the way of all heavenly things? Perhaps all that remains is some mode of natural piety, such as the shudder before the mortal mysteries (with Goethe), or the felt ecstasies of springtime (with Wordsworth). Surely this is a lot, and unsettles the mind from its human habitudes. But is there more?

>>><<<

Any positive answer must emerge with care and patience. No honest theology can ignore what we know and experience as moderns, or relegate this to some separate cognitive sphere. Theology must take account of the full spectrum of our lives—from birth to death, with all our hopes and fallible hearts. Nor can it ignore the experiences of other peoples on the earth, as if what was theologically pertinent for one group had no bearing on others, or that somehow the sufferings of the stranger were irrelevant to one's sense of theological truth. Accordingly, the first task of theology is to provide a perspective that would place one firmly upon the earth and set forth a framework for the entirety of existence—such as humans may know it in their life-realms. We are not one kind of person when we walk on the earth feeling hunger or love, and then an entirely different sort when we listen to music or talk about theology and religious experience. We are always one and the same; we are always mortal creatures living in this world. So how might we proceed?—Perhaps by paying closest attention to the concrete realities of our lives, as we experience them on earth; and by rethinking how we constitute our daily existence through thought or action, and how we fill in or explain unsettling events that occur all around. Here below, in the vast phenomenal world, the project of theology must begin with a wholly natural attitude to the things and happenings of experience. There is no other way. If it founders here, it founders altogether; and if there is no opening here, there is no opening to speak of whatsoever.

What does this mean?

I would put it this way, by way of introduction. Like all matters human, theology must be grounded in earthly experience and understood from within its forms. The phenomenal world is all that we have. This is the sphere that lies before us in our everyday existence; it conditions the products of aesthetic perception; and it provides the sphere for theological experience and reflection. However, it would be folly to assume that we experience this world the same way in each of these mental modes, or to deny that different types of surface and depth are disclosed thereby to our consciousness and understanding. For to do so would be to reduce these modes to one type of experience, and disregard the diverse character of worldly appearance or the way "something more" of reality is disclosed through the world by art and theology than it is through one's ordinary (or even extraordinary) experience of things in the natural world. Much (perhaps everything) depends on how we situate ourselves toward the interpreted world, and therefore also on the relationship between the self, who receives the phenomena, and that which is given to perception. In certain circumstances, there is a foreshortening of the depth of "the given" for pragmatic purposes; and that is the everyday world we negotiate our entire lives. But in other circumstances, the stable (or stabilized) depths are transfigured, and either reconstructed through the artistic imagination, or deconstructed into the ever-more receding infinities of theology. But for theology to be theology, and not merely a species of human experience, these infinities must be intuited as more than a trace of the elusiveness of experience, but somehow also as the given (or "shadow") of an unsayable, and insensate, and utterly transcendent Giving, to which we can only orient ourselves in silence. Theology provides language for that orientation, bending in humility to its own limits.

To more properly sense such an unfolding of the Godhead into world-being, so to speak, or to perceive or intuit its penetrations therein, we must first return to our ordinary experiences. What follows, therefore, is an attempt to trace something of the character of our sheerly human reception and transformation of the world—in different modalities. It begins with the natural world and ourselves as natural beings (which we ever are), and proceeds thoughtwise to the aesthetic sphere and our artistic constitution or reception of existence, and from there to a sense of the (overarching and inhering) theological dimension. Our lives are thus grounded in worldly phenomena, but there is conceivably something more that we may hope to intuit and bring to thoughtfulness. In doing so we become theological beings, even from within our mortal naturalness.

Three Domains of Human Being

THE NATURAL WORLD ALL AROUND

Primary Realities. Our lives are grounded in the natural world. It is our primary sphere of existence. As natural beings we are, in the most elemental sense, coextensive with this realm: our bodies are composed of it, our stomachs take in and digest its matter, and we traffic with this world all our days until we die and are decomposed into its elements. Thus, if this world is also experienced as something separate from our vital nature, it is because of various types of resistance or limits that we encounter: the hardness or softness of physical things we touch; the emptiness of hunger or the sensation of pain; and the impact of impressions that swirl around us daily.

We also experience the world as distinct from ourselves for another reason, and that is because the world we process through our consciousness is mediated by the symbolic structures of language. We are not only vital entities linked to the organic and animal realms, but self-conscious beings who respond to and re-formulate our reality through thought and speech. In Western civilization since antiquity, just these features have been understood to be the special soul element of the human species. Hence we "have a world" not only through the inchoate feel of tactile sensations and impressions, but also through a developed sense of intelligence and verbal articulation. Indeed, it is especially our forms of language that bring the world we experience to cognition and expression. Language is thus both a symbolic form that abstracts us from the "brute" facticity of things, and the means for their "spiritual" appropriation and internalization. It is therefore our most primary rationality, giving our minds their most basic mindfulness. We weave our lives into a web of words, like spiders who spin their creations from within themselves and trap reality in these very meshes—from moment to moment, in both silent monologue and social discourse, and across the divides of time, as we learn about the past and communicate it.

Our lives are thus shaped by varied patterns of communication from the outset. First felt as primary impulses, the sounds and sights of existence slowly assume a meaningful order and significance. Simply think of the primordial processes each childhood repeats. The whir of noise and the blur of shapes are sensate, eerie elements from the very start, and are only gradually routinized into sensible patterns by the touch of parental care and the wave tones of intimate sounds. For surely the sights and sounds of being are felt long before they are understood, and eventually understood precisely because they are felt in regular rhythms. Body and sound are thus conjoined in diverse loops of meaning, expanding and contracting in range. As we develop, we begin to think through our sense of hunger and wetness, and through the sensation of care or abandonment. These are primary fields of consciousness and memory, around which vocal patterns attach themselves as accompanying vibrations. Bodily smells are also part of this process—perceived initially from the odors of parental skin or breath, and experienced in certain oscillations that become the ever-anticipated signifiers of personal significance. These and other factors variously communicate and provide meaning long before they "make sense." In time, the tonalities of vocality are specified, and the great mystery of language and expression once again becomes a living reality.

The intimate rhythms of sound and sight also weave the reality of relationship into the fabric of sentient life—a warp and woof enhanced or broken, repaired or nurtured, over and over again. We attune ourselves to patterns and possibilities, discovered in the doing and hearing; we learn to attend to signs and their significance, uncovered in the course of life; and we build correlations between ourselves and other persons, through the right words and gestures or their repair. In short, the vast phenomenal world is the setting for ongoing interactions between the private self and the many public happenings we encounter from moment to moment. This context of interconnections marks the dyadic form of human experience: the compresence of the single self and that worldly feature which appears to be happening or evokes attention. In communication with other persons, it is particularly a dialogical dimension that may open up; for it is here that one learns about partnership and difference, and our language constructs spheres of stability for ongoing social life. Language thus channels the flow of a sometimes inchoate reality, and coordinates the patterns of sight to rhythms of sound. In this way the subject develops a sense of self, both in relationship to worldly things and to other persons. In so doing, we build a life-world within the vastness.

Each successful communication imprints trust in the power of words to carve a sphere of sense out of the limitless "whole." Indeed, every word or phrase that is confirmed by another person, and each syntactical pattern correlating a subject with an object, is, so to speak, a primordial narrative of world-building— a metonym of every expanded "creation account" found in culture. Similarly, every successful act that accompanies these words and phrases engenders confidence and trust in one's relationship to the world, and thus constitutes a primordial "drama of life." Myth and ritual, as cultural forms, are thus the developed codes of meaningful narrative and action, and are ultimately grounded in the most basic human forms of *mythos* and *dramenon* found in speech and act. Only when words and works break down for one reason or another, or for no apparent reason at all, does the vastness return as a terrifying reality and we doubt our capacity to make sense of the world through language and deeds. At such times, the authoritative myths and rituals of one's culture are performed with greater intensity, as if thereby to affirm that the roiling upsurge of the vastness is only a mistake in the proper use of words and deeds, and no real indication of the true and brute nature of things. In such a way, the outrunning vastness is momentarily dispelled through an exertion of the imagination, and one returns to the belief that the given cultural order safeguards life from disorder and danger. Such is the masque of life. Forgetting the great vastness "out there," we blithely return to settled habits and routine, and a sense of control.

The natural world we so arrest and order is thus harnessed to *the care of the self.* I mean this in the most primary sense. As humans, we are vitally concerned to care for our survival and sustenance, work for our safety and well-being, and cultivate our environment so that it will be a safe haven for the flourishing of everyday life. But I also mean this in a more secondary sense. We are also concerned to build up a meaningful order of social value, so that systems of justice will protect the self, and the culture predicated upon its forms will create a sphere for the enhancement of human relations and institutions. All this may happen through a careful regulation of life and a dutiful care for language and its meanings. We need not always be thinking about thinking, or the ways that we make a world through thought and speech. But by doing so, we also show our care for the world; for this kind of philosophical attitude opens the world to reflective wonder, and such thoughtful wondering promotes an ongoing sense of duty and responsibility. The natural world we may inhabit with mindless endurance can thus also be lived in with a concerted mindfulness, focused on the very nature and meaning of our worldliness. This too is a fundamental component of our natural selves and self-care—since we are both coextensive with the natural world and distinguished by mind and consciousness.

Rupture and Revision. Let us now return to the ruptures of routine and experience that unexpectedly undermine our ordinary lives—and for good reason, since these occasions open a distinct space for reflection about the natural world and religious consciousness. As already noted, the "care of the self" with which we invest our existence is geared to make the world a dependable place, and to allow us to establish workable patterns and dependable perspectives. For this reason, one of the central functions of culture and tradition is to convey what works to future generations so that each life cycle may benefit from the tried and true of the past—and that is a good thing. But the transmission of conventions can also contribute to a mindless malaise, with the result that our world becomes a series of cues directing our actions in one direction or another. The sights and sound of existence are then so many flickering matters of fact, the less felt the better—and that is hardly beneficial for spiritual existence.

But then it may happen that the thoughtless ordinariness of daily life is jolted and gives way to a more elemental specificity. Suddenly something occurs that claims us with an overwhelming intensity, and floods our sensibilities without any accompanying thoughts of its human meaning. Rather, the sense of rupture is all, and it seems as if primordial energies have burst from the depths and ripped the veil normally stretched over things, concealing them in blandness. Such moments may occur within the bounds of nature, as with the uprush of some overwhelming vista or sound; they may happen in the human world, as with the unsettling impact of sudden death or love; or they may happen through the creations of culture, as with the capacity of certain compositions to propel us to the edge of sensibility. We then shudder before what is given to us from the fullness of phenomenal existence, manifesting mysteries of the surge of things at the core of world-being. Just here is an absolute "somethingness," pulsing in elemental specificity—for we suddenly sense the raw plenitude of existence; but here too, simultaneously, it seems, is a revelation of primordial "nothingness," yawning like an "inconceivable chasm of invulnerable silence in which cataclysms of galaxies rave mute as amber"—for we also sense that the event is in excess of human meaning. In time we come back to our normal selves, and when we do we more knowingly confirm this happening and ourselves as well, answering the ever-present question "Where are you?" with the confession "Here I am—just here." On such occasions, consequent to the restabilization of consciousness, a renewed subjectivity is aroused in us (the "here *I* am"), together with an awakened sense of the great immensity in which we are suffused, now experienced at a particular time and place (the "just *here*").

These experiences may fundamentally change our lives; for though the primal depths may close over, and we return to more regular experiences of the world, the "sense of depth" may remain in mind. And if so, one is infused by an awareness of a twofold dimension to reality—the pervasive superflux of existence that underlies our lives, and its more delimited nature on the existential surface of things. Along with this dual sensibility may come an awareness of our role in circumscribing the boundless and naming what exceeds all terms. This hyperconsciousness need not put us at odds with things, for we are also natural beings, and adapting ourselves to the world of nature is part of our acculturated naturalness. But by becoming aware of this matter, we realize that the world is not just there as "a world," fixed and final (like some substantial datum waiting to be disclosed), but is rather a happening, ever coming into actuality through human inventiveness; and that the self, for its part, is not just "a self," fixed in nature and proclivity, but a self-consciousness, ever attuned to itself and its worldly involvements. In this way the eruptive, caesural event is kept in mind by a new attentiveness to the contingency of experience, and an attunement to the deeper nature of worldly existence. As this double dimension of existence is infixed in consciousness (as a bimodal *mentalité*), our subjectivity and life-world are transformed.

It is the particular poignancy of the caesural moment that changes us and may induce a new mindfulness. For though the initial experiences silenced human expression, the sense of being overwhelmed by the event may give way to a sense of being claimed by it in a fundamental way. It is just that more conceptual (or self-conscious) sensibility which marks the moment with axial significance and calls the person to change their life. This is therefore not only a cognitive insight, through the perception of primordial forces underlying experience; it also carries a value component, through an awakening to the contingency of existence and the command to respond. When the precipitating moment is an elemental event of nature, such as an earthquake or flood, or the cycles of birth and death, and even when the occasion is a historical fact, such as some monstrous evil of deed or neglect, the charged moment palpably calls to our elemental nature and conscience, directing us to: Remember, Do Something, or Have Sympathy; and to the extent that one can fix these revelations in one's mind through rituals of action and recollection, their moral charge remains, and the claim is continuous and does not fade. How we collect such events in our personal lives, and how we keep them alive, determines the nature of our character; and how a culture does this through education and the selection of events for public recollection affects the moral shape of society.

Think for example of the classics of culture, and how they present *the conjunction of the elemental and the everyday*; and how they, by bringing us to this nexus, teach the complicated but ever-new balance between the two. Myths and epics of origins do this in especially notable ways—taking one into the primordial depths themselves, where the world or culture comes into formative shape, or can lapse into an inchoate swirl, again and again. The old Babylonian creation account (*Enuma elish*) dramatizes this struggle for structure and equipoise against the forces of disorder and willfulness. Chaos is presented as a disabling feature at the core of existence, and it takes savvy and strength to contain it and transform it into orderly forms—first of all *in illo tempore*, in olden times, but repeatedly in world-time: the world is built in the pauses of victory, even from the substance of the unruly elements. The text displays this matter, and the culture recites it in order to keep such teachings in mind. Knowing the fragile underpinning of things is thus not mere information to be stored in a cultural database, but essential knowledge that cuts to the quick of values and vigilance, if we would ever have a sustainable world. Forgetting these matters would be the beginning of chaos. The right balance between elemental forces and their conversion to values must be struck anew at each moment; and this principle must be kept in thoughtfulness for the sake of culture itself.

The *Iliad* emphasizes a similar consideration, when it meditates on the paradoxes of culture and its survival. Homer sings of valor and friendship, and of noble genealogies and patrimony; but he also recites verses coursing with violence and revenge, and with berserk behavior that threatens one's peer group and ignores elemental fellow feelings. There are thus powerful emotions at the heart of life, for companionship and family and survival; but these can be perverted into vanity and pride and self-destruction. Homer brings the listener to the interface of these primary elements and dramatizes their use and abuse so that one can fix them deeply in mind, and not forget the tensions and consequences of certain choices. Most poignantly, this dramatization is often found in the very midst of specific actions, as when two heroes recite their patrimonies and mutual regard, just prior to engaging in mortal combat, which will cut off lineages and lifelines forever; or when a warrior such as Achilleus, gone mad with grief for his dead companion, hesitates at the cry of a father who begs him not to shame the body of his son, who had done the killing, and then proceeds to enact the most brutal travesties imaginable. The listener is brought into these pauses in order to contemplate the nature of limits and the outrages of revenge—and to consider just how they emerge in the course of nobler concerns, and thereby realize the complexities of passion, which can save a culture or destroy it, and sometimes do both at the same time.

>>><<<

Through such literary creations cultures bring their members to the juncture of the elemental and the human, and open a space for contemplating this double dimension. These works are thus sanctioned ways of rending the veil of everyday life and bringing the qualities of existence suddenly to mind and thought, against all forgetting and the natural tendency just to "get on" with things. But without the sudden call to attention, and the rehabilitation of awareness, we are all but dead in the midst of life. The teachers of culture and the creators of its elemental instructions know that this too constitutes a fundamental care of the self.

And we may know this as well: that *attentiveness to the double dimension, at the crossing point, is a first prefiguration of theology.* Not merely huddled beneath the surface of things, unknown or silent, untold depths bespeak their presence to our hearing ear—and we are awakened. It is a disclosure from the vastness of reality, where all things are enfolded in their own right—and for their own sake.

THE AESTHETIC IMAGINATION

Meaning-making is for the sake of life. Our interpretations function habitually at the most basic levels of earthly care, and even when we are jolted unexpectedly into new modes of consciousness, we usually respond to these matters through reflexive types of explanation and understanding. But our interpretations of reality may also be employed more intentionally, in ways that creatively widen the arc of awareness. It is to a consideration of these matters that we now turn—for their own sake, and as another step toward theology.

>>><<<

In the natural realm we try to enter into accord with the sights and sounds of existence, and respond to their impact on the basis of what seems tried and true. At this level of experience, the world is a primary datum—not a semblance of itself; and when disruptions occur, they happen despite our care for continuity and control. For this reason such moments are filled with dread, even if the experience itself has an uncanny fascination or even strange beauty.

The artistic imagination and its creative forms are different. They more consciously engage the imprints of existence and transform them into new impressions of the world. Such acts lift us out of the mortal round of things, and put us into more spiritual spaces. The common world is now deliberately stripped of its habitual crust, and unfathomed depths of sensation are revealed, in and through the artistic representations. Three forms of the aesthetic imagination may be especially highlighted for the way they reshape the sights and sounds of existence: one is painting, which reenvisages our worldly sights; another is music, which recreates the sounds of things; and a third is poetry, which integrates sight and sound (via image and tone) to renew our sense of reality. Thus, from the infinite vitalities of existence, finite works of expressive coherence are "made"; and through these creations aspects of the boundless are given form and evidence. The artistic imagination thus involves intentional acts of rupture, opening caesural spaces against our worldly habitude. In this way, it attempts to *cultivate the self.*

Painting. In painting, the artist brings the world to mind through visual images. These images do not somehow inhere in the natural world, merely needing to be exhumed; rather, they are artistic semblances of the world, portrayed upon the one-dimensional surface of a canvas. The creator thus stands at the intersection of the outer world of sight (the common world of nature) and an inner domain of vision charged by an uncommon pathos. During the praxis of painting, insight and sight interfuse, in dialectical relationships. For some, the external world comes into view through the projection of an internal vision and sensibility; for others, it is the primary perception of external color schemes that dominate, and are only secondarily accommodated to the world-forms of common experience. Hence there is no fixed, external reality that is "just there," like some backdrop through which we move. On the contrary, the artistic vision helps us to see that we see constructively, and to perceive that the world is always coming into focus in numerous shades and angles. As viewers of the artistic portrayal, we are thrown back upon ourselves anew, and thus the contingency of seeing the world becomes transparent to our consciousness. Normal routine and thoughtlessness often dull this sensibility, and lead us to suppose that the world is somehow "ready made," and we must "deal with it." But painting restores us to fundamentals and helps us realize that even common sense is not something fixed, but may shift as light shines and plays upon the eye. We come to see that, in the deepest sense, no one time of day is like any another and that no one perspective can take it all in. Standing near or far, we may suddenly perceive the world as interlocking patterns of color and texture, with depth and volume, or as a complex of geometric shapes and superimposed planes, a conceptual interfusing of several perspectives at once—seen through the gift of visual memory.

The painter descends into the elemental primacy of seeing with the vibrancy of lived experience, and produces images out of the hues of a palette ground from the pigments of the earth. In the process, form is reconceived, as it is relived; texture is represented, by being perceived anew; and light bends differently around natural things, because our eye is reborn. There are no words here and no naming; only presence made present. The painter reformulates something of the great vastness of existence by descending into its inchoate possibilities; and in the making of images and emblems the artist responds to the vitality of Being, ever given in excess of every human formulation. The result is thus the manifestation of vibrant "shapes of value," real presences of worldly vitality, which seize our hearts through our naked eye. And when fortunate, at such moments we may perhaps also be given to perceive something more—a trace of the elemental inhering in things, in forms of matter before matter took form.

And if the painter might add words to this process, thereby providing an account of artistic seeing and its realization on a canvas, they would perhaps sound somewhat like these remarks by Cézanne (written to a disciple): "Nature reveals itself to me in very complex forms . . . One must see one's model correctly and experience it in the right way . . . To achieve progress nature alone counts, and the eye is trained through contact with her. It becomes concentric by looking and working." For this artist, there is no simple self plus the world; nature *is* what the artist takes it to be, since the artist's eye has become a receptor of its reality and truth. And if the artist often sees things quite differently from common sense, we can hardly deny that reality or truth, for such is reality to the painter—just as we, concomitantly, also have perceptions of the world based on our own sense of its tones and valences, though our reduction of its colors to some common sense drains it of vitality and helps us forget how much we contribute to the quality of its appearances. A comment by Matisse is instructive in this regard, as it underscores the interplay of forces that make up an expressive visual presence. "Expression," he emphasized, "does not consist of the passion mirrored upon a human face or betrayed by violent gesture. The whole arrangement of my picture is expressive. The place occupied by figures or objects, the empty space around them, the proportions—everything plays a part . . . In a picture every part will be visible and will play the role conferred upon it, be it principal or secondary . . . A drawing must have a power of expansion which can bring to life the space which surrounds it." Or consider further the reflections of Juan Gris: "The technique of painting is flat, coloured architecture . . . It is based on the relationship between colours and the forms which contain them." And not only this. "Technique is the sum of the relationships between the forms and the colours they contain and between the coloured forms themselves. This is the composition and culminates in the picture."

Is it possible to see in such ways, when inspired by great artists? Might one actually feel the brooding atmospheric depths in Rembrandt's paintings, or the modest effulgences shining in the canvases of Vermeer? At the least, their wondrous achievements may open us to new spheres of sight, through the shock of an elemental seeing—bringing us to a deeper sense of what is seeable and our role in its manifestation. The artwork then instructs and addresses the soul: See this here; Attend! As the images communicate their patterns to the mind, the cognitive apperception may assume a moral quality as well, and we are called on to relate to that image and its perceived import. This might be a new sensitivity to a face and the way it reveals feelings, or a sense of the curves of the world and the human bodies we must care for. Perhaps the images of suffering before us transfix our eye and reshape our hearts, as happens when the figures of Picasso's *Guernica* cast their spell, and we are confronted with its raw shapes of brutality, where the caesural is life itself, stripped of the veneer of civilization.

Such are thoughts given to us by painting, and the ways it affects our view of things, as well as our subsequent behavior.

Music. Music offers something else, and that is the phenomenon of sound wrought from the vastness of the world. This sound is not the drone of things around us, or the clang of human activity; neither is it the buzz of crickets at nightfall, or the waves of air that may ring in our ears. All this is part of the natural world. Music is different. It is the deliberate making of sound, in diverse patterns and variations: it is a human form, transforming the vibrations of nature and its rhythms into distinct tones and fixed intervals; a creation of the spirit, producing registers of sound and their interplay, degrees of volume and their intensity. From the stretched skins of animals, the beats of existence may pierce the human ear; from the dried reeds of plants and human breath, languid vibrations and volume may result; and from the guts of dead animals, the tones of the world are brought to life. The composer hears the timbres of sound itself, as it were, and gives them expressible formulation; and the performer puts hearing into our ears in ever-new ways. The temporality of music carries one note into another, so that we hear not only sound as such but also the effects of its echoes and continuities. Thus music makes sound something enduring—not a momentary rush of air, but a finely wrought combination of tones that engage our internal rhythms, now set in motion. Music is, so to say, sound set free and purposive: it is set free of the instruments, whether sacred or worldly, as angelic realities as such; and it is purposive in the context of its unfolding logic, implying new tones and combinations within the timbre of every note.

Music makes sense beyond human words, for it makes the elementariness of sound sensible to the body and mind—an infusing flow of ringing tonalities that carve out a realm of pathos in our hearts. In the process, creative artifice becomes human beauty, and the world-buzz from which music arises puts us in mind of the vast inchoate undertone and potential of all expressions. Shaped by this new (or renewed) consciousness, we are thus called upon to: Hear, and Listen with care!

Responsiveness is all, and it is cultivated through sound and its sequences. Speaking in this vein, about music as an aspect of the human spirit, Copeland commented: "Music is designed . . .

to absorb entirely our mental attention. Its emotional charge is embedded in a challenging texture so that one must be ready at an instant's notice to lend attention to what is most required so that one is not lost in a sea of notes." Music is thus a training in attentive hearing, a cultivation of a certain mindfulness. But it is not that alone; for by virtue of its "harmonic tensions and expressive timbres," music penetrates the depth of our psyches, and is thus a dual cultivation of the spirit. One theorist even characterized the conditioning beats of music as "sounding forms in motion." And thus we somehow experience time in the rings of sound, and learn thereby to perceive rhythm and its intonations. For the human subject, so often caught in the blur of noise, the majesty of music can therefore also serve to restore one's hearing to the hearable, and attune our sensibilities to its unfolding processes. How we hear overtones and silences is fundamental for our human being; and it is music that may restore these qualities to us in all their timbre and significance.

We should therefore not ignore the moral or value dimensions here either. No less a person than Beethoven remarked, in a conversation reported to Goethe, "It takes spiritual rhythm to grasp music in its essence . . . All genuine [musical] invention is moral progress. To submit to its inscrutable laws, and by virtue of these laws to overcome and control one's own mind, so it shall set forth the revelation: that is the isolating principle of art." In this way, music may instruct the self in a patient attunement to the hearable. This is an artistic retrieval of the most formative elements, in their very elementariness.

Poetry. This brings us to poetry, which, through its combination of images and tones, may also galvanize a renewed sense of the world. By means of assorted conventions or techniques, older habits are challenged and thinking may be reborn. One may thus regard poetry as a superordinate expression of the aesthetic imaginary. It is not only grounded in the natural world, with its sights and sounds; but through their transformation into verbal figures, readers may see and hear things differently.

This being so, how may we understand the work of poetry as a creative form?

Poetry interrupts the daily flow of language, with its various utilitarian objectives and habitual significations, and gives each word an uncommon effect or import. The common world of sight and sound is suspended in poetry, and something artful is fashioned from the phenomena in figures and sonorities. Hence the poet does not so much imitate the world as remake it with words. To be sure, the ordinary life-world that one inhabits on a daily basis is recognized in the words and images of poetry; for otherwise the content of the poem would seem alien and not make much sense. But the poet only makes this common world just recognizable enough, and does not try to describe it in a merely factual way; and that is because the deeper intent of the poet is to interrupt the regular patterns of speech and evoke (through the seemingly known) something of the greater vastness of sound, sight, and sense. Consider the following lines from Wallace Stevens's poem, "Reality Is an Activity of the Most August Imagination," which depict a sudden manifestation of light on an evening drive home. The poet registers this occurrence as a vision of

> An argentine abstraction approaching form
> And suddenly denying itself away.
>
> There was an insolid billowing of the solid.
> Night's moonlight lake was neither water nor air.

The poet's words burst forth in image and sound, transfixing our inner eye and ear. Neither at the onset of this poem nor at any line or word are we set among the chatter of the everyday world; nor does the poet allude to any earlier conversation or speech. The space before the poem is not a pause in some prior discourse, but an eruption from silence itself. It is a new beginning—one that speaks forth and takes shape in our deepest self.

Thus the poet speaks, and something new comes into presence; and this happens again and again, with each recitation of the poem. But this *novum* does not happen all at once. Much living and feeling condition the work of poetry, which arises out of silence and hovers songfully over the void. And we readers must similarly try to make this particular creation our own, through the resources of our own living and feeling. We too must pause in silence before its vocables, and must work patiently to let the poem make sense. The opening words of the poem are neither orienting nor disorienting in their initial effect. At the onset, the reader does not yet know where the words are headed, and ponders haltingly at many points. The initial experience of reading poetry is thus one of being called into attentiveness. We are first infused by the silent aura of the poem as an unvoiced figuration before us; and then sound happens as we enunciate the chain of words with our breath (in fact or imagination), and meaning begins to unfold. With deliberate regard, we try to follow the poet's voice as a world is made manifest through an emergent concatenation of sounds and images.

The experience of poetry is thus accompanied by a special sense of time, different from the one we know in our everyday lives. This is because the poet does not normally use regular syntax, such as would approximate the movements or sequences between things we know in the "real world." In poetic diction (called poetic license) the parts of speech may occur in irregular patterns, and words are suffused with tones that leave them somehow suspended in sense. Moreover, the felt absence of sound, first sensed retrospectively with the onset of the poem's enunciation, recurs in the gaps that surround each and every word. One hears familiar sounds and terms, and tries to create their meaning through the particular combination of words. This means that the poet (and the reader, in turn) is constantly recreating the renewal of the word. Thus a poem is more than a world unto itself; in fact, in the poem, each word becomes an event in its own right. We are therefore quite far from our common world of speech and communication. The true poet is always at the precipice of verbal possibility, and both from the beginning of any poem, and repeatedly with each of its words, speaks from this borderland.

It is this great gift that we are given through poetry—beyond every specific meaning that may be derived; for with poetry we are given a poetic sensibility, so distinct from our routine daily attitudes, but also so fundamental to our self-cultivation as humane beings.

All this is the call of the poem as a deliberate event of words. Through it a zone is opened in the vastness and a verbal creation rivets us to reality. If our everyday language simply uses words as tools, and depends on their capacity to make sense of things in the world, the language of poetry reveals it as a sphere of verbal happenings, where events occur in and through language. What is more: with poetry we are also brought into the realm of the becoming of words—into the vastness of tonal possibilities from which language emerges again and again. Thus poetry takes us into a dimension where we can somehow experience the "eventness" of verbalization; or it even makes us feel, as so powerfully in the poems of Celan, their words' pre-syntactic and pre-logical core. Indeed, in his works, the caesural is revealed as the disconnected void of existence.

And when we are also affected by the images of poetry and their content, cognitive musings are replaced by teachings of value. Think of Rilke's object-poem about a great, caged tiger, seemingly oblivious to all human stares, absorbing them into its thick pelt and giving the viewer a disarming sense of silent sullenness. When unexpectedly:

> as if awakened, she turns her face to yours;
> and with a shock, you see yourself, tiny,
> inside the golden amber of her eyeballs
> suspended, like a prehistoric fly.

The poet has suddenly grabbed our hearts, after lulling us into the languor of casual perceptions. All at once the most elemental depths are revealed through an image of primal power and the terrifying reflection of one's unhinged finitude. As readers, we too are caught in the eye of the image. And we are also seen and shattered and addressed at our deepest core—like Rilke, once again, who, when looking at a sculpture of Apollo, feels the stone "glisten like a wild beast's fur," and fix him within "the borders of itself," addressing his soul with an imperative, which he recites to us in his poem: "You must change your life."

>>><<<

Such aesthetic moments provide a second prefiguration of theology. Different from the unexpected experiences of the natural world, which involuntarily open our hearts to the elemental depths of Being, artworks are deliberate acts of the creative imagination, forming sights and sounds from the surge of existence, and thereby transforming the sensibilities of their recipients. Through these aesthetic acts we are affected by new experiences of the vast elementariness of existence, and the fragile world we construct on a daily basis. Perhaps more radically than myths and epics, which seem somehow to be inlaid in the depths of Being, the art forms we have considered (painting, music, and poetry) throb with a certain secondariness and the aura of their artifice. They shriek against our chatter and flash in the darkness of routine—*transient creations stationed at the interface of elemental infinitude and the forms of culture.* They are witnesses and reminders of what we do not readily bear in mind. In and through their agency, we are implacably seized and thrown toward the void—silenced by the silence beyond words.

This brings us to theology.

THE THEOLOGICAL DIMENSION

Theology happens in the world of persons. It is a human truth projected into the mysteries of God's truth. Theology is a construct of thought and imagination. It arises within mortal finitude, but yearns for more. In its exuberance, theology has often soared on the wings of abstractions and bent the mysteries of existence into the shapes of logic. Such excesses do not speak to the modern mind and sensibility. Something different is demanded, and it is this: a theology that is no more and no less than a "speaking about God" out of the thickness of human existence, through the vitalities of one's breath and body in the course of life, on the way to death. Accordingly, our first task is to *think* about theology and its concerns, and this is for the sake of *living* theologically and enacting its truths in the midst of life.

>>><<<

We may take our bearings from the previous discussions; for theology is a striking integration of our lives in the natural world and the resources of the aesthetic imagination. As with our lives in the natural world, theology is grounded in everyday reality—which includes both our normal experiences in time and space, and those caesural moments when something elemental breaks into consciousness. Moreover, as with the aesthetic imagination, theology is a symbolic form which takes our experiences in the natural world and reshapes them, so that their special qualities and depths may be brought to mind. We have noted that poetry in particular is a deliberate attempt to refocus our attention on daily happenings and their extraordinary dimensions or character. Theology tries to do this as well, but in an altogether unique and intensified manner.

I would put it this way. If in our ordinary experience caesural moments seem to happen against our will or expectation, and artwork tries, both willfully and expectantly, to create experiences of an elemental character, intentionally disrupting our normal habitude and common perceptions, *theology tries to transform this perception of elementariness into a sustained way of life and thought.* This does not mean living at some abnormal edge of experience, out of touch with our regular sense of things. It rather means taking a particular stand where the elemental and the everyday intersect. In ordinary life, the everyday is generally habitual, and when the elemental breaks through it overwhelms one totally; thus their crossing point is not so much an element of consciousness as the place of a radical opening of awareness. By contrast, the artwork tries to create a fabrication of the crossing point so that one may experience the sights and sounds of existence in a more primary way, and thus allow the elemental to cleanse our rudimentary perceptions for the sake of life. The artist therefore tries to jolt one into perceptions of the elemental so that it will challenge casual consciousness. Artwork is a response to ordinariness, and to the sealing of the abysses through routine mindlessness.

The ideal of theology is different. It tries to stand in the natural world where we live our everyday lives, and to experience all its happenings as points of crossing, where the elemental depths come to some phenomenal perception. Theology thus seeks to orient the self to a twofold dimension: to the numinous qualities of unsayable origin inhering in every moment of existence. So understood, all our worldly experiences are prismatic revelations of a deeper elementariness, the worldly shapes of primal forces received as sensations on our bodies and stimulations in our minds. It is thus through a wholly natural attitude toward the world that a deeper phenomenality is disclosed. A task of theology is therefore to *attune the self* to the unfolding occurrence of things in all their particularities and conjunctions, and help one remain steadfast at each new crossing point where raw elementariness, radically given, becomes human experience.

Theology is thus situated at the border of the known and unknown, of the manifest and the concealed. It is at this nexus that the self seeks God. For just here there is both a sense of happening and the excess of all happening, extending to the utmost depths of Being and beyond. Theology gathers the import of this awareness and attunes the heart to it, directing one's attention beyond the perceived appearance of things to the intuited and imagined vastness of all existence, ever generated from the ultimate Source of all things (and actuality). This most primal Depth (beyond the Beyond of all conception), so infinitely disposing, is what we haltingly bring to mind by the word *God*. We thus gesture the thought-image of a supernal Font of Being; and with it also this more paradoxical, corollary notion: that if all existence is not God as such, it is also not other than God, Life of all life.

It was with such matters in mind that I spoke earlier of theology as a spiritual practice, whose principal task is to guide human thought and sensibility toward God. As the exercise of theological thinking unfolds, it directs the human spirit toward an increasingly focused awareness of God as the heart and breath of all existence, and tries to sustain that focus throughout the course of life. Put differently, theology seeks to cultivate an abiding consciousness of God's informing presence in all the realities of existence, the infinite modalities of divine effectivity. Hence the world is both what we "take" it to be, in all the moments of ordinary experience, and what we must "untake" it to be, when we relate all things back to their ontological and primordial ground in God. Slowly perhaps, or in flashes, one may even be able to intuit some of the deeper dimensions of reality, inhering in a realm of God-fulness where our human distinctions fall away. Spiritual attunement to this divine domain is an attentive God-mindedness in the course of life; and it is a task of theology to cultivate this attunement so that one may live in the everyday with God in mind. Considered this way, the goal of theological consciousness is the cultivation of a multiform spiritual awareness in the midst of life: a "Jacob's ladder," so to speak, ascending from the inner heart (and common world) to the heights of heaven—which is, in truth, no "other" realm but that which lies roundabout us here on earth, in all its holy depth and fullness. Living this way, our thoughts would be like angelic couriers running between the self and God, exalting in wonder: for God is in *this* (earthly) place . . . and *it* is the Gate of Heaven.

And if we may hear an address from these depths, it is the primal claim of Yes and No. The "yes" is the positivity of reality, as it makes claims of presence and thingness; it is the "yes" that is the fullness of all things, again and again, no matter how we name them; it is the "yes" of the panoply which envelops us, pulsing with expansiveness and contraction. But the changing face of things also opens up a depth of "no"; for we intuit the "yes" as the phenomenal tip of the unfathomable, and thus the "no" is the ever-receding abyss, where our names ring empty before the ineffable source of their being, and our sense of what we perceive. But as we strain to some higher positivity through the name "God," we draw God into connection (through a negation of their ultimacy) with the vast realm of ever-namable worldliness. And thus we must unsay or negate this "yes" of No, so to speak, so that Divinity shall be (truly, to the best of our saying) No-thing—a correlate of absolutely Nothing.

>>><<<

Some speculations of R. Azriel of Gerona (a mystical philosopher of the thirteenth century) provide a more concrete expression of the theological musings just set-forth. For R. Azriel pondered the mystery and depth of infinite Being, and even tried to imagine the very borderline between the unknowable realm of Absolute Reality and all that might be humanly conceived or known by human minds. In his discourse he calls the first realm Naught (or *ayin*), because it is wholly beyond thought and thus virtually Nothing; and the second he deems Aught (or *yesh*), because it is the realm where knowable (or discernible) reality becomes and is. But the point of transition is truly neither the one nor the other, but both: it is neither wholly naught, insofar as there is a gathering toward existence (where things are nameable and determinate), nor is it wholly aught, since this domain is still characterized by the naught (where no thing is named or differentiated). At this borderline we have something else. What we have is some imaginable sense of aught grounded in naught; that is, a sense that the all-unfolding reality and being of existence, whose source is God, is ultimately effaced in the depths of God's Godhood. And though we may not follow R. Azriel in his particular mystical ontology of divine emanations, we may nevertheless strain to understand his teaching as a great truth of theology—still pertinent for our lives. For what he conveys through this meditation is that whatever may be humanly sayable about God and existence is ultimately grounded in and a manifestation of the Naught. To bring our minds toward this realization is the task of theology. This holds as much for our common view of everyday reality, where the Aught rightly pre-vails and predominates, as for our sense of God, where the Naught is the ultimate reality wherein all mindfulness is eclipsed.

R. Azriel charges his discourse with the terminology of *Naught* and *Aught*, and thereby puts his speculations in the language of older, Neoplatonic philosophy. But he also employs the language of scripture, and in so doing also attempts to connect his specu-lations to the matrix of ancient divine revelation. This striking hermeneutical achievement may help us as well as we move to-ward Jewish theology, insofar as we are now given some tradi-tional terms with which to think. Specifically, the master states that the truth he has presented philosophically is also encoded in Isaiah 25:1, which speaks of "Olden counsels, steadfast faithful-ness" (*etzot me-raḥoq, emunah omen*). In a cryptic manner, he asserts that the word *omen* denotes the realm of Naught and *emunah* the realm of Aught, thereby leaving us to understand the passage as an esoteric hint of the truth that the "primordial counsels" (or ultimate spheres of divine reality) are the Aught of God's Naught—the "faithful and true" (*emunah*) realizations of God's "steadfast and sustaining" (*omen*) Godhood. That is to say, the realm of *emunah* is presented as an ontological reality effec-tuated by God, and it indicates that whatever we understand as Being is, ultimately, grounded in and faithful to God's most ulti-mate truth of all-sustaining steadfastness. Once again, though we moderns may not share R. Azriel's own mystical metaphysics, his striking choice of this biblical passage may nevertheless provide a rich resource for contemporary consideration; for it suggests that human "faith" (*emunah*) could be understood not as some cognitive suspension of ordinary consciousness, but rather as the concern to attune oneself faithfully to the divine Source, where the seeds of all Being are sown and sustained—faithful to God's own truth. Theology would then have the task of cultivating this spiritual attunement so that a person might live in *emunah*—that is, in living faithfulness to God's *yesh* (or Aught), such as it is and unfolds in worldly existence, where the human self may receive it and bend it to thoughtful and sustainable ends.

This theological task is crucial, and infuses the entire enterprise with spiritual and moral value. For the individual may also be deemed a channel whereby God's effectivity, arising primordially and ceaselessly in the ground of Being, is actualized in the earthly realm—alongside the myriads of forms through which God's divinity is activated throughout nature and the knowable cosmos. It would, accordingly, be the spiritual and moral task of each person to become a fit vessel for modes of God's realizations on earth. Such a channeling of God's Aught would thus come through human hands and eyes, through mortal mouth and speech, and through earthly body and action as the self lives with other selves and beings and things in the vast physical universe. So conceived, all the impulses of human desire and conation emerge ultimately from the font of God's steadfast giving in a plenitude of worldly possibilities. This is God's bounty and faithfulness, such as we may imagine it; and it is a task of theology through thought and tradition to cultivate this matter and guide the diverse pulsations of Divinity into the pathways of human culture—for the sake of righteousness and with reverent regard for the gifts we have received.

There is no guarantee that theology will perform this task well, and help persons to actualize God's Aught in ways that abet a responsible human flourishing. But this is an ideal. For theology, I may now also suggest, is a species of precisely that mode of "faithfulness" noted above: it is just that attunement of sensibility which seeks to promote a bond with God's infinite gifts of world-being *and* to guide their earthly realization through human life at all times. Wherever this theological project becomes stultified or unresponsive to the moral or spiritual tasks of life, a vigorous reinterpretation of its texts and ideas is necessary. One must remain alert and act accordingly; for the revision of convention does not normally happen on its own, and the exegetical imagination is often needed to help religious cultures remain honest and keep their best priorities intact. Sometimes native resources do not prove sufficient to the demand; and then one might seek out other religions and cultural projects for instruction. In such instances, knowledge of the "other" may reveal gaps or inurements in one's own moral and spiritual life, or elicit agendas that have faded with time. It will then be the task of one's particular theology to evaluate these external factors and, to the degree possible, guide them into the formulations of one's own culture—appropriately transformed and even speaking the native language of one's "faith."

Every actual theology must thus appear in a specific cultural language. In this way, life is infused with an inherited intimacy of purpose and vision. But this said, it must never be forgotten that *theology* itself, as a "discourse about God," has the primary duty of serving God alone—not some particular religious formulation or tradition. This means helping make the world "God-real" or God-actual (in Buber's terms) by thoughtful realizations of the many modalities of divine effectivity, even when these acts conflict with one's personal or social interests. So conceived, theology must serve the divine realm faithfully, especially when human nature gets the better of God's Godhood and runs its effluxes into the ruts of small-mindedness or routine. Theology and its guardians must therefore be diligent in their duty. I would even suggest that such vigilance is the sacred trust of theology, and provides a prophetic beacon against spiritual torpor.

From General to Jewish Theology

RESTATING THE TASKS OF THEOLOGY

As we come to the conclusion of this chapter, let us consolidate our reflections about human experience and the place of theology in that domain.

The vastness of existence impinges upon us everywhere and at all times, and the theologically minded take their stand within this reality—not to carve it up into verbal objects for practical use, but to participate in its ongoing manifestation. The ever-happening effluxes of God's effectivity are mute and meaningless until we speak. Only then does the world become a *creation*; for with this human activity of naming and knowing, the mystery of divine actuality appears as a manifest presence. The process is interactive. There is no self-evident vastness unmediated by persons and their perceptions; and there is no human imagination that is unaffected by the impulses of reality born of God. Human speaking brings something of the ineffable divine truth to expression, even as that truth ever constitutes the self in all ways.

These two factors interrelate and constantly oscillate. It is the human self's perception of the great vastness that first evokes our human speaking or naming; and reciprocally, what is brought to light transforms the speaker and what is now seeable and sayable. Divine truth and human truth are correlated; and in this correlation the vastness of the world becomes a creation for human habitation and a sphere of instruction. This constant disclosure of portions of God's full truth may be deemed the *revelation* of its meanings for human beings. The depths of these teachings vary, depending on who does the disclosing; and the particular situation (and speaker) affects its perceived authority. Individuals and groups collect records of these disclosures and hold them in sacred regard; they constitute the wisdom of experience and tradition.

Insofar as theology directs attention to the vastness, it cultivates the divine-human correlation of its disclosure. This correlation is also the basis for what is experienced as sacred and treated as ethical. For in the event of human speaking and acting, a given individual stands before a worldly occurrence that has never happened or been manifest in just this way or just this time. The unique shapes of world-happening come to consciousness as traces of the primordial as such; and insofar as they direct the self to thought and action, they also have ethical effects. One is thus brought into an attunement with elemental things; and a living theology tries to cultivate this sensibility and direct it to God. In time, and under the guidance of teachers, patterns of behavior are formulated in order to regulate the sanctity of existence. Within the framework of this earthly sanctity, God is a cultivated presence and theology its handmaiden. One should not forget this. But one can, and then it is the task of theology to reawaken persons to this truth and guide them toward its realization.

A primary task of theology is thus to direct an ever-new attentiveness to the manifold impingements of sight and sound which happen roundabout; in response to these effects one may bring God's all-encompassing effectivity to mind. Everything depends on one's focus or attention. To lose attention is to slip into a mindless habitude that disregards the mystery of the vastness; whereas to regain one's focus is to reprise the world as a sphere of value. The loss of attention is more than a deadness to the life-forms in our world. It also betrays God—the effective ground of all existence. Living theology regards this as a sin of omission. By cultivating an attentive consciousness, theology cultivates the soul and turns it toward God.

I would emphasize three foci of attention cultivated by theology through the resources of one's culture. These are, first of all, the *names* or terms by which we call the vastness into particular zones of presence, articulate values, and speak of divine matters. Second, they are the *persons* in our world through whom we confront the vagaries of character and the challenges of a common existence. Third, they are the *phenomena* (of existence) by which we perceive the great bounty of the world, to which we are ecologically bound on this planet.

As regards our use of names and words: here our very souls are at stake; for how we speak affects who we are and become, and it conditions the character of our consciousness and concern. One must be attentive to this. Words may build and destroy, articulate and ossify, and also invoke or conjoin all sorts of realities. They appear in the mouth or in a text, in values and in evaluations. Words can have a finality; but they need not be final. When words are used mindlessly, or fade and die, the world we live in may become a sphere of rote rituals—or worse. And when this happens, words, and ourselves with them, must be radically revised in order to serve the highest ends of life. This is our ongoing hermeneutical task. We must be sure that the vessels of language mediate the vastness of possibilities emergent from God's effectivity, and that they do so with moral sensibility for what may be called into being. Where necessary, we must clarify or correct our speech with other persons, reinterpret our sacred texts and traditional formulations, and adjust ourselves to what is being said to us in the present or formulated by writings from the past. We do all this for God's sake, for our words provide living habitations for Divinity in the world.

Persons provide another vessel for divine indwelling. We may live on automatic pilot, as it were, or may sharpen our consciousness with respect to what is happening in the human realm; we may live with unsettled spirits, or may strive for some inner balance and composure; and we may live inured or immune to the distinctive pulsations of existence, or try to resonate with these factors and adjust ourselves accordingly. When persons are regarded as embodiments of the effusing vitalities of Divinity, we must seek to nurture their sacred presence by attuning ourselves to their being. This should also be done for God's sake; and it is a task of living theology to keep one alert to this imperative.

And finally, there are the innumerable phenomena of life and existence that occur around us as we live our everyday lives—seeing and hearing, ignoring some things and responding to others. Here too habitude may reign, or we may awaken to a new consciousness of our activities. The resources of tradition may help us focus attention on these events and enable us to receive them in their special sanctity. For the sake of such attunements we must prepare ourselves in readiness, and thus be able to respond in a proper manner. Theological attentiveness will thus be geared to the minutiae of our lives—all the time. In this manner, we may confess at each moment: "Here I am," living thankfully among God's gifts.

Insofar as we may attune ourselves to the inhering formations of God's effectivity, and strive to enhance the life-forms we

encounter and connect them with ever-larger units of reality—
then, in a manner of speaking, we are doing the work of *redemption*.

>>><<<

One should not minimize the difficulty of these theological
practices or mistake their importance. The possibilities of engaging the world as a sphere of sacred values hang in the balance. In the course of time we may perceive fragments of God's
truth in this world, if we attend to the happenings of existence
with humility and alertness; and only in the course of time may
we perhaps understand just which aspects of that truth may be
of human and life-enhancing value, and pass these on to others as forms of tradition that must be protected. How human
awareness makes sense of the vast eros of existence, pulsing out
of its divine sources into life-forms of every sort, and how one
integrates this sense with the perception of decay and the deadening dimensions of thanatos, are the work of culture—guided
by theological integrity. Retreat from this challenge may be due
to a sense of futility before the confusions of life which can prey
upon our minds. The readiness to stand firm in the vastness of
existence is the spiritual alternative. It may be deemed a high
task of living theology to teach this readiness, and to cultivate a
livable sense of reverence before the mystery and reality of God.

Jewish theology must rise to this task, in its own particular
way.

INTRODUCING JEWISH THEOLOGY

What then is Jewish theology, insofar as we can state it at this
point?

First and foremost, Jewish theology is a particular instantiation of theology more generally, as I have characterized it in the
previous discussion. It too is grounded in our life in the natural
world and comes to expression through the forms of the creative
imagination. But Jewish theology will invariably give distinctive

faithful.

tones to the theological orientation as such, and to the ways that it perceives the happenings of the world as crossing points of God's all-encompassing effectivity. Stated succinctly, Jewish theology will provide *particular cultural forms of this truth*, out of the resources of its inherited traditions and ongoing thoughtfulness.

Second, Jewish theology is hermeneutical in a special way. It is not only characterized by the interpretation of experience, grounded in the divine Naught, and its adjustment to shared human values. It is also marked by the accumulation of Jewish interpretations of God's reality and their claim on personal and social life as these have been expressed by inspired individuals and gathered in special collections of sacred writ (scripture) and tradition over the generations. Such interpretations provide the unique character of Jewish living and thought (the Aught of tradition). Each generation must do this work anew. In the most fundamental sense, then, Jewish theology is a *hermeneutical theology*.

Moreover, Jewish theology is a living practice, expressed in deeds and actions, and focused on their character and implications. The moments of human life bring the vastness of existence into focus, and these are acknowledged by particular performances which function as specific sanctifications of God's effectivity. Jewish theology cultivates these behaviors with great seriousness, and tries to inculcate a sense of justice and right insofar as possible. This is an ongoing task, conditioned by inherited traditions and their ongoing transformation or accommodation to new realities. In this further sense, Jewish theology is also a *performative theology*.

And finally, to the extent that performance has a human character, it ascends in significance in proportion to the attention or thoughtfulness given it by human beings. Whatever be the value of certain actions as such, theology is a particular symbolic form of the creative imagination and develops a self-consciousness with respect to its own activity. This consciousness is cultivated by theology so that one may live with the fullest mindfulness before the vitalities of God's reality in this world. Human nature being what it is, such a consciousness must be ever alert to the integrity and character of its deeds, and labor for its ongoing cultivation. A modern Jewish theology will provide particular formulations of this ideal. For this reason, Jewish theology may also be deemed a *transformative theology*.

>>><<<

When we think of Jewish theology and its various components, we are put in mind of its most central statement of principle. This is stated in scripture and has been repeatedly interpreted over the ages. That statement calls us to attention:

> Hear, O Israel, the Lord is our God, the Lord is One!
> And you shall love the Lord your God with all your heart and all your soul and all your might. Let these instructions with which I charge you this day be upon your heart; and teach them to your children, and speak of them when you are at home and away, and when you lie down and when you arise; and bind them as a sign upon your hand and a symbol on your forehead, and write them on the doorposts of your home and on your gates. (Deut. 6:1–4)

Such is the theological charge: to affirm God in one's life, through mind and heart and deed, through teaching and interpretation everywhere; and to cultivate a mindfulness of this duty through signs and symbols, so that one will always be reminded of the sanctity of the body and its actions—in the home (as the domain of one's family and future generations) and in the city (as the domain of society and the sphere of interpersonal values). A modern Jewish theology will do this in its own distinctive way, resonant with our contemporary sensibilities and mind-set.

A Jewish Hermeneutical Theology

Sinai and Torah

Jewish theology begins at Sinai. This is its axial moment—the occasion when, according to scripture, the people of Israel were called to accept God's world-historical dominion and live within the framework of godliness. Judaism acknowledges the centrality of this event (called *matan torah*, "The Giving of Torah"), and places its teachings at the core of religious life. For Jewish theology, there is no passage to spiritual responsibility that does not in some way cross the wilderness of Sinai and stand before this mountain of instruction.

BIBLICAL FOUNDATIONS

For scripture, Sinai is primary and its words are primary. It is foundational in every sense. At this place, the entire people stood before God and received their central theological principles. They were called upon to accept God absolutely ("I the Lord am your God . . . You shall have no other gods besides me"; Exod. 20:2–3), and to worship with integrity. No earthly form could represent

God or depict God's reality ("You shall not make for yourselves a sculpted image . . . You shall not bow down to them or serve them"; vv. 4–5). God was not something to be seen, but solely a voice of instruction ("You heard the sound [voice] of words; no form did you see: only a voice"; Deut. 4:12). Human dignity and life were also fundamental to this instruction: no harmful acts or destructive desires were condoned. Thus says the Decalogue, which forms the matrix of covenant values and the many commandments and duties that shaped the nation and its character. This is first delineated in Exodus 21–24, where absolute demands combine with conditional ones; civil laws are conjoined to capital cases; and ritual practices (offerings linked to the seasons or special occasions) appear alongside ethical ones (norms linked to the broad spaces of everyday life). Repeatedly, justice is combined with compassion: the evildoer must be censured and the needy cared for, and the audience is exhorted to be attentive to the needs of all persons—neighbor and stranger alike. Sinai set the standard. It is a metaphor for cultural *nomos*. It is an axial moment of consciousness.

The event of Sinai was intended to yield a comprehensive commitment, infusing loyalty to God and God's commandments into every area of life. Accordingly, ongoing tradition linked many other rules to this foundational moment—saying, for example, about an altogether independent collection of legal materials, "These are the laws, rules, and instructions that the Lord established, through Moses on Mount Sinai, between himself and the people Israel"; Lev. 26:46). Or in yet another instance, the complex of old and new legal materials found in the book of Deuteronomy (chapters 12–26) is presented en masse as a repetition and explication by Moses of the teachings first given to him by God at Sinai. The terms employed are significant: "It was in the fortieth year . . . that Moses addressed the Israelites in accordance [*ke-khol*] with the instructions that the Lord had given him for them . . . [Then] Moses undertook to expound [*be'er*] this torah" (1:4–5). Listen well to this notice, and its discernible trace of a hermeneutical revolution. We are now told that one called Moses, without divine revelation, explicates some portions of the older instructions for a new generation, and the result is simply called torah. In such a manner, *Sinai* was carried forward into different times as a living word of instruction. This process was not limited to comprehensive formulations. It recurs in more limited ways as well. Many prophets clearly echo the religious spirit of Sinai in their rhetoric, when admonishing the people to return to its theological principles of divine loyalty; and some of them even allude to the Decalogue itself (Hosea 4:1–2; Jer. 7:9), or to assorted religious norms and social ideals (Amos 5:4–15; Isa. 1:17; Ezek. 22:7–12). Moreover, when the nation returned from the Babylonian exile to its homeland, they were guided by one like Moses (Ezra), "who set his heart to inquire of the Torah of the Lord, and to do and to teach statute and judgment in Israel" (Ezra 7:9)—these latter being "the words and the commandments of the Lord and his statues for Israel" (v. 10). Episodes of such Torah instruction also served as the basis for the restoration of the covenant and reconstitution of the nation at this time (Nehemiah 8–9). In a striking manner, these are the external shapes of a theological piety shaped by Torah values and the ongoing study of its texts. But in a more vital way, they also express the deeper spirit of the hermeneutic revolution found in the book of Deuteronomy. In the exhortation cited earlier (Deut. 6:1–4), all who would love God are told to expresses this devotion through observance of the commandments and by teaching them morning and night. Such is the ideal; and then suddenly, in later generations, these spiritual seeds burst forth and the teachings of Sinai become an ever-present theological reality. According to one psalmist, true joy awaits one "whose delight is the Torah of the Lord" and who "studies that teaching day and night" (Ps. 1:2). And more remarkable, not only could a person show devotion to God through ongoing Torah study, but the Torah itself became an object of spiritual love. "How greatly do I love your Torah," another psalmist intones, "it is my study all day long" (Ps. 119:97). These words attest to a second hermeneutical revolution, even a new mode of theological living. They attest to a life transformed by the words of Sinai repeated "all day long" as an act of loving devotion. Focused on God's teachings, and their meaning, the adept was ever bound to the foundational moment of Sinai and its theological core. Later generations developed these ideals and supplemented the teachings of Sinai with the interpretations of ongoing tradition. Different teachers emphasized different topics and values; and various seekers sought the core of Sinai in different intellectual or spiritual principles. But *Sinai* always remained primary. One might even say that there is no authentic Jewish theology outside this covenant core, however diversely it might be conceived or elaborated. For it is the Sinai covenant that has shaped Jewish life and thought over the ages. The many tasks and values of Jewish existence, the diverse images and ideals of divine instruction, and the far-flung conceptions of cultural origins and goals all flow from this scriptural matrix.

Sinai is thus not a one-time event, but for all times; it is not only grounded in the historical past, but hovers in the living present. Sinai stands at the mythic core of religious memory, and the explication of its teachings is a sacred ritual for Judaism.

"On this day they came to the desert of Sinai" (Exodus 19:1). Now did they really come on *this day*? Rather [learn from this] that when you learn My words they should not be old in your eyes, but as if Torah was given today; for Scripture does not say *ha-yom* ("on the day") but *ba-yom hazeh* ("On this day [they came to . . . Sinai]").

>>><<<

I shall demonstrate this process of study below, and present it as a primary element in the generation of ongoing theological consciousness. But since we are only now turning toward Jewish theology, it is first necessary to ask: What is the theological center of the Sinai event? If Sinai is the beginning of Jewish theology, what is the beginning of Sinai, and what is *its* core? This last query is less a historical question than a hermeneutical one, and it addresses anyone who would still hope to stand at Sinai, in new times and circumstances.

I would begin an answer this way: Jewish theology begins with Sinai, but God was before this event. The mysterious vitality of divine effectivity was endlessly named long before Sinai; and it just as endlessly exceeded these many formulations. Humans search and sift the happenings of life for signs of vitality, order, and power—and try to locate and denominate these benefactions, calling them gods while inducing their favor. Standing at the surface of life, the sources are ever hidden and presumed, pulsing mysteriously into the rhythms of existence. In the ongoing human attempts to give an account, there thus emerge the many Named Ones, divinities large and small, and the perceived or imagined activities that seem to create little "bonds" with Being, ever so elusive, moment by moment. At the very least, such naming attempts to habituate the illimitable vastness of existence and its mysteries so that one can get on with some degree of order and control. We name things and thus try to "have them" in our grasp; and we transmit these matters to others. One could hardly begin anew at every moment, and fortunately there is no need to do so. We rely not only on our own formulations but on those of others as well, gathering them together in bundles of information. Tradition transmits what seems to work, and marks off the imagined dangers; teachers teach this inheritance, and try to show how to think about its implications; and narratives report events worth remembering, and also invent literary types for idealization and reflection. The more such matters are repeated, the more the formulations are stabilized and the instructions appear self-evident. The fragility of inventiveness gradually fades from view, and our theological constructions seem like matters of fact, seemingly part of the nature of things.

Cultures grow along these pathways, and every achievement is a triumph of the human spirit. But the vastness remains, always eluding our syntax and mental vigor; and this truth must be borne in mind, lest the little victories of the human imagination become a mask of self-delusion. We may have faith in our use of

names (for gods and things); but we must remember that they
have been wrought from the unfathomable unboundedness for
human use, and thus do not reflect the ultimate truth. To forget
this is folly. The covenant helps focus on such essential matters.

It takes much living to be ready for the covenant, and much
courage to live in its truth. The life-tracks emerging from Eden
wander along the hardscrabble of the earth, with its tasks of labor and sustenance and mastery. The little portion of knowledge
wrested from Eden seems just enough to bring confusion and
domination, and the conviction that destiny lies in the coherence of the generations, the traditions of the ancestors, and life
in a safe haven on the earth. This belief is even deemed a blessing. Who would deny it? But it also hunkers after habit and a
god of predictable promises. Scripture gives evidence of this—in
its depiction of many lives and beliefs and attitudes in the long
years prior to the spiritual breakthrough of a covenant worthy
of God's truth, and not one that merely satisfies human needs
and desires. Some trace of this religious revolution happened at
Sinai, and scripture also provides an account of it. We must therefore try to approach this textual record for the theological moment
it expresses. Gradually, we might even enter its circle of language
and shape our understanding through its formulations. And then,
perhaps, the heart-flash of its words will be revealed to our souls
and we too may stand before that olden moment and be instructed
anew.

Such is our hermeneutical hope; it is a process grounded in
humility.

Why was the Torah given in the desert? To teach you:
that if a person does not hold himself as unpossessed as a desert,
he does not become worthy of the words of the Torah.

TWO PARADIGMS

Jewish theology begins at Sinai and makes a claim on a community. But the decisive turn to Sinai is made by the solitary spirit.

Indeed, it is in the individual soul where the truth of Sinai and its actuality are first formed.

Two moments in the life of Moses are pivotal and paradigmatic. Through an interpretation of their scriptural account, we can reflect on the core of the covenant as a theological event, both for individual persons and for religious communities. The first moment marks an awakening from the mindlessness of habitude, and through it we may perceive a first intimation of what covenant attentiveness might mean. It occurs in the wilderness, amidst the labors of sustenance and routine, in an endless terrain of sameness.

> Now Moses, while tending the flock of his father-in-law Jethro, priest of Midian, drove the flock into the wilderness, and came to the mountain of God at Horeb. An angel of the Lord appeared to him in fiery flame from the midst of the bush; and he looked, as the bush was all aflame, yet the bush was not consumed. Moses said, "Let me turn aside, and behold this wondrous sight; for why isn't the bush consumed?" When the Lord saw that he had turned aside to look, God called to him from the midst of the bush, saying: "Moses, Moses!"; and he replied, "Here I am." (Exod. 3:1–4)

Here then is Moses, defined by his work and family affiliation, driving a flock of sheep into the wilderness. The narrator presents this scene in a matter-of-fact way, for just this was the nature of Moses's life: it was simply matters of fact and easily portrayed in natural terms. The circumstance is all silence. And suddenly it happens: from out of this stupor something uncanny appears to the shepherd's eye. At once everything is seeing and looking and appearing, and hardly matters of fact. The common has become spectacle, and there is a caesural opening in the viewer himself, who decides to turn from his everyday tasks and behold the wondrous visage—at first out of sheer curiosity. It all occurs unexpectedly. A manifestation takes shape out of the vastness, revealing something of the mystery that can transfigure the natural world and set it off as holy. Stopped in his tracks by this vision, Moses then hears a calling out of the depths. Now all is voice, addressed to himself alone; he is called by name, for only he is spoken to. Transfixed, Moses is entirely the person called. His response of "Here I am" is all subjectivity and all presence. He confesses to being just there, at that moment. This call is a call of destiny and demand. Out of the silence, Moses hears the appeal of commitment. It was similar to the call addressed to the ancestors, Abraham, Isaac, and Jacob, in generations past, which instructed them to guide the people to their land of promise; and now Moses understands that he too has been summoned to step out of his everyday routine and see his life as part of a larger destiny, unfolding beyond his personal purposes (Exod. 3:3–10). Now all is mission, consumed by the consciousness of being sent.

But Moses somehow knows that something more specific will be demanded by the people, when he tells them that he has been sent to Egypt at the behest of the ancestral God; and he also knows that for humans the claim to authority and the assertion of authoritative agency require a name. And so he asks the God who has addressed him to disclose the Divine Name; and he is told to tell the nation that "Ehyeh-Asher-Ehyeh has sent me to you" (v. 14). The meaning of this phrase is something like "I shall be as I shall be," and serves as a statement of God's ever-effectual Godhood—not nameable as such. Thus, remarkably, no nameable name is given to this primordial divine manifestation; for what is stated is merely an epithet of unconditioned occurrence (a transcendent, world-effecting "thatness"). But truly, nothing else could more significantly underscore this event and its theological character. Out of the depths the Divine breaks into human consciousness, but it cannot be fixed or formulated; it can only be attested to as a compelling presence, coming to be as it will be, again and again, and changing a person's life. The connection of this name with the fiery configuration that addressed Moses was momentary; but the truth he experienced went beyond this particular occurrence. From the divine side, God "shall be" as God shall be, we are told, and one can say nothing further about it. Whereas from the human side, a person must simply be

attentive to the vastness all around, for it is just here that God's
effectivity inheres; and it may be experienced with such acuity as
to seem supernatural to one's normal sensibility. The correlation is crucial. The divine "I shall be" requires a living human attentiveness for its realization as an event of earthly
significance; for it is only through such a human attentiveness, so
disruptive of normal perception, that the vastness appears invested
with an uncommon presence, and its nameless mysteries, incom-
prehensibly effectuated by God, erupt as a call to the individual
self.

Thus something transcending the person Moses is revealed
through this ancient narrative about his spiritual transformation
into a man of destiny. As a call to respond to this encounter and
be faithful to it, Moses's experience (so elliptically formulated in
scripture) provides a first intimation of the nature of covenant. It
has broader implications for us as readers; and we must therefore
try to attend to them and give them voice. In this way, the old
scriptural report of a theological experience may also become a
religious event in its own right—a word of living instruction to
subsequent generations.

I would put it this way: this initiating induction of Moses
into a covenant with God (Exod. 3:15) calls its readers to the
need for attentiveness to the ever-new "I shall be" of Divinity
throughout earthly existence. Such a mindfulness gives value to
each element in one's daily experience; for in every feature of
the world something of the unseeable face of God may be perceived, and something of the all-unsayable name of God may be
named. But this sacred perception must be had with a humble
discretion, as Moses himself understood when he concealed his
face from God's felt presence (v. 6). For there can be no unmediated seeing of God's actuality in the vastness. The same holds
for every attempt by language to depict worldly modalities of the
Illimitable. The "I shall be" is infinite and ineffable in its happenings; for the One Who says "I shall be" is the Ground of the
actual potentiality of that which shall be at every moment. This,
we are told, is the truth of the holy tetragrammaton YHWH

(which verbally denominates the One Who "shall be" forever; v. 15). Indeed, scripture itself would give us to suppose that this very Name (YHWH) is a reformulation of the personal epithet EHYH ("I shall be"), and refers to God as the primordial reality: "Shall-Be."

Perceiving this wisdom somewhat, one enters a covenant with God—establishing bonds with the divine effectivity as it is and happens in the world. But this remains an individual truth, focused on singular moments of religious consciousness. It is not yet the communal reality of Sinai. Hence the first experience of Moses only provides a model for theological reflection about the primariness of covenant living in one's personal life; and it is only with Moses's second experience that we can derive some insight into the way a covenant may also establish a social structure for God-centered living. It is the foundation of this form that is so primary for biblical religion and theology; and its ongoing revision is of absolute centrality for Jewish theology and its various life-forms.

Come and hear.

THE COMMUNAL EVENT

Many lives must be lived before Sinai is possible; and many teachers have to stand in the vastness before God's infinite "Shall-Be," pondering its truth and its implications for human life, before Sinai becomes a reality. The lives of the ancestors make up this chain of experiences, as do their perceptions of divine efficacy and protection; the character of the ancestors also makes up this chain of tradition, as do the accounts of their virtues and failures. Finally, the actions and beliefs of strangers are linked to this great chain of wisdom as well, and contribute to new ways of thinking about life. One must therefore sift the deposits of living transmitted from the past, discerning the import of their cultural experiences; one has to think widely about the importance of certain acts, and wonderingly about their consequences; and one has to be aware of the teachings of other peoples, and register the value of their achievements and the patterns to be avoided. In short: real knowledge of birth and death, of slavery and freedom, and of wandering and despair must enter the hearts of many people, and especially the leaders and teachers among them—and then Sinai is possible. For Sinai is the result of an accumulated wisdom, however incomplete in itself, and however much it is in need of ongoing supplementation or revision. It first happens only after a certain flowering of the human spirit—not before.

The life of Moses provides a second moment of paradigmatic importance for reflecting on the event of Sinai (portrayed in Exodus 19–24), and on Jewish theology as well.

Something gathers in a person like Moses, accumulating out of the great past and present of the nation. Something gathers in him through a spiritual consciousness transformed by insight into the infinite possibilities of God's "I shall be" in the everyday, and especially by the specific tasks of leadership, whereby heeding this watchword requires an ever-changing but focused persistence. Bits and pieces of a gathering wisdom collect in Egypt as Moses learns that he must instruct people who could not readily attend to his new words, because "they are crushed of spirit and the weight of bondage" (Exod. 6:13); as he learns to understand suffering and stubbornness, and the importance of freedom and worship to express dignity and identity; as he also perceives the power of rituals to memorialize the past and to sanctify time (Exodus 12 and 16); and as he is able to learn vital cultural information from others, even foreigners—in this instance about establishing judicial procedures and a hierarchy of responsibilities (Exod. 18). All these matters gather as a series of personal insights; but they do not yet constitute the immediate conditions for a national covenant.

These conditions only unfold somewhat later—once again in the wilderness, and once more near a mountain of God (Exod. 19:1–2). In the course of the people's journeys, at their collective encampment near Sinai, the man Moses was again singled out and summoned.

The Lord called to him from the mountain, saying, "Thus shall you say to the house of Jacob and declare to the people of Israel: 'You have seen what I did to the Egyptians, how I bore you on eagles' wings and brought you to me. Now then, if you will truly hear my voice and keep my covenant, you shall be a special treasure to me among all the nations; surely all the earth is mine, and you shall be to me a kingdom of priests and a holy nation.'" (vv. 3–6)

The scene is set in the course of daily existence. The narrator captures this by locating the moment at a stage in the national travels. "After having journeyed from Rephidim, they entered the wilderness of Sinai and encamped in the wilderness" (Exod. 19:2). The accent is on movement in space, nothing more. And then a theological event happens: God calls to Moses and tells him what he should say to the people. The stress is now on speaking and hearing; there is no vision, and the sole reference to sight actually marks memory and experience. But that is not all. The text focuses on the nation's destiny and its transformation through hearing and obeying the divine voice. This is the conditioning factor. "*If*" they heed the covenant, *then* they will become "a kingdom of priests and a holy nation." There is thus a call to attentiveness filled with consequence, emphasizing that a divinely guided life requires ongoing commitment. The details are not specified, but the communal aspect of the covenant is. When God tells Moses, "[These are the words that you shall speak] to the house of Jacob and declare to the people of Israel" (v. 6), the reference is to the overarching demand for national allegiance, and the assurance that covenant living can lead to holiness. The event of Sinai becomes possible at this point; for not only is the ideal of the covenant enunciated, but all the people say as one, "All that the Lord has spoken *we* shall do" (v. 8). This is a commitment to the overall principle: one must live life in a special way and with a dutiful awareness. The specifics await another occasion.

That moment happens three days later. We must attend to the literary depiction of that scene in order to derive its theological implications. The event doesn't happen in the blankness of the silent wilderness, but as a numinous event erupting in the natural world: "there was thunder, and lightning, and a dense cloud upon the mountain"; and there was "trembling" among the people in the camp as "the whole mountain trembled violently" (Exod. 19:16–18). "Smoke rose like the smoke of a kiln" as God appeared "in fire" and roared like "thunder." This was an unapproachable event, a shuddering of the surrounding vastness, and an unleashing of its fearsome forces. There is nothing stated here of duty and task; and nothing of religion and morality. There is only violent storm. And this too had to pass through one like Moses for him to be a leader and a teacher. Hearing and seeing all this, "Moses spoke, and the Lord answered him in thunder" (v. 19). This is not any kind of human communication—not yet; it rather lets the violent vastness pass through the self as an awesome divine truth. Moses must first embody something of the fullness of Being (God's "Shall-Be"), beyond all social value, before he can speak truly as a teacher for life and godliness.

Slowly things took shape in his mind, and "Moses went down to the people and spoke to them" (Exod. 19:25). What follows is not a terrifying roar, but a divine instruction in human terms—a verbal articulation of the details of commitment and action (Exodus 20). As earlier, this is referred to as "all these words." But this is more than a general exhortation; it is an overall adumbration of the conditions and consequences of obedience. For now there is a clarification of principles and a specification of duties. Some of these elements are stated with absolute finality as unconditional commands; these include the command to worship God alone, and not to make images of God from anything imaginable or seeable on the earth ("You shall have no other gods besides me . . . You shall not make for yourself a sculptured image, or any likeness of what is in the heavens above and the earth below . . . [and] bow down to them"); and they include the norms of parental honor and the value of human life and property ("You shall honor your father and mother . . . You shall not murder . . . [or] commit adultery . . . [or] steal . . [or] covet . . . anything that is your neighbor's" [Exod. 20:12–17]). Other elements are presented as the conditioned details of life. Thus the overarching "if" of Exodus 19:5 (bearing on the performance of divine duties) is reformulated into a frequentative "if," dealing with the possibilities of life. *If* you do this or that, *then* such are the consequences. Included are the attempts to formulate a life of justice and righteousness, in order to enact the sanctity of life. Much is specified and much qualified: the possibilities of injury and theft are specified, as are robbery and accident; untoward behaviors are detailed, as is improper speech; the values of persons and property are evaluated, as is concern for the neighbor and stranger; and repeatedly, one is charged to guard against falseness and disregard and cheating. These are the "ifs" and "thens" of everyday life. And with changing circumstances these "ifs" and "thens" are further qualified and extended, and new matters taken into consideration. There are initially the rules of the covenant in Exodus 21–24; and then there are other rules on similar or new topics in Leviticus 18–25, as well as the revisions and explications in Deuteronomy 12–26. "All these words" embrace the fullness and extent of lived life—at first in principle, through principal topics; and then over time, in annotated detail and through secondary specifications.

This is the covenant: the great vastness of world-being is shaped into a sphere of religious instruction and duty for communal life. Moses begins the theological process. As he stands fast in the God-effecting, swirling howl, and communicates religious norms for the people, he exemplifies a kind of spiritual living. Language is now a shaping of the illimitable into viable speech, articulating values and pious living. Moses had to stand firm in this divinely wrought vastness, and experience its many interfusing possibilities, so that he could knowingly speak about a God who could not be imagined or portrayed; and he had to stand firm in the amoral welter of world-being, and know its inherent indifference to human plans and purposes, so that he could thoughtfully craft norms and values over this void. Something of God's all-illimitable truth passed through him at Sinai so that it could then become a human instruction—providing an ongoing religious ideal on earth.

Moses thus exceeds Job and Elijah. In stirring scenes, the latter two individuals variously endured the caesural vastness and the storm of divine reality, which so unhinges small-minded and self-centered formulations; and each of them succumbed in silent submission. Surely in this rupture of sensibility both Job and Elijah undergo a change of religious subjectivity; and therefore the example of their lives is instructive and of value. But neither of them formulates a covenant with this God-infixed whirlwind—certainly not by humanizing it or molding it to human pretensions, which would be folly; but by trying to forge a life of holiness in its midst. This however is precisely what Moses tries to do; and just this is the different model he offers. Standing in the divine storm, he bends this caesural event into forms and values for communal existence. In so doing, he offers an ideal of a covenant life that is cognizant of the thunderous vastness and its terrors, and sees religious life as a shoring up of deeds of holiness and justice in this setting. In some cases, natural potentialities deriving from God were strengthened for the empowerment of human life; but in other instances, spiritual values were formulated to counteract raw natural urges, and thus strengthen other God-given gifts. And because he knew the raw facticity of God's "Shall-Be," Moses would always allow the great plenitude of divine reality to affect the ongoing character of covenant existence. This is evident in the continuing revision and development of the norms themselves; for these changes happen only insofar as one is not merely the bearer of inherited practices, but remains attuned to all that overflows them in the fullness of existence. All those who would inherit this theological wisdom—the dual awareness of an all-illimitable divine reality *and* the human task of shaping it into forms of human value—must likewise bear this need for ongoing attunement in mind and cultivate it.

"A THREEFOLD CHORD": TYPES OF TORAH

Over time, Judaism has formulated ways of thinking about these matters.

The Torah provides a rich record of the shaping of the divine thunder into a human voice and viable human terms. This record, which includes traces of the ongoing revision of the norms, has been referred to since rabbinic antiquity as the *torah she-bikhtav*, the Written Torah, and has been revered as a canonical corpus. In it, the originary voice of covenant living has been inscribed; for it has become a scripture, fixed in form and sacred in character. Instructive in their own right, the letters of this Written Torah are infused with the spirit of ancient Israel.

But the words were also infused with the ongoing spirit of Jewish living, and founded upon its principles and formulations. The emergent record of this infusion (which includes traces of the vast revisions of the Written Torah as legal norms and theological teachings) has also been named since rabbinic antiquity, and referred to as the *torah she-be'al peh*, the Oral Torah. This is the multifaceted witness to ongoing covenant living and thinking, and characterized as something spoken through study and sustained by the ongoing articulations of tradition.

Why does this voice arise? One reason is surely the perceived need to understand and explain the Written Torah. But then the Oral Torah would only be a series of glosses and meager annotations. So something "more" must occasion this massive achievement. Put theologically, I would say that this "something more" is God's illimitable investiture of Being, the far-flung vastness of divine effectivity, pressing upon human consciousness on a daily basis.

This divine reality precedes the Written Torah, as said earlier, and may be designated as the *torah kelulah*, the Torah of All-in-All—an infinite enfoldment of all that could ever be in our world. Only this Torah truly comes from the mouth of God, forever and ever, as the kiss of divine truth upon the vastness of world-being. This kiss seals all existence with the touch of divine presence; and it breathes into existence something of the actuality and effectivity of God, for this kiss and this breath are, so to speak, the primordial and ever-happening saying of God's ineffable Name: a saying that is an actualizing and effectuating of the Illimitable. Only those who can hear an imaginable echo of that Name (and Naming) resounding silently through all the orders of Being, and who bend their hearts to it in attentive love, can sense an imaginable something of God's true Torah and witness to it with their lives. Such masters may perceive in the divine Name some imaginable something of all the sounds and shapes that resound throughout existence, and may thereby reveal, through their attentive hearts, such sounds and shapes as may guide human life. These formulations are revealed out of the cloud of Sinai as a Torah *from* God. But it is not the absolute Torah *of* God, the *torah kelulah*, whose reality throbs around the letters and words of the Torah from Sinai—and reminds those with ears to hear that the immense "Shall-Be" of God ever exceeds the written "just this" of scripture. "This" artifact may indeed be something like "the Torah which Moses placed before the Israelites" in a time long past (Deut. 4:44); but it is not God's primordial Torah, the *torah kelulah*.

Moses our master knew this when he first shaped the Torah of All-in-All for the specifics and values of earthly life; and he never forgot this theological truth in his lifetime, as he repeatedly reformulated his initial instructions, variously attuning the Torah of Sinai to this quintessential reality—as he grew in wisdom and experience, and as times and circumstances changed. Thus the *torah kelulah* preceded Sinai (it being an expression of the utmost divine primordiality); and it pulses throughout Being as a whole. This is also the theological reality to which the disciples of Moses respond, knowingly or not, when they bring the exigencies of life into the domain of the Written Torah, and transform both scripture and life reciprocally. The result of such attentiveness is the Oral Torah—ever changing and ever expanding, because it is ever lived in the depths of the *torah kelulah*.

This is covenant living, the product of covenant theology.

Jewish theology thus begins at Sinai—but it is hermeneutically so much more.

Torah and Hermeneutical Theology

What is hermeneutical theology? How may we understand it in the context of Jewish theology?

As I have begun to present it in the preceding section, hermeneutical theology grounds religious thought in texts (scripture) and in life (the *torah kelulah*). Thus thinking theologically about scriptural passages like Exodus 3 and 19 orients us to deeper perceptions of life, engaged and decoded hermeneutically, and may even sharpen our attention to a perception of its religious vitality; reciprocally, our (interpreted) life-experiences keep our readings of scripture rooted in the everyday and guide us to interpret its theological dimensions in the light of truths known to us in the course of life. I would put it this way: we interpret scripture and life for the sake of scripture and life. To the extent that scripture is responsive to our interpretations of life, ever repeated and always open, the sphere of Sinai is expanded; and to the degree that our lives are responsive to the texts and life-paradigms of scripture, themselves subject to hermeneutical attentiveness, they are illumined by its spiritual expressions.

The relationship between the received text and life-situations unfolds in the course of interpretation. The teachings of scripture become known only through exegetical engagement with their concrete expressions—not through any abstract deliberation or reflection. This is an essential principle of hermeneutical theology. The cultural archive must become a living voice, and the written formulations must become direct address; one's life and the life-world presented in the text must coincide in a dynamic way. Simply applying correlative information to the text is a mere archeological enterprise, a task of gathering and sorting. It is only when the textual content is humanly appropriated as a living truth of existence that our own life fills out its exegetical spaces, and its linguistic features infuse our consciousness with challenge and possibility. Then the scriptural text offers models of theological living, of life lived in the context of God, and we live a citation-centered existence.

Scripture may thus provide literary forms and expressions to help think about life, and also expand its theological threshold; similarly, our lives may offer modes of experience for thinking about scripture, and thus give its theological elements a more direct or personal dimension. The literary forms of scripture are diverse and multifaceted, and include types of narrative and law and discourse. Our human life-forms are also multifaceted, and these may correspondingly include accounts of experience, legal depictions, and dialogues. Interpreting texts well and carefully may benefit our lives, and vice versa. Hence the task of a hermeneutical theology is to interpret sacred scripture in ways that sharpen our religious awareness for the sake of a God-centered life, and to allow our reinterpreted lives to disclose ever-wider and deeper spiritual realities of God's *torah kelulah*. Becoming ever attuned to the alphabet of creation, for the sake of serving God's creative happenings, is the ultimate aim of hermeneutical theology.

A religion that can serve this goal can serve the truth.

And insofar as Judaism fosters forms of reading as a spiritual practice in order to cultivate a God-centered life, it too may serve this goal.

We now turn to these matters in closer detail, and shall see how one may be more theologically attuned to the mute syntax of things and persons through different modes of scriptural interpretation. In this way, scripture may again provide a dynamic matrix for thought and value—coordinating our fractured consciousness in altogether different life-circumstances. In this way too, scriptural study may also provide caesural openings into the vastness of life and its inhering and ever-imponderable divine depths.

MODES OF JEWISH SCRIPTURAL INTERPRETATION

Jewish thought has developed four principal modes of scriptural reading, which variously train the mind and heart for a life of spiritual alertness in the world. These hermeneutical activities cultivate different types of religious perception and consciousness, even diverse theological orientations and ways of living with God in mind. Separately, these modalities of interpretation have been designated by the following terms: *peshat* (the so-called plain or contextual meaning of scripture; the direct and ungarnished sense, so to say, insofar as we can know it); *derash* (the far-ranging theological and legal reformulations of scripture; providing more indirect and mediated meanings of the text, in response to the ongoing challenges of religious life and belief); *remez* (the assorted hints or allusions of scripture, insofar as its words and phrases may be decoded to reveal moral or philosophical or psychological allegories); and *sod* (the intuited spiritual or mystical dimensions of scripture, inseparable from the cosmic and supernal truths of divine Being). Taken altogether, this exegetical quaternary has been denominated by the acronym *PaRDeS* (a term that connotes the "paradise" or "garden" of scriptural senses). This designation also points to the multifaceted truth of Jewish tradition, which can sponsor diverse meanings and truths simultaneously.

We shall consider each of these modes in turn, focusing on correlations between forms of reading (and interpretation) and forms of living (ethical and theological). In this way, we shall hope to see how a sensibility (or various sensibilities) cultivated by scriptural study may serve life and theological consciousness. Following this exploration of the four types, thoughts about their conjunction as a complex truth shall be offered.

>>><<<

The ensuing discussion will thus engage one of the essential tasks of a Jewish theology: to show how Judaism (through scripture) fosters various forms of God-consciousness and spiritual awareness. In the process, I shall speak in terms that make sense to our modern mentalities (as adumbrated earlier). Starting from our lives in the natural world, each mode will move from this primary ground to its own theological horizon, such as we may imagine it and give it expression. Scriptural study mediates between the two—as befits an authentic Jewish theology.

Peshat. One of the great sages of medieval Ashkenaz (in northern Europe), Rabbi Solomon ben Isaac (known familiarly as Rashi), once referred to his sense of the *peshat* as the concern to interpret the words of scripture as they fittingly unfold within their own contexts, and as the teachings of tradition fit sensibly into this same literary frame. In formulating this (dual) understanding, Rashi utilized a phrase from an old biblical proverb, "Like apples of gold in a filigree of silver *is a word fitly spoken*" (*davar davur al ofanav*; Prov. 25:11, my emphasis). The original figure of latticework provides the vehicle for speaking about the fitness of a specific linguistic turn or formulation; and thus, in its adapted use as a principle of interpretation, it specifies the need to read the words of scripture rightly as they fit together in their primary context. One may think further about this phrase, and thereby enter it as a mind space for hermeneutical reflection.

Reading for the *peshat* sense involves a subjugation of the self to the words of the text as they appear, both singly and in syntactic combinations. At first glance, the words are the terms of ordinary discourse, which one uses in the common world, and by means of which one is oriented in space and time among the persons or elements that constitute this realm. But almost immediately the reader is caught up short: the words on the page or scroll (as read or recited) are not the words spoken by living persons in the ordinary world, for all their apparent worldly character and seeming naturalness. This is because the accounts and discourses are not occurring among the events of interpersonal life, where the human voice is actual in one form or another. They rather occur as second-order constructions of the literary imagination, as creative transformations of the terms of ordinariness. Thus, for all their apparent similarity to the language of everyday speech, the words of a text, such as scripture, are semblances of life-acts and speech. This need not mean that these semblances are fictive or designed to deceive. It only highlights the fact that the words are intentional acts of composition, produced after an event or with some measure of reflective deliberation. Moreover, they are mute signs on a page and remain dormant until filled with human phrasing and emphasis. They thus rise into actuality through the role of a reader, who calls them forth in the process of reading. In just this way, the "world of the text" is built up. But the words do not answer back. They remain silent in their scriptural realm, and by virtue of this fundamental silence constantly remind us of their otherness. Accordingly, the text never indicates that it is being misread; and it is only we the readers who perceive gaps or ambiguities, who struggle to make sense of uncommon usages and complex syntax, or who try to determine whether a word should be heard with a certain overtone, and whether it should be construed in terms of nuance or verbal play. A reader determined to disclose the *peshat* of a text must therefore proceed from word to word, building up successively larger networks of sense, in order to determine what a particular word may mean in context; what some phrase denominates elsewhere; and so on. We even align emergent readings with subsequent ones, trying to make sense as we go along. Such creations of meaning are therefore cumulative, the meaning of the text being the spectrum of possible meanings that unfold in the process. As readers we come to the text with a presumption of coherence, assuming that, as the expression of a human mind, it is fundamentally intelligible—no matter how long it may take to get the hang of it.

The process of reading at this level thus trains one in patience and care before a given textual phenomenon. It also trains one in the need for attunement to the distinct rhythms and pace of a text. Scripture, for example, is filled with words; but it is also filled with spaces and elisions and archaic deposits. Accordingly, the reader must enunciate the speech forms silently or aloud; and in so doing it may even help to adjust oneself to the perceived breath units of the passage. For to the extent that the written text is some semblance of human life in language, these units may also establish the verbal rhythms of the text and provide some help toward understanding its message. Hence the careful reader will be attentive to the dynamic relation between verbal articulation and breath—an articulation that splits open the silences between the words, and gives them shape and quality; and a breathing that works in and through the words, carrying its distinct tonalities, but also carrying one word into the next. Tone and timbre resonate within the silence of breath; and breath itself becomes audible in the patterns of sound that constitute the words of the text.

A reader attuned to these matters will realize that there is no one *peshat*, but that this sense is variously constructed in the act of reading, in the act of speaking with other readers, and in the act of building up a context of meaning for the words of the text—first and foremost from within the document itself (its signs and putative significations), but also within the context of other texts (with related terminology and topics) from a similar time and place.

Let us take an example from scripture.

> Jacob left Beer-sheba, and set out for Haran. He came upon some place and stayed for the night, as the sun had set; and then took one of the stones of that place, and set it under his head, and lay down at that place. He had a dream: Here now: a stairway was set on the ground and its top reached to heaven; and now: angels of God were going up and down on it. And now: the Lord stood beside him, and said: "I am the Lord, the God of your father Abraham, and the God of Isaac. The ground you are lying on I shall give to you and your offspring; and your offspring shall be like the dust of the ground; and you shall spread out to the west and to the east and to the north and to the south. And all the families of the earth shall bless themselves by you and your offspring. And now: I shall be with you: I shall protect you where-ever you go and shall bring you back to this land. I shall not leave you until I have done what I have promised."
>
> Jacob then awoke from his sleep and said: "Surely the Lord is in this place, and I did not know it!" Awestruck, he said: "How awesome is this place; this is none other than the house of God: the gateway to heaven." When he arose in the morning, Jacob took the stone that he had set up under his head, and set it up as a pillar and poured oil upon its top. He named that place Bethel; but previously it had been called Luz. (Gen. 28:10–19)

Having read the passage, we ask, what is the plain sense? What would constitute a *peshat* reading of this episode? How do its words "fit" together?

Let us enter the reading process. The beginning is abrupt: it starts with a personal name (Jacob) followed by a verb (left) and a place-name (Beer-sheba), the point of origin; next there is a phrasal verb (set out) and then another place-name (Haran), the destination. The emphasis is on movement and direction; and the text continues with a volley of verbs that give the narration a swift pace and an emphasis on action. Internal states are not indicated. The abrupt beginning does not state the motivation for the journey, and the reader must remember the two reasons mentioned a bit earlier: Jacob's mother had told him to flee to Haran, because of the wrath of his brother Esau, whom he had deceived (Gen. 27:42–44; the negative motivation); and his father Isaac told him to return to his ancestral homeland in order to marry within the native clan (28:1–2; the positive motivation). Isaac went on to offer the prayer that the clan deity El Shaddai make him fertile, and that he receive the blessing of many off-spring given to Abraham, and inherit the land promised to him (vv. 3–4). This last matter is clearly alluded to in our text, which also speaks of the ancestral blessing of land and offspring; but the reader will also be struck by the more specific echoes of Genesis 12:2–3, including its reference to all nations being "blessed through" the patriarch. One will also be surprised to note that the divine Name given here is YHWH (the Lord), since that particular name had not yet been disclosed; in fact, when scripture does specify this disclosure to Moses (in Exodus 6:1), we are told that it was only at this later date that the name YHWH was revealed, and that the patriarchs themselves only knew God as El Shaddai. Surely the strong hand of later tradition has impacted the language of our text. A first-time reader of scripture may not know this; but this same reader will nevertheless be puzzled by the difference between Isaac's own statement of the divine bless-ing and the one recorded in our passage.

The text emphasizes the fact of place (*maqom*); this anonymous spatial designation is repeated both at the outset of the unit, be-fore the dream, and later, after Jacob awoke and named the locale Bethel. The repetitions of this word thus frame the dream se-quence, as do the references to the stone set up as a pillow under his head. This place marks the site where the external movement stops, along a horizontal axis; and there is a shift to the internal state of a dream, featuring the vertical axis of the stairway and the up-and-down movement upon it. In the outer world, Jacob is alone, while his dream is filled with divine images.

The dream state happens abruptly. It is marked by sudden appearances, shifting scenes, and interior speech (all repeatedly marked by the word *ve-hinneh*, "and now"). The opening scene of ascending and descending angels appears to be symbolic, but it is not interpreted in our passage; rather, it serves to give a sense of transcendence to this earthly event. For this reason, one might perhaps be inclined to understand the reference to the Lord standing "near" Jacob as indicating his presence "above him" (the preposition *alav* is deftly ambiguous, simultaneously marking divine intimacy and distance, immanence and transcendence). In any case, the divine speech is all promise and blessing, joining Jacob to a line of ancestors; and it is all assurance and assistance, stressing help and guidance: the Divinity YHWH is all promise and all protection; God's human wards are not alone.

This dream unit ends with Jacob's awakening, and is marked by his immediate confession of awe, acknowledging that the place where he lay was a sacred site, linking heaven and earth; and then, soon thereafter, also by his dedication of the place through an act of ritual unction and by renaming it Bethel, a "House of El." The reader can only by puzzled by this designation, since it was YHWH who had appeared to the man Jacob, not a deity named El (Shaddai), who was mentioned earlier as the god of his father Isaac (all this being another hint to the reader that the text is no mere report, but a product of tradition). In any event, the ritual dedication of the stone marks an act of memorialization. Significantly, the external stone, which had been interiorized in the dream state as a stairway "set up" (*mutzav*) on the earth, with "its head" (*rosho*) reaching to heaven, now becomes the symbolic embodiment of this vision of elevation; and lest we miss this point, the narrator says that Jacob set the stone as a "pillar" (*matzevah*), and poured oil on "its top" (*rosho*).

These textual elements make us consider just how much we readers are guided by the narrative voice and its presentation of the events. At the level of plain sense, the descriptions move seamlessly from the external world of appearances to an internal state of vision and back again, with the clear sense that both dimensions are real, each in its own way: dreams and divine visions are as real here as any worldly circumstances, and can be even more compelling for human behavior. Our text marks this point through the pillar. It signifies the superior reality of the dream imagery over mere earthly matter; indeed, it is precisely the interior state of the dream that gives the worldly elements their meaning and significance.

Let us now leave this specific act of reading and return to our larger reflections.

>>><<<

Reading (scripture) to discern the *peshat* is thus an exercise in attentiveness to the details of the text and its modes of presentation; and it is an exercise in the patient subordination of the self to the otherness of the language which has been selected by the author, but which requires one's readerly engagement to come alive. Determining the *peshat* sense thus requires the reader to attend to the life-context presented in the text: it is dependent on us, for the text does not speak by itself; and we are dependent on it, for the text is not our own speech. Just what is being named and said in the passage?—is the inherent query that propels the reading forward, word by word; and just what is being expressed or verbalized here?—is the great wonderment that fills the reader's heart and unfolds through the process of reading. The reader can never recapitulate the creative event of the composition as a primary articulation and revelation, or become one with its intentions and aims. But there may nevertheless be some recuperation of that unique event through an attentive listening to the words of the passage and a silent recitation of them within one's mouth or mind. Such an attuned responsiveness to a text may be called the ethics of the *peshat*. It is a distinct shaping of consciousness through the act of scriptural interpretation—for the sake of life and theology.

First, life.

We cannot ignore the names of things and persons. They are given to us through the language and tradition of those who bring us into the world and help make it a habitable domain. These names help distinguish one thing from another as points of reference and specification; and the names of persons and things are often virtually indistinguishable from them: for when we call a person by his or her name, or refer to something by its name, we call that person or thing to mind and to presence—just that person or thing, and no other one. If we stand before some visual field, and it passes before us as a series of images, there is a kind of mindlessness about our mental state. But when we name what we see (verbally and explicitly, or silently and implicitly), the persons or objects become something "other." And this otherness gives them moral qualities. The gap that is opened may be derogated as some alienation from immediacy (ecstatic or otherwise); but this does it a grave injustice; for in the consciousness of difference, characterized by names, a person is called upon to make judgments of value and distinction, and to recognize that this individual or that thing is an entity in its own right. How I "read" the world depends on this manner of thoughtfulness.

The names of things call them out of their mere "thingness," and give them presence as "identities" at one level or another, whether as objects to be utilized or entities within specific contexts. In a living engagement with the world, there is always an attempt to read the context of these configurations and adjust oneself to what is required in order to function in this domain, or to embed oneself in this domain in what seems to be an appropriate manner. I would go further: in such living engagements with our environment, there is an ongoing attunement of the self to its clues and terms, and to what is not said. All this varies with the degree of proximity or distance, and of familiarity or strangeness. It will also be decisively affected by persons. In such cases, attunement is not only a patient attentiveness to what is disclosed or may be inferred; it is also a more active subjugation of oneself to the interpersonal relationship that may unfold, verbally or silently. There is now a sharing of words and breath, and of context and life-realm; and now one must realize that this particular person, with just this name and character, who is speaking and acting at this time, is distinct from any other one and must be related to accordingly. Of course, one will inevitably inject past experiences into this new moment as one tries to interpret it and live with it understandingly. But a sphere of otherness must also be allowed to open up so that one may try to read the situation on its own terms as much as possible.

There is no one simple plain sense: the *peshat* of things is never simple or simply given; it is always constructed word by word and action by action, again and again. All this gives me and you a shared world, even a multiplicity of life-worlds. As different names and naming disclose different persons and things, one may stand firm in covenant readiness: ever repeating in the depths, "I shall do and hear" (compare Exod. 24:7) to whatever is called forth or appears. These are "all the things" and "all the words" of divine speech happening in the everyday (the infinite expressions, so to speak, of the *torah kelulah*). In my attentive attunement to all this, the world is revealed as a vast and diverse creation—as a reality of distinctions, and a manifold of diverse kinds. The budding of buds and the speaking-breathing of persons are their own inherent "good," or *tov*, each "according to its kind," always and again; and in responding to this great bounty, always according to the particular nature of each manifestation (trees ever being trees; and persons, persons), the far-flung vastness becomes a creation for human consciousness, an overflowing excess of vitality, or *tivyuta*. In such a way is God, the Name of all names, and Life of all life, "good" for all the All—*tov la-kol*.

This is the theological dimension that unfolds in human life: a mindfulness for each and all, and a binding of oneself to all the specific names and contexts in our world, disclosed in the vastness of God's effectivity, insofar as we can be aware of it. Attentiveness to the permeability and fluctuation of these appearances opens the heart toward the unfathomable depths of Divinity, so utterly beyond all human imagination. And a dwelling in the silences of speech, which pervade the nameable and the sayable, keeps a sacred witness to God, whose true Name is ineffable—though resounding through the expressions of all Being and speaking through all the languages of humankind. Not to name the world or read it in the course of one's life by acts of attentive regard would therefore betray this truth; and not to seize one's context with strength and restraint would likewise betray our human responsibility for living in attunement to the sounds and silences of God's illimitable vastness. The process of reading scripture for its *peshat* sense helps to cultivate such a way of living theologically in the everyday.

Derash. The phrase cited earlier from Proverbs 25:11, *davar davur al ofanav*, may yield another sense: "a word that is said according to its turns of expression." By this interpretation we are put in mind of the play of language and its manifold aspects: how it unfolds in diverse combinations through its own inner logic and the spirit of its speakers—revolving in all directions, like wheels within wheels, directing the heart and mind to ever-new realities of the imagination. Within the textual space of scriptural interpretation, this exegetical creativity entails a restless inquiry into the words of the Written Torah (the *torah she-bikhtav*), and the ongoing revelation of its potential meanings constitutes the reality of the Oral Torah (the *torah she-be'al peh*). Jewish tradition calls these acts of textual inquiry and creative exposition *derash*, and engagement in these processes cultivates a distinct path of spiritual mindfulness. The *derash* does not displace the *peshat* or demean it; but neither is the process of *derash* constrained by the determinations of the *peshat*. To what may the *derash* be compared?—to the wings of the cherubs that rise above the ark of the covenant, sheltering the tablets of stone with a divine spirit and bearing them aloft in ever-soaring possibilities, as the old words are carried from Sinai into new life.

A reading of scripture oriented toward the *derash* turns away from the discursive contexts of the text, and the concern to disclose its meaning as a document of antiquity. The new turn is toward the contemporaneous meanings of scripture as a document that speaks to ongoing receivers, who believe it to be ever meaningful and renewed for post-Sinai generations. This type of reading is less a subjugation of the self to a given scriptural sense than an active engagement with its inner eros—that is to say, the attraction of the words of scripture to one another, beyond their immediate context, and the meanings that may be discerned from such intertextual activations of the components of scriptural language. The reader is thus involved in new conjugations of the old words of the text in order to reveal through the human self the ongoing voice of Sinai. The *derash* thus focuses on the duration of Sinai in time, at each and every moment of its creative reception. Such a mode of reading restores the textual inscription to a living voice.

The primary sphere for the acts of *derash* is scripture, the *torah she-bikhtav*. But now it is not the syntax of a given sentence that helps determine the sense of its words, but the inner resonance of selected words or phrases with others in the larger canonical whole. The context of reading thus shifts from specific words within a chain of words in the same sentence, to specified words conjoined to others deemed similar to them, by virtue of a chain of associations located within scripture as a whole. The reader is crucial in a very particular sense; for it is the reader who opens new pathways in the texture of scripture, and reveals new patterns in its warp and woof. The interpreter is like a new Moses, standing within the words of scripture and enunciating new revelations from its midst. Just this is the *torah she-be'al peh*.

What, then, are the exegetical measures by which a reader engages in the act of *derash*? On the one hand there is the imaginative attention to similarities between words and phrases in scripture, but on the other is an attentive examination of their differences. This allows for correlations and discriminations as one explores the implications of scripture concerning certain values and actions. It also allows for gradations of inclusion and exclusion, and patterns of analogy of various types as one considers diverse frames of reference. In these ways, the life of scripture is extended to the life of ongoing religious culture. Scripture is deemed an ever-flowing fountain with diverse meanings expressed through the mouths of its teachers. This sage said this, and that one that; another person transmitted this teaching or that one, and from all this new possibilities are disclosed through creative combinations or reformulations of scriptural language. Nothing so much characterizes the rich collections of theological *derash* from late antiquity as the recurrent phrase "another example" (*davar aḥer*); for the voice of Sinai was ceaseless, unendingly turned over and over to find all that is in it.

>>><<<

Let us return to scripture and demonstrate the point.

There is first of all the plain sense of Genesis 28:10–19, our primary passage; but as we now put one ear to this passage and another to scripture as a whole, we may attune ourselves to its wider resonances and teachings. The guiding query is, what does this come to teach us? This is the ever-present impulse of *derash*.

We read that "Jacob left Beer-sheba . . . and came upon some place [*va-yifga ba-maqom*]." The initial departure seems quite regular, and appears as an ordinary itinerary; however, the concluding locution is odd and calls for interpretation. Normally, the verb *paga* indicates something like a hurtful or injurious encounter (as in the phrase *va-yifga bo va-yamot*, "he hit upon him and he died"; 1 Kings 2:25). But what could such an engagement or smiting mean here? Surely father Jacob was a peaceful "man of tents"—a sage according to rabbinic tradition, and it was Esau his vengeful brother who was a violent "man of the field"; and surely, also, one hardly hits upon "a place" like some animal or sword. So what does scripture mean to say? If we are not quite certain, we might find a hint in the noun *ba-maqom*. At first glance it too is odd. After all, Jacob left Beer-sheba and set out for Haran—but did not arrive there. What then could it mean that he came to "the place," without further specification? Later on, Jacob calls "the place" Bethel, for it had specificity; but would we not have expected an expression like *el maqom eḥad* (he came "to some place")? But then we remember a similar passage. When father Abraham took Isaac to be bound on an altar, he looked up after three days "and saw the place [*ha-maqom*] from afar" (Gen. 22:4). Here, again, is a reference to a place, but without a specific nomination. Later rabbinic readers could not believe that scripture would waste words on such a mundane observation, and therefore presumed that Abraham, the man of faith, had a vision of God at that point, and proved the matter by reference to the standard rabbinic epithet for God as Ha-Maqom (The Place). That is, Abraham raised his eyes and "saw *God*," the One Who had bidden him to undertake this trial in the first place. So could not the word *maqom* have a religious-theological meaning here as well? If so, then surely Jacob, a pious ancestor, could have engaged God through a spiritual act, such as prayer. Just such a supposition could be proved by linking the verb used here (*va-yifga*) to its usage in Ruth 1:16, where *tifge'i bi* means something like "entreat on my behalf." And thus one might midrashically infer that Jacob also was involved in an act of divine entreaty while fleeing from his brother and hoping for safe passage to Haran.

It matters not that the same verb in Ruth 2:22 means to "encounter" or "meet"; just as it matters not that the epithet Ha-Maqom is rabbinic and not biblical. For the purposes of *derash*, we hear what we need to hear, and in this case what is needed is a mode of rabbinic piety that transforms Jacob (future father of the nation) into a religious model. Scripture, it seems, has chosen its formulations deliberately; for *derash* deems scripture a book of spiritual instruction, not just a record of events, and as such it is a work for the generations. And if you should also wonder at the timing of this act of prayer—at sunset—this too must be noted, for ancestor Jacob is most certainly one of the founders of the Jewish practice of prayer three times a day. Thus just as Abraham "arose early in the morning" (Gen. 22:1), thereby providing the model for divine service at daybreak; and similarly, just as Isaac "went out to walk in the fields towards evening" (Gen. 24:63), and the rabbis assumed that the verb *la-suaḥ* could hardly have the trivial sense of walking for a pious man, but must have the liturgical sense of "speaking" or "praying" (*siaḥ*; as in Psalm 77:4), thereby establishing the institution of afternoon prayer, as daytime turns "towards" dusk, Jacob now fits the same mold, and his entreaty at "night" when "the sun had set" is taken to found the prayer service at eventide.

As this example shows, the acts of *derash* swing far and wide and gather textual citations into a vortex of instruction. With one phrase, a network of associations is invoked: Jacob serves as both a theological model for pious prayer and a founder of a traditional halakhic practice. Intertextuality is the key. Deftly, through such acts of *derash*, the Written Torah yields the Oral Torah; or, to put this more rabbinically, through midrashic interpretation the Oral Torah is revealed as a species of the Written one.

Other interpretative initiatives disclose different dimensions.

Take another verse: "He [Jacob] had a dream: Here now: a stairway was set [*mutzav*] on the ground and its top reached to heaven; and now: angels of God were going up and down on it. And now: the Lord was standing [*nitzav*] near him" (*alav*; or also: "upon it"—the passage is redolent with ambiguity).

Reading the passage in a straightforward manner, we simply have a fragment of a dream sequence, quite fantastical to be sure, but still quite comprehensible in its series of phrases and images. But is this all? If this is a divinely inspired dream, and if Jacob (soon to be renamed Israel) is the future father of his people, is it conceivable that the imagery only refers to him and his adventures, so that the angels going up and down on the stairway would merely suggest his own journeys to and fro? Is there any hint of what would happen to the nation in the future? Is it possible that scripture is silent about this? To the religious mind, bound to scripture, the matter begs for interpretation. So what is one to do?

The answer: Listen well to the words and the sequence as a whole, and you may well discern the deeper communication of the passage. Perhaps you will conclude with Rabbi Bar Kappara that "there is no dream that has no solution," and that this dream sequence is actually referring (in its imagery and terminology) to the future institution of temple sacrifices. As he says: "'And he dreamed: and now: a stairway'—this refers to the ramp (upon which the priests ascend to sacrifice); 'set (*mutzav*) on the ground'—this refers to the altar, (as it says), 'you shall make an altar of earth for Me' (Exodus 20:21); 'and its top reached the heaven'—this refers to the sacrifices whose aroma ascends to heaven; 'and now: angels of God'—this refers to the high priests; 'were going up and down on it'—for they would ascend and descend (the altar) on it; 'and now: the Lord was standing (*nitzav*) upon it'—(as Scripture elsewhere says:) 'I saw the Lord standing (*nitzav*) upon the altar'(Amos 9:1)."

Or perhaps these correlations miss the point of scripture. If so, listen instead to how "the rabbis interpret [them] with respect to Sinai." "'And he dreamed: and now: a stairway'—this refers to Sinai; 'was set (*mutzav*) on the ground'—(this alludes to the gathering of the people there), as it says (in Scripture): 'and they stood (*va-yityatzvu*) at the base of the mountain' (Exodus 19:17); 'and its top reached to heaven (*ha-shamaymah*)'—as it says (elsewhere in Scripture,) 'and the mountain was consumed with fire up to the heart of heaven (*ha-shamayim*)' (Deuteronomy 4:11); 'and now: angels of God'—this refers to Moses and Aaron: 'were ascending (*olim*)'—(note:) 'and Moses ascended (*alah*)' (Exodus 19:3; 'and were descending (*yordim*)'—(note further:) 'and Moses descended (*va-yered*) the mountain' (v. 14); 'and now: the Lord was standing (*nitzav*) upon it (*alav*)'—(as Scripture says:) 'and the Lord descended upon (*al*) Mount Sinai' (v. 20)."

Is this then the event implied by scripture? Have these two sets of interpretation rightly construed the textual references of the passage, by proper correlations of its images and verses? Most likely, these striking typological patterns, linking phrases from Genesis 28:12–13 to sacrifices or to Sinai, were propounded in old sermons, and demonstrate the sages' sense of the omnisignificance of the Written Torah. Or perhaps they are inspired scholarly speculations into deeper networks of meaning. For to the midrashic mind nothing in scripture is just there, like some rhetorical flourish. How could it be? Is it not a work for all generations and bearing on all events? Does not scripture itself say that the covenant was given "both to those who are present with us today [of the old generation] before the Lord, our God, *and also* to those who are not with us here this day" (Deut. 29:14)? Should you be skeptical, just listen to all the other interpretations of our passage produced by Resh Lakish, or Rabbi Joshua in the name of Rabbi Levi, or Rabbi Berekhya, or Rabbi Ḥiyya Rabba. They too (and many more) have been collected in the great anthology of *derash* on the book of Genesis (*Genesis Rabba*) in order to satisfy all possibilities, and to show latter-day readers how the masters of interpretation put their minds to work and their ear to the sound of scripture. The Written Torah is a living text for all times. Perhaps Genesis 28:12–13 might even be referring to the exile and restoration of Israel, or also to Jacob's (or anyone's) spiritual life, with all its ups and downs of consciousness (between a normal earthiness and experiences of uncommon sublimity)? Only an attentive reading and the resonance of one's heart can decide.

One could proceed further in this manner, word by word and phrase by phrase through the byways of our passage, and take any number of associative detours to similar words and phrases found elsewhere in scripture. But the foregoing cases sufficiently exemplify the way interpretative acts of *derash* lock on to specific terms in a text, and then interpret scripture by means of scripture, for the sake of expanding religious life and thought. Any textual point can serve as a matrix, drawing other passages to it and yielding new clusters of insight.

>>><<<

This said, we now return to our principal question concerning the relationships between scriptural reading and ongoing life and theology.

It has been observed how, according to the midrashic mode of interpretation, scripture provides the comprehensive context for the determination of meaning. For just as the Written Torah is the primary covenant context for the unfolding of the Oral Torah, the Oral Torah is itself shaped by readers with changing historical contexts, and this larger setting also speaks through their mouths. Scripture is thus read with the legal logic and moral ratios sanctioned by interpretative tradition at different times as it attempts to mediate between the text and issues that emerge from ongoing life-situations and new values. Accordingly, the Oral Torah is infused by the *torah kelulah*, and in this way remains alive to the voice (or: world-expressions) of the living God. As these matters are passed through the cultural forms of the Oral Torah, and joined to its values or evaluated by them, the sphere of the covenant is expanded and transformed. Just as one should try to be alert to all the verbal nuances of scripture and bring these into life, one should attend to the wide world of occurrences and bring them into covenant life. The two affect each other reciprocally. Let us consider this further.

Among the human virtues that the practice of *derash* cultivates is, first of all, an attentiveness to relations and correlations through discriminating speech. This practice constitutes the ethics of the *derash*, and cultivate a distinctive mode of consciousness with bearings on life and theology.

We again begin with life.

Humans are thrust into the vastness of the world with its apparent givens and formalities. So much is this so, that we may easily forget how much we bear responsibility for the way we construe things and interpret purpose or behavior. Nothing is just there as a matter of fact. Even so-called matters of fact are "matters" of "fact" because we determine them to be so in this or another way, based on assumptions and correlations taken from within the texture of the world. The same goes for our relations to persons. It would be misleading to assume that the notion of a human being is something self-evident, as if it were some kind of physical given and not a cultural ideal to be determined and realized in ever-new ways. When we say that a person can "become human," or that education "builds character," we imply as much and more.

But we forget this in our habitude and the thicket of accepted meanings. This forgetting deadens the world of appearances, which pass before us like the shades of existence, until some caesural moment occurs and we become transparent to ourselves as makers of meaning. The world may then become alive through our self-conscious determination of the words we use. How we make a word relevant to a given situation is our human business in the living practice of interpretation; and how we construe what we are listening to is also our responsibility as we try to put things into the right context. In so doing, we expand our thinking beyond immediate occasions, and use thoughtfulness as we employ words in a dialogue. As with scripture, life may be disclosed again and again as a sphere of engagement and invention and value.

The act of *derash* is an inquiry into matters of sameness and difference. This cultivates a mindfulness of discrimination and judgment, and an ethical responsibility for the decisions made. Thinking about similarity is no simple matter, and involves some measures of difference. Even carbon copies are not entirely one and the same thing: for there may be two types of likeness, or more. Parallel lines in poetry are similar, yet different; and even the same word in a different place or rendered with a different tone is different. We can never escape these comparisons or correlations, and we may cluster them to determine just what makes them alike or different for other groupings. Such acts are always based on the comparisons we make from what we know. We are always explaining one thing by another in an attempt to be clear and precise, or to instruct someone who thinks in a different way. If an abstract thought is rendered by a concrete example from the world, we are thinking with similitudes and engaged in acts of interpretation. Here, as with the midrashic process of correlating phrases of one passage with those of another, we also establish orders of similarity; and if we are thoughtful about how we build up meaning in one sphere, we can instruct ourselves about their impact in others. The distinct "I am" of each thing is an interpreted "I am," whether we like it or not; it constitutes an ongoing covenant with the world we make and have. There is therefore much gravity in the statement: "We shall do and we shall hear" (Exod. 24:7).

The tasks of doing and hearing are distinctly unremitting imperatives when one stands before another person. Just what is the likeness that is emphasized or discerned, and what is the nature of the differences? One cannot rely on abstractions or generalities. Moral life is bound up with concrete determinations and the ongoing explication of norms and ideals. This has particular force when one is dealing with the language of precedent or tradition, and one must be mindful of the way terms are carried over and applied to others. Some (such as the framers of the Declaration of Independence) might declare, "We hold these truths to be self-evident that all men are created equal, that they are endowed by their Creator with certain inalienable Rights, that among these are Life, Liberty, and the pursuit of Happiness." This formulation offers a great bundle of possibilities and assumptions and ambiguities. Our moral lives must be more precise if we are ever to live with the implication of our terms. What is really being said about similarity and its limits (insofar as it asserts a universal equality), or about authority and its application (insofar as it is a natural human statement of a divine quality)? Is this proclamation of rights held as "self-evident" through stark reason or religious belief; and what does the qualification "certain" mean; and are there rights that are alienable, and what might that mean? Moreover, what can or should be determined from this passage about women and children and slaves and their rights? And further, what does the "right" to life mean here, and how does it bear on the unborn or the criminal or the enemy; and how much and in what manner can one pursue personal happiness as an inalienable right? For those with political concerns, all this may evoke some Aristotelian practice of happiness for the greater social good; but there is room to suppose some other interpretations which move in the opposite direction, espousing more self-centered values and culminating in the notion of an inalienable right to personal benefit or pleasure.

Surely, the work of *derash* obtains here in all its needs for comparison and correlation; in all its requirements for thinking about the words, severally and together, and then establishing meanings that have value and worth; and also in its need to move repeatedly from the written text to its oral explication and activation, based on changing circumstances and on the life-practices that might give us guidance. Reading well and thoughtfully may help us live well and thoughtfully, and vice versa. Formal education is largely predicated upon the first assumption, and thus privileges certain texts as carriers of cultural values and ideals. By contrast, the culling of experiences "on the road" is often predicated upon the notion that life has a lot to teach, and that this should take precedence. But texts do not teach on their own; neither does life. There is no mere matter of fact.

Much depends on how we look at another person and say, "I am like you in this way, but not in that." For we must be ever mindful of the many cruelties that have been perpetrated on the basis of presumptive human differences. When we look at another individual, can we say anything other than "This is a person 'as myself' at the most physical level—who bleeds like me, who is mortal like me, and who with me shares the same air and earth of the world"? Do we dare formulate more essential human differences and live with the consequences? Our ethical lives depend on such judgments of sameness and difference. Moral mindfulness is grounded in the capacity to say, "You too, like me," and to linger reflectively in the implications of this *likeness*. By contrast, mindlessness is the swamp of evil, mired in inappropriate assertions of sameness or unjust difference. One must therefore be on guard to read each situation with deliberateness and vigilance and care.

There is yet another area that depends on the character of our interpretative acts, and that is speech between persons. A space of difference opens up in speaking, with different explanations of the meaning and implications of words; and one must try not to pollute that gap with vain projections, but to fill it with care and clarification. When words go stale or become ambiguous, or they are misused, we must nevertheless continue speaking, in the hope that new meanings may be added to old phrases for common purposes, and that patient explications may result in healing. The alternative is the abyss of misunderstanding. The nuance of terminology is not just there or self-evident, but the result of living interpretation. In this manner the contexts of life expand, and more of the *torah kelulah* is received and lived and given a human dimension. God's illimitable effectivity passes through all persons, and their cultivation of their own "human *being*" gives it one direction or another. Moses took matters only so far; the interpreters of scripture take them further. To receive the world as an expression of Divinity is a grave covenant task; for these expressions always pass through our entirely *human* being.

We thus come to theology. A mind shaped by *derash* takes all these imaginative constructions (of scripture and of life) with the utmost seriousness.

Think about it. Are all the mythic correlations of God with the powers of nature, or the workings of culture, or the personalities of humans merely to be shunted aside as so many childlike crudities—the products of misplaced (and even blasphemous) concreteness, or gross (and jarring) projections onto Divinity from the world of human feelings and experience? Might they not rather be perceived in more positive terms: as the work of the creative imagination, endlessly trying to depict God and express what are sensed or believed to be God's multiform connections with the world? Indeed, might they not be regarded better as the articulations of humanly experienced or imagined modes of divine vitality in one's life? Sometimes these (scriptural and common) images are stated explicitly, so that God is said to be "like" one kind of being or another (perhaps a lion or a person); while at other times the medial terms of likeness are dropped and the conjunctive force of the image is increased (saying that God "is" a consuming fire, or gracious, or near). In the process of such image-making, a whole range of existential values emerge and congeal. Some are noble, others trite; some are enunciated with sophistication, others simply crass; and some are offered with a certain self-consciousness, while others are crudely fundamentalistic. Nonetheless, they all (in their kinds) attest to moments when the human spirit senses a divine presence within or behind the phenomena of the world, or some notion of influence (whether material or spiritual) that is conceptualized through images drawn from the world of form and force. Each of these images of divine likeness thus opens up different realms of theological reality, entirely distinct ways of conceiving God's vitality in human terms.

To speak about God with likeness in mind is to retain both a sense of divine vitality *and* the work of the human imagination; to forget this is to slide toward metaphors that begin to seem self-evident, and then ultimately become verbal idols. To speak of God with likeness in mind (and some interpretative transparency) is to remember that there is no direct seeing of God from the cleft of the rock, within the obscurities of our human nature; there is only the hint of God's presence through our reflective consciousness of it, a meager sense of the glory that has somehow, apparently, already passed through and beyond. Our similes try to capture something of this mysterious touching and turning; and when they work there is a sense of likeness and unlikeness, simultaneously, in different degrees of expressive dominance.

Images of God emerge, then, through the bold figures of scripture itself, and those they also catalyze for ongoing reflection. The creative mind seeks to find the right balance between these two aspects (likeness and unlikeness), where the unsayable is said in human language. Boldly, the poetic drive formulates hybrids for thought—always seeking something beyond mere common sense. But the religious seeker remains cautious, for the integrity of one's soul hangs in the balance. For that reason, every likeness must be unsaid by the heart even as it is spoken by one's mouth. Images may direct the mind, but they must not fill it.

Remez. Another great medieval sage (of Spain and Egypt), Rabbi Moses ben Maimon (known familiarly as the Rambam or Maimonides), was a master of textual insight: for he was able to perceive in the language of scripture stylistic significations of more hidden truths of pure thought (philosophical and spiritual). He spoke of these verbal signs as providing a *remez*, or hint, of these supersensual ideas, and found just the biblical phrase to make his point: the first clause of the same proverb used by Rashi to promote the *peshat* sense. For the Rambam, the image, "*Like apples of gold in a filigree of silver* [*ke-tapuḥei zahav be-maskiyot kasef*] is a word fitly spoken," conveyed just that art of concealment that he discerned in the composition of scripture. The fitly wrought word or image, he taught, was a double communication: it conveyed a surface sense and a deeper one, the first being like a stylistic trellis which covered a figure set within or behind it. The deeper understanding was like an apple of gold, perceivable to the discerning eye without disturbing the field of vision. As sight is to insight, so is *peshat* to *remez*. One simply has to know what to look for and how.

The way of *remez* seems at first glance to be both paradoxical and trite. The paradoxical aspect is because it appears to invert the hermeneutical process and turn the act of interpretation into a self-fulfilling event. The reader begins with a body of truth claims from some other realm of inquiry (such as philosophical teachings about the hierarchies of reality, or psychological assertions about the multiform structure of the soul), and this matrix is then presumed to operate as the deep (and true) structure of the text—a presumption confirmed by the exegetical disclosure of verbal markers or sequences that are said to allude to this very structure or matrix. The circle of inquiry is thus self-confirming, so that the task of reading is to draw the correlation between the surface level of the text (a word, a phrase, or even an entire passage) and its deeper sense (an idea or a pattern of truths). This process seems trivial and routine as well, even if the ideas disclosed thereby are profound and transform the temporal discourses of scripture into the eternal truths of philosophy. According to this latter perspective, the exegetical mystery of *remez* lies in its assumption that truth lies beyond appearances, and that meaning is more than meets the eye. So viewed, truth is always a spiritual insight.

But this is not the whole truth about *remez*. In the hands of its most profound adepts one may also discern an attentive regard for how the *peshat* hints beyond itself, that is, how an exegetical attentiveness to some crudity or contradiction at the surface of the text is sufficient to make the reader take note; and knowing (or believing) that such formulations do not befit a divine work such as scripture, the savvy reader is inspired to gather up the textual clues from the plain sense in order to infer from them the real truth about what is intended. This turns the paradox of such so-called parabolic or allegorical readings back on themselves and reopens the circle of inquiry. Now everything depends on how scrupulous one is in perceiving the hints in a given word to its own-most (that is, its philosophical) truth, and how one understands the human character of human language. If the language of scripture is altogether like human language, and we should read it like any literary product of the human imagination, one could then say that the textual references to a divine arm or eye refer to those physical features known in the natural world; and if a person comes to a place and has a dream, and that dream includes a stairway and angels, we should recognize the stairway for what it is in the real world and the angels for whatever kind of creature they would constitute in one's culture (all this being one way to construe the old rabbinic dictum "Scripture speaks like human language"). But if scripture necessarily and ineluctably speaks like human language (because it has been formulated to make sense to human beings), but is also a rich or special language that can operate meaningfully at several levels simultaneously, then, when scripture makes reference to a divine arm or eye, one should be circumspect and not take such depictions too literally or get stuck on their surface sense. It would then be a sign of wisdom to penetrate beyond the external wording of the text to its deeper truth (this being quite another way to construe the foregoing dictum, in line with *remez*). From this perspective, the outer figures of scripture are tropes, verbal vehicles that carry a more profound sense. It would thus be folly to think that the outer carriage is the real motor.

If all this is so, the exegetical procedure of *remez* is hardly trivial at all and requires the utmost attention to textual details. In certain cases a human eye is an eye and an arm just an arm; but in other instances this would be a concrete or silly reading of a text ("I'll keep my eye on you" connotes care, and not necessarily direct sight; and the sentence "Take my hand if you need to" can indicate emotional support in addition to physical clasping). And if this is the case with respect to human body parts, and the way human language may use physical features as figures of speech, how much more is this so with respect to scriptural statements about God when portrayed in human terms? We should thus think twice before interpreting references to divine sight as denoting eyesight and not regard, or thinking of a mighty arm in terms of its strength rather than some expression of guidance or protection.

Such reflections can bring us to stairways and other worldly things used with respect to divine beings. Here too one should pay attention to the textual details. For example, in Jacob's dream it is said that he envisioned that "a stairway was set on the ground and its top reached to heaven; and angels of God were going up and down on it. And the Lord stood upon it." What is conveyed by this trope? According to Maimonides, this a "kind of prophetic parable" (a type of *remez*), in which each of the words or phrases, like "a stairway" and "set on the ground" and "its top reached to heaven," refer to distinct subjects and are conjoined into a pattern of meaning to be discerned ("Thus every word occurring in this parable refers to an additional subject in the complex of subjects represented by the parable as a whole"; *The Guide of the Perplexed*, introduction). Maimonides determines the meaning of the clauses by giving careful regard to other words in scripture, and then drawing certain larger inferences based on his understanding of this work as a book about philosophical wisdom and its pursuit. Accordingly, if the word *nitzav* is used with respect to God being set upon the stairway, and this verb elsewhere means a certain firmness and permanence, he reasonably supposes that the dream refers to God as a Being who is "stable, permanent, and constant"; further, if one also observes that the word *angel* is used elsewhere to refer to a prophet (Judges 2:1), then the same line of interpretation will say that the reference in our text is also to prophets (or intellectual adepts) who ascend toward God (the pinnacle of true knowledge) in heaven; and finally, if the dream also refers to the descent of these angels to the ground, then, in consonance with the whole narrative complex, this must presumably mean that they (the adepts) descend level by level (as on the steps of a stairway) in order to govern and teach the people on earth (*Guide*, 1.15).

This interpretation may succeed as a reasonable inference, particularly if one starts with the notion that the stairway indicates the gradations of knowledge, and that one moves between gross matter to higher spiritual realities in the course of developing a true comprehension of the nature of things. Such a construal of the textual hints is closely connected to the words of scripture. But what happens if one reads this passage through the lens of rabbinic *derash*? Then the topics and themes will vary and the conclusions change, as is the case with Maimonides himself, who used rabbinic dicta to determine the cosmic size of the stairway, the number of steps upon it, and also the number of angels and their nature. In so doing, he is brought to a whole new series of speculations about "physics" and the cosmos (2.10). And his interpretation is also different from the *remez*-type speculation of another Spanish sage (Rabbeinu Baḥye ben Asher), who goes on to tell us that "the ladder [stairway] is a *remez* of reality," which is divided into three parts (a fact we learn from a certain reading of Psalm 103:20–22): the "world of angels" (designated as such in the dream), the "world of the spheres" (designated by the steps of the stairway), and the "lower (material) world" (designated by the ground); and then he also says that by the image of the Lord set upon the stairway on high, Jacob was informed about God's rule and providence over the whole business (of reality).

Hence even the wise can't be too sure about the import of the passage: you take your cotext (scripture or rabbinic exegesis) and determine your hint; and you know the larger reference of the hints of scripture from philosophical tradition, and a peek or two at Aristotle and some others. But you can always be sure that scripture will be concerned with ultimate truths; and thus, however dogged the search or the variations in explanation, reading for the *remez* cultivates one's higher self. As a result, despite some slippage and inconsistency, this manner of interpretation is deemed by its practitioners to be a whole lot better than getting muddled in literalism and verbal crudities—since this can only activate our base desires and cheapest needs. Indeed, for the philosopher-in-the-making, the very act of trying to determine the clues of spiritual truth from what seems to matter on the surface is itself a process of intellectual self-cultivation and an overcoming of one's earthly nature.

>>><<<

At first blush, this manner of reading texts in terms of fundamental truths operative in reality seems quite far from the modern temper, and at odds with the empirical spirit of inquiry, insofar as it measures matters in terms of prior "countries of the mind" (as Sir Francis Bacon dubbed the allegorical method). In addition, this search for latent truths by means of predetermined configurations of significance seems to project ideas onto things with something smacking of hegemonic imperialism. But let us not be too quick to judge. After all, any number of modern ideologies (concerning psychological or social process) are routinely imported into the reading of texts and then shown to preexist there, and this method is even said to deconstruct our gullible nature and give us more truth, not less. Indeed, we are often caught up in a vicious circle, with one presumption chasing another. It is also not uncommon (and for some the methodological fashion) to look for deep structures in literary sources or the natural world and then consider the more surface elements distorted or developed expressions of them. Similarly, we even assume that other, similar phenomena are traces of the same truths or essential components. Is all this so very far from allegory and its ideational paradigms?

Let us therefore learn from this, and in the search for clues that might support an initial paradigm of thought be ready to find other patterns of significance. Hypotheses are the offspring of thoughts based on certain readings of the evidence, and we would hardly proceed in our thinking about the world (and its manifest and hidden matters) if we didn't bring our speculations to what we see and think about; but this must be an ongoing process in the mystery of the vastness, and not calcified. There is nothing more disconcerting than to see a hypothesis morph into an unexamined truth after repeated use. The search itself, and whether we have drawn the right hint from things or properly assessed its implications, is a matter for constant reflection. Such alertness and critical judgment comprise what we shall deem the ethics of the *remez*. This activity cultivates the mind for an accounting of the world and its inhabitants, and, beyond that, for theological musings about the traces of God within and beyond appearances.

Let us begin again with the world and our lives therein.

As we look out on the world, our sensibilities are beset by a great array of images that flicker and pulse. We try to discern figures and patterns from the whole, and then make sense of them for ourselves. We may do this on a trial-and-error basis, sensing that this event or matter hints at something worth noting, or that another matter hints at the first, and the two should be somehow integrated; or we may build up, through personal memory and tradition, clusters of meaningful clues and information, and use these to evaluate clues and fragmentary impressions in other parts of our lives. We do not do this every day, and we are not always conscious of this way of reading the world. But this is our condition, for better or worse. We are ever attempting to determine just what is significant evidence within the ongoing flow of things; and we are constantly searching for evidential paradigms that might make sense of experience and existence. Our ideas become templates for thought, and our thoughts help us see things in new ways. The ancients called this procedure divinatory, and they constantly revised their hypotheses and assumptions based on new evidence. This too is a mode of reading one thing in terms of another, and one thing as a clue of another. It is allegory by another name. We may chafe at the term, but we live the reality. It is therefore essential that we be ethically on guard at every moment for the way we read clues from the surface of things, or make assumptions from appearances about all that still lies in deepest concealment.

And if all this is so with respect to things, what may be said of our relations to other persons? Perhaps this: that the human being before us is a divine image of life, a life-form wrought from the infinities of God's *torah kelulah* and inscribed with earthly particularity, like the Written Torah. In the course of a lifetime, this person is also inscribed by memory and hope, by experience and possibility, by patterns and confusions, and by words and silences. As we come to know this person, we try to "read" the emergent life-expressions with all this in mind, and attempt to perceive in such appearances or manners of speech something of the deeper self not explicitly expressed; and as we speak with this person, in the hope of drawing forth information, so that the relationship will not be based on assumptions or projections, there unfolds something like an Oral Torah. Every *remez*, or hint of meaning or intent, must therefore be checked and discussed and considered as we live with the signs of a person's life and try to assess their sense and significance. Such a mode of living is a double envisioning of the other one—as surface and silence, and appearance and allusion—as we try to attune ourselves to the Written Torah of that other self (the "other" as an inscription and series of signs), and to the Oral Torah only partially revealed (the "other" as a speaking soul of interpretations and self-understandings). To live in this way is to stand at Sinai in the midst of the everyday: it is a hearing and receiving, and a binding of oneself to an ever-new covenant that is no longer an "if you will hear" but an "I am" now. In the process, our own selves are even inscribed with the expressions of this other one.

When this happens there is no mere difference or otherness, but a covenant connection: the two lives are bound by interaction and reciprocity—by doing and hearing—and the duties that unfold are the obligations of love.

Where else might we speak of God than in such allusions in the everyday, in the marvel of appearances and their openings to vitalities beyond? This is not God as God, but God as we may orient ourselves to the vastness which Divinity makes possible, in an attitude of humility and reverence. On this reading of existence, the signs of things and persons become hieroglyphs, sacred configurations of the vastness of divine reality—not so much to be decoded or even interpreted as to be sealed in silence upon one's heart.

Sod. The proverb we have been pondering does not fail us here either as we try to give voice to something of the mystical dimension of scripture; for its words ("Like apples of gold in a filigree of silver is a word fitly spoken") put us in mind of the truth that language both reveals and conceals, and often does so at one and the same time. Sometimes this is by verbal accident or because of human limitations; but at other times this type of complex communication is more deliberate, as when we speak with innuendos or write with dense metaphors and allusions. The case of scripture is different still, since, from a mystical point of view (derived from esoteric tradition), scripture is regarded as the earthly manifestation of the most supernal truths of God. Indeed, according to classic kabbalistic lore, the creative emanations of divine Being, and their transcendent interactions and modalities, are believed to be refracted and encoded in the language of scripture. Hence this literary work may have all the appearance of a national record of cosmic origins and historical life, or of religious institutions and divine teachings. But that is its outer garment and corporeal shape. In truth, the inner soul of this language and the depictions of scripture embody dimensions of Divinity, since the external manifestations are verbal symbols of the supernal realities and pulse with their esoteric energies. Hence, from the perspective of *sod*, there is no gap between the hidden mysteries and revealed scripture; they are complex variations of one another. The supernal dimensions of Divinity have their lower, earthly aspects, and what scripture contains is not only a series of figurations of these higher expressions, in all their perfection and complexity, but also records of the ruptures or repair of these dynamics, insofar as these are induced by human behavior, so intimately bound to that ultimate reality.

For the human being to read scripture properly as *sod*, it is necessary to seek a spiritual alignment with its language and the energy of its images. As one does so, the divine structures and dimensions of the self may reciprocally penetrate the structures and dimensions of the text, which, as noted, constitutes an aspect of God's supernal reality; and then these divine aspects of the self will be activated, and one may ascend into the higher realms in deepest contemplation, or embody this wisdom in worldly acts. Both results strengthen God. For as a worldly image and expression of Divinity, the human self is entwined and correlated with God. The *sod* of scripture is thus not so much a level of reading as a mode of reality and being. Reading is a spiritual rite of passage into this truth so that it may be enacted for God's sake, in the most ultimate sense.

>>><<<

Who would dare speak off-handedly about such matters, or turn them into cultural chatter? Even the silences and blank spaces of scripture are supernal elements, expressions, we are told, of the primordial light of Divinity, shining in radiant effulgences from God's face.

Every teaching of *sod* should therefore be by allusion or suggestion, as the ancient masters advised. At the borders of speech we should guard our tongues, out of respect for what can hardly be said, and out of fear for its trivialization and misuse. I shall therefore give but halting voice to *sod*, and let any readers who may catch its echoes fill in the gaps from the wisdom of their hearts, silently.

Scripture says: "Jacob left Beer-sheba and went to Haran." The plain sense of this verse is readily established; it depicts a journey from the land of Canaan to Aram. But what more might we perceive of a spiritual nature, for those who know that scripture portrays not merely one's passage in the world, but also one's inner reality and the supernal realities of Divinity? Come and perceive what scripture really says. In this leaving and going there is a journey, to be sure; but it is Jacob's quest toward wholeness and integration, on his way to becoming Israel, a person of up-rightness with God, as this name may mean. He was a favorite child of his mother and received a blessing of bounty from his father. This was the sense of fullness, or *sova*, that filled the well of his life; but in order to be spiritually whole he needed to know "other" dimensions of being. And so (he did not so much leave Beer-sheba for Haran as) he left the Well of Seven-Fold Bounty, *Beer-sova*, and entered an Other (*aḥra*) realm, the realm of lack and even anger (*ḥaron*). That meant that he had to relate to the earth in a new way. Thus he lies down upon the ground, and in doing so the truth is revealed to him in a vision. He now per-ceives the dual aspects of Being, the material and the spiritual, not as two distinct elements but as points on one spectrum. God is set above this unity, which is the Whole truth of God's All-Being. But this is no external or heavenly truth; it is the truth of the interconnections of all aspects of Being, which Jacob can ascend or descend through the divine or angelic aspects of his own being, with increased or decreased levels of spiritual con-sciousness, as he goes about his life.

And not only this: the ladder of the harmonic scales of Being, in which all is interconnected, is within Jacob himself; for he is an embodiment or microcosm of the whole, if only he would realize it. Does not scripture express this secret mystery? Does it not say that the angels were going up and down *bo*? Surely that word could mean not just "on it" (the stairway), but really and truly "on *him*" (Jacob himself). And you can confirm this further, because the stairway of spiritual wisdom, the one Jacob could ascend through the various aspects and modalities of Being, is said to have "its top" (*rosho*) in heaven. Certainly we may perceive here a further indication of Jacob's heavenly dimension, with "*his* head" (*rosho*) in the supernal realms. What was briefly alluded to at the outset, concerning Jacob's journey for integration of oppo-sites, is now confirmed more fully in the vision, where the brute otherness of things, resistant and sometimes violent and cha-otic, is linked to more spiritual orders of being in one mysterious bond. It is not easily comprehensible, even when portrayed in a vision; and the ascents and descents of the angels suggest that even Jacob, despite this insight, will struggle repeatedly for inner balance during his lifetime. But the vision concludes with God's word of promise, suggesting that though this journey will be in and out of different realms, this truth (of the unified whole of all Being) will be "with" Jacob, like a sign of remembrance between his eyes (compare Zohar 1, *Va-yeitzei*).

When Jacob awakes he is transformed by the wisdom and truth revealed to him. And so he cries out, "Surely the Lord is in this place, and I did not know it." And where is "this" place? Is it just there at the site of his dream? Jacob tells us: "This is none other than the house of God." This world with all its fullness is a habitation of God; it is, so to say, a house of the wholeness, but not the "whole" itself, and just as surely only a modality of God's All-Being. And Jacob then adds: "[And this is] the gateway (*sha'ar*) to heaven." Through each point in the world, one can touch something of the mysteries that pervade all Being. The passageways are everywhere, if one opens (elsewhere called) the "estimations of one's heart" (*shi'urei libba*)—these being the gates of spiritual imagination and consciousness.

>>><<<

We return to our hermeneutical inquiry. How might the exegetical modality of *sod* help cultivate the reader for the tasks of life and God-mindedness? Put differently: with this modality in mind, might we also find a way, suitable to our modern temperament, to develop some kind of ethos of *sod* in and through the phenomena of the world? How might we engage scripture so that its words might open our hearts to the unthinkable vastness, and its verbal constellations reveal more interior universes, through silent hints of unsayability?

Here is a suggestion. At the level of *sod* the self moves beyond the expressible sense of scripture (be it of fact or wisdom) to a more metacommunicative dimension, to ways that the process of reading scripture can shape one's spiritual awareness and sensibility. Four domains shall be considered. Each cultivates a different aspect of God-consciousness for the self, this being the ultimate aim of *sod* for the spiritual reader, medieval and modern alike.

The first domain is the *eye*. At the level of *sod*, for a modern, the text does not resonate as a series of esoteric symbols or coded content. Something else is required. And it is this: while reading, one's eye passes along the curve of the letters and the shapes of the words. This focuses attention on the iconic figures of the orthography, not their figurative content. In the process, one may concentrate on the play of light that shines around the letters as graphic configurations. The eye is thus directed to the changing patterns that come into view, while the mind is withdrawn or disengaged from routine cognition. In this meditative state, one develops a new sense of having an eye. Initially, we may simply be more attuned to its natural function, of the fact that our eye is a receptor for perceiving the world as a successive cluster of images and forms. But deeper insights may also come to mind; perhaps first the awareness that these graphic configurations both delimit and enable the knowable world, and then also that the phenomena of perception arise to view from deeper and unfathomable depths of Being. This sensibility may even put one in mind of God, the ultimate effectivity of all world-being and a modality of its actualization. For the spiritually attuned, there are moments when the events before our eyes seem like the prismatic refraction of Divinity itself: like a radiance from the Source of all illumination. This wondrous conjunction of our inner eye and physical perception produces what the religious mind calls revelation. Our experience of the world in this way is—always—a miracle.

The appearances of the eye occur immediately. When we look, we see and perceive. The particular sight does not so much "become," or gradually develop from inchoate perceptions; it is rather just there, fully formed, and this happens repeatedly as we behold a scene. Thus the eye verifies the world as an ongoing immediacy. This realization may open the mind to a sense of the renewal of creation at each moment as we participate in its perception and sense God's primordial efficacy in the ever-happening present.

Such seeing is not natural, and does not directly serve our everyday actions; but it is a form of perception that may be cultivated out of our naturalness, and this is the aim of *sod* as interpreted here.

A second domain in which God-consciousness may be cultivated is the *ear*. As one recites scripture aloud (or listens to its chant), one hears the enunciation of sound and the buildup of tonal patterns of various lengths. We naturally try to construe the meaning of these verbal cues as they resound, whether we are listening to the plain sense or shift to other modalities of comprehension. But when attending to scripture in the mode of *sod*, as we now construe it, the self will bypass the worldly meaning of the words and intone or hear the sounds qua sounds; that is, simply as tones and vibrations that impact the ear. In this meditative state, when one does not try to "make sense" of what is being heard, one may even hear the happening of sound out of the depths. Such a hearing state is thus not something mindless or vacuous. Rather, the mind is entirely filled by sound and the hearing is itself a meditative harmonic. This state may also put one in mind of God, whose ineffable Name symbolizes the absolute fullness of sound and expression that variously conditions and constitutes all the living tones or vibrations of our world. When we hear sound in this way, we may realize concretely that sound happens independently of its meaning and our limited construal of its tones. In itself, we may say, sound is the very mystery of God's voice. Is this not a truth also found in scripture? Recall that at Sinai there were at first only sounds, the awesome rumble of thunder and crack of lightning; and only thereafter, through the agency of Moses, were these experiences transformed through his being into the words of our world. Hearing the sounds of Moses's words meditatively, as sounds wrought from the infinite *torah kelulah*, one may perhaps also be brought to a sense of this primordial Torah, and to the *sod* of God—beyond the god of words.

Different from seeing, the revelations of sound happen successively and carry the listener along the arc of tonality. We are thus put in mind of duration as such. This consciousness may be cultivated in the hearing of hearing. In this way we may even perceive (in our mind's ear) the ineffable which resounds from the depths of Divinity. Hearing scripture in the mode of *sod* (as we now construe it) may cultivate this sensibility and spiritual consciousness.

A third domain is the *mouth*. When reciting scripture, we enunciate its sounds and vocables with our life-breath. We do not always attend to this; but it underlies every scriptural articulation or secular speech we utter. What is more, the words are enunciated in specific breath units. These are usually quite natural demarcations of meaning; and as we feel comfortable with a text we gain a sense of its phrasing and the turns that characterize it. New passages may cause some hesitation, as does listening to a new person speak. In such instances, ever-greater attentiveness is required so that we may rightly pick up the cues of sense and feel confident about the pace of language.

Our breathing keeps us in a life-rhythm with the world, with our mouths at the border between internal and external realities. As we breathe in, we inhale a dimension of the world; and as we exhale we may express meaning through the letters and words emitted. All this takes place in the first (and primary) instance within the natural world, of which we are an integral part. What then may we say about the modality of *sod*? How may our breathing and enunciating words in the process of reading fit into this spiritual type? Perhaps in this way: as we withdraw our attention from the words of scripture as articulations of meaning, and focus on breathing itself, we may be put in mind of the way meaning happens through the shapes of human breath; and how breath draws from the world and gives back to it in ways that surpass any human or social sense (think of photosynthesis); and that our breath extends to the widest extent of the planet, and in infinite loops returns to our mortal being in one form or another. Mindful of this, one may be put in mind of God—the Source of all the vitalities that fill our lungs and bodies, along with every other living thing from sea to sky. At this spiritual level, consciousness of the act of breath attunes one to the pulsations of the organic nature of reality. This is a meditative awareness arising from our naturalness; but it extends throughout existence, above and below our thresholds of awareness. In the process of this increased mindfulness, we participate consciously in the mystery of Being.

As breath happens, life happens, moment by moment, in continuous duration. In and through our mouths and breath something is enunciated out of the ineffable sounds expressing God's Name. As we inhale and receive this reality, or exhale and return it to the world (with every breath and speech), we express something deeper: we say "yes" to life, through our entire being. Thus, to wound or harm another life by cutting off its breath—in fact or by interruptive speech, or through deceit and ruse—is also to refuse its "yes," to deny its essential claim to existence. Who would separate *peshat* from *sod* here? They are deeply interconnected. The breathing "yes" I give to divine reality is expressed in the "yes" I extend to persons and events in all my daily actions. Though the *sod* aspect of breath may be cultivated as a spiritual practice, it cannot remain a private act, but must enter the plain core (or *peshat*) of all that we do.

The final domain to be considered is the *body* as a whole. One reads scripture in an act of bodily presence. Ideally, one should feel oneself totally engaged in the recitation of the text: there are the attentions of the eye, the hearing of the ear, the speaking of the mouth, the rhythms of breath, and the full realm of tactile sensations involved in touching the text or sitting before it. Our reading is thus accompanied by a sense of embodiment in a most primary way. But there is more. In reading scripture, and the way it reports lives that have been lived, or depicts actions that have been (or should be) performed, we may perceive diverse patterns of human embodiment passing before our mind's eye. And then, withdrawing from the expressed content of these actions, and attending to their configurations alone, we may be put in mind of the way bodily gestures and deeds gather the elements of Being, give them human shape, and infuse them with qualities and values. This sensibility to the phenomenon of our human being is a meditative attunement to the ever-pulsing reality of life itself. This consciousness may even give rise to the sense that all these human happenings, emergent from God's creative effectivity, are, in truth, finite modalities (or images) of God. For as we activate the fullness that we are, and shape it into life-forms, we are not only vibrant nodal points in the universe, but unique human realizations of possibilities of unimaginable divine origination. Such types of spiritual consciousness may be developed through reading scripture in the mode of *sod*.

All this occurs moment after moment, throughout our lives. It is a giving oneself over to God, and a living with God-mindedness as much as possible. In cultivating this spiritual attitude, one affirms the ineffable mystery that inheres in the world. Standing firm within it, one's entire body and being say, *"Amen ve-Amen"* (Yes and Truly). In this "self-expression," through the varieties of our lives at all times, we verify our being in Being—our lives in the Life of the universe, and our godly possibilities as vessels of God's creative pulsations. Saying *amen* in this way renews a covenant with the Giver of the *torah kelulah*. And binding oneself to all that happens with spiritual attunement transforms one's life into a living proclamation that "God is One."

It may take a lifetime to achieve this breakthrough of consciousness; but it is a sacred task and the ultimate goal of theology.

PaRDeS

The different types of thinking and theology cultivated by the four forms of Jewish scriptural interpretation are not inherently mutually exclusive. At different times and in the hands of different teachers, one mode of reading might be emphasized over the others, which are either silently shunted aside or actively criticized or rejected. Some medieval grammarians, such as R. Abraham ibn Ezra, championed the *peshat* mode above all else, and privileged the fine-tuning of one's linguistic or grammatical comments while lambasting the *derash* because of the creative, philological liberties it takes with the text. But this is a captious attitude and unnecessary to boot, since, as we have noted, these modes of reading serve different ends and activate distinct aspects of the imagination. Similarly restrictive is the attitude of other exegetes, such as Rabbeinu (Jacob) Tam, who contended that the only interpretative mode of real significance is the *derash*, since it provides the scriptural basis of traditional religious life and practice; and even that the only words of scripture one needs to know are those either cited or invoked in rabbinic literature. Such an attitude obviously limits cultural information, and valorizes one curriculum to the exclusion of all others. By contrast, if some philosophers or mystics gave exclusive attention to the modes of *remez* or *sod*, they did not necessarily mean that the other types of reading are folly or to be transcended; rather, they gave this emphasis because they were concerned to cultivate their own spiritual sensibilities through a preferred method of study, since to them reading scripture fosters special kinds of insight and self-transformation.

The emphasis on certain interpretative modes did not exclude their incorporation into more synthetic or hierarchical or graded attitudes toward the scriptural text. The synthetic type is integrative and appreciates different exegetical modes for what they are and do; and it may even try to blend several types of readings into one discourse. Thus, while Rashi could recognize differences between the grammatical aspect of *peshat* and the theological or moral issues of *derash*, he also attempted to integrate straightforward readings of the sentences of scripture with materials drawn from the literature of rabbinic *derash*, where that could fall in line with the flow of the passage. Maimonides, on the other hand, exemplifies a more hierarchical model of interpretation, whereby the *peshat* and *remez* are distinct levels of reading, each true in its own right, insofar as each is geared to different modes of consciousness: the ungarnished plain sense for the untutored person, impressed by images and feelings, and the more parabolic way of allusions for the philosophical type, engaged by abstract ideas and thoughts. And finally, there is the approach that emphasizes a graded sequence of meanings. This type is represented by mystical works like the Book of Zohar. Its emphasis is on multiple modes of reading, dynamically correlated, and part of a process of spiritual development. Reading scripture is hereby more akin to a religious pilgrimage or rite of passage, whereby an individual successively proceeds through the four levels of textual meaning, moving toward the goal of spiritual wisdom. In this way, reading scripture is a rich path toward different modes of God-mindedness, each with its own truth but bound together in a progression of significance, culminating in the most supernal of truths—conveyed through the *sod*.

I would like to build on these latter insights in a modern mode.

In the preceding discussion, we observed how different types of reading practices can sponsor different types of sensibility, which serve different ways of living thoughtfully in the world, and can also cultivate different types of theological attention and attitude. Reading may therefore be a site of reflection, and its processes can contribute to one's life-process. I would thus suggest that each one of the four modes of interpretation is a kind of rite of passage, whereby a reader is inducted into different types of understanding of the ways that we make meanings in life—in the natural world all around us, for the purpose of practical affairs, and also in the world of moral values and spiritual apprehensions. These may variously interact and affect one another; or they may be kept apart as distinct sensibilities. There is no one pattern. Each person, at different moments of life, can activate and integrate these modes in different ways. Still and all, one always stands on the ground of the *peshat*. The ancient rabbinic sages put it this way: "Scripture never loses its plain sense." For them, this dictum meant that, when all is said and done, one always comes back to this base line. For us it means that we always walk on the earth, and must first hone primary skills for understanding the basic sense of words and things in our natural environment. But this is not the whole of life; our initial understandings are quickly taken up by other matters, since we also live with moral values and spiritual concerns. These latter fold back into the everyday world and infuse it. Not bound by the exclusive importance of any one mode of reading and thinking, or by fixed hierarchies of value, we may live with the awareness of a more complex simultaneity of meanings. How these are activated or discerned is part of the larger rite of passage that constitutes our lives on earth. Here is one possible way of understanding these matters in a theological context.

First and foremost there is always the *peshat*, our world of common sense. It is always there as the foundational level of religious consciousness. In this realm we name people and things, act and talk, and share a public realm. This is the sphere in which the self is embodied and joins with other persons, where we eat and suffer and die, and where we love and struggle. This is the world of goods and evils, in which the covenant is forged and expanded, or changed and revised. It is also the realm where interpretations are proposed and realized, or rejected and scrutinized. All our words and acts in this world of common sense reveal new aspects of it, even as they may also conceal others from view. We need one another to keep the fullness of speech and perspective alive for the sake of the flourishing of human life. In such ways we honor God; for by our actions the vastness of divine vitalities is humanized, and the world is no mere natural or neutral realm, but is revealed, part by part, over the course of human civilization, as a creation. It is not always a creation, for the features of this realm can be obscured by habitude and disregard, or distorted by mean-spiritedness or evil. But it *can* be the context for a creation. By focusing on the everyday, the *peshat* fosters a mindfulness of the details of life, and thus treats with sacred trust and deed the humanly perceived fullness of God's illimitable effectivity.

What does the *derash* dimension add? Just this: it opens our minds to the constructed nature of our common world of language and value, and to the possibilities that may reshape our common world with new thoughts and purpose. This is the domain of the Oral Torah, which keeps our minds and perspectives fresh, and challenges all routine and idolatry. The mindfulness of *derash* is the mindfulness of the play of language and its creative possibilities, and also the realization that we are the custodians of language as well as its priests. Language constitutes both the gifts offered and received, and the offerings whose substance is always transmuted in the world of persons and values. To cultivate a theological mind infused by the qualities of *derash* is to cultivate an ongoing mindfulness of our responsibilities for how the living God is realized and named in the common world. Here then is a delicate simultaneity: the *derash* guards against the stultification of the *peshat*, while the *peshat* grounds the *derash* in the common world; the *derash* is a prophetic voice decrying fundamentalistic reductions, while the *peshat* keeps counsel with the basic truth that circumstances require choices about values and meaning. In the fullest sense, the *derash* helps God remain God in our world by keeping the vastness of possibilities alive through the Oral Torah; but just as vitally, the *peshat* of the common world reminds us that we must always act in the here and now, and that this is the domain where Divinity may become actual and humanly real. Both factors must be held in mind; both are truths of a living theology.

And what more might the mode of *remez* contribute? It may keep us attuned to the flash of possibility, suggested in some way or another, *and* to the fact that all hints are rooted in human discernment and judgment. As such they may be helpful or not, wise or just plain folly. We build networks of sense out of hints at all levels of our perception, for there is no mere matter of fact. Who is to say if there is really something there beneath the surface, or whether we are just bumbling along thinking that we have discerned a deeper meaning? The phenomenon of *remez* should cultivate an attitude of humility before the so-called clues and allusions we proclaim as we make decisions about people and events and writings, as well as the larger "meaning of things." Even the hints we gather in tradition may get our minds stuck, as Job came to realize in the course of his life. One must therefore always proceed with caution, and a readiness for reconsideration. New hints may compel an overhaul of one's thinking, or put some things in abeyance. There is no easy way. The miracle is that we actually do build our world out of hints, and find ways to let them dilate and join with other allusions, and thus create patterns for our thinking and judgment. The flicker or flash of insight may smash an idol of thought or belief that has hardened in our hearts. On such occasions, *remez* serves God and truth.

Ultimately, the three levels just considered participate in the *torah kelulah*, and give it a human voice. Consciousness of this superordinate dimension is the work of *sod*. It opens the domain of mystery, and of possibilities beyond imagination. But it must be brought to mind and kept in mindfulness. The kind of complex religious consciousness that I have adumbrated here, cultivated by four (separate and interactive) levels of scriptural interpretation, would stand in the common world amid its needs and obligations, ever mindful of the divine depths below and beyond. Such an orientation may also develop a mindfulness infused with humility and care before the fragility of life fashioned out of the whirlwind. Each point of consciousness is a holy shining through the darkness of our unknowing, the thick cloud through which God is revealed to our mortal minds.

Religious Practice
and Forms of Attention

Preliminary Thoughts about Living Theologically

A central task of theology is to bring its ideas and values into the everyday of life, where they may be enacted and put to the test. Without this dimension theology is a mere cluster of speculative abstractions and traditional assertions—of cognitive or conceptual value at best; but with it, theology assumes a concrete immediacy, and thought and life may be variously integrated. Considered this way, religion is the gravitational settling of thought into behavior; and concomitantly, it is the nexus where physicality becomes spirit, infusing the forms of worldliness with transcendent dimensions.

Having such matters in mind, we observed earlier that an important feature of theology is to provide modes of self-cultivation, whereby a person might develop spiritual perceptions and be guided toward types of God-mindedness in the course of life. To exemplify the issues, four classic types of scriptural study were discussed and shown to sponsor corresponding types of world-perception and religious consciousness. Demonstrably, theology and life go hand in hand: one's religious life is cultivated in tandem with one's awareness overall. Becoming attuned to diverse hermeneutical modes of awareness (while interpreting scripture) is thus a ritual process of ongoing self-development, whereby one may become more attuned to the multiform diversity of life itself as well its dimensions of all-effectuating Divinity. Just as we seek to find a balance point for making sense of a textual passage, we similarly hope to find a balance point for our world-intending sensibilities, caught in the meshes of clues and mysteries that always exceed our understanding. Each moment is a throbbing of divine everlastingness, of ever-new shapes of sound and sight that assail our mortal consciousness. They pulse and flicker, elide and fade—seemingly unfixable by thought and mocking our meager abilities.

Still, something must be done. The theological task is to rise to this challenge: to live wholly engaged in the divine covenant, as alert and responsive to God's initiating "I shall be" as possible. Moses is our master here. It is he who first taught the nature of this commitment; and it is in his voice that its ongoing character and consequences have been taught. Insofar as Jewish theology continues to learn from this teacher, a twofold task presents itself: to receive the vitalities of Divinity in all their variety *and* to forge a life of piety from these worldly elements. There is thus a "greater" and a "lesser" covenant. The greater, or more comprehensive, of these two is the *overall commitment* of the self to the truth of God's ever-happening "I shall be," by means of the fundamental (and life-shaping) assertion "We shall do and we shall hear." This involves a total subjugation of oneself to the divine "Shall-Be" of existence. The smaller covenant involves the transformation of every *specific moment* into events of spiritual value, so that the individual is always responding to the manifestations of God's "I am" with the human confirmation "Here I am" (ready to try to hear and do what is required). Sinai symbolizes this junction of heaven and earth. Living within the covenant, we are challenged to actualize the principles of Sinai at every moment, through the bonds we forge with persons and things in the course of life. In this way we may live at the intersection of transcendence and immanence—the transcendent immanence of world-being perceived as (actualities of) immanent transcendence. The resources of tradition and the demands of integrity set the terms and guidelines for response.

>>><<<

In the opening chapter of this work, I suggested that the awakening of consciousness from the routines of life begins with the confession "Here I am." We now can see that this existential assertion is also a statement of religious commitment. An additional element is likewise involved in that the assertion is also a fundamental act of testimony. For with the statement "Here I am" in the context of life, the self confirms God's "I shall be" throughout the vast particularities of existence. This is the core of the covenant. It can only be lived and enacted. No dogmatic piety can serve as a substitute. In covenant theology, the world becomes "God-real."

"You are my witnesses, says YHWH, and I am God." Thus spoke the prophet (Isa. 43:12). His words are built on distinction and difference. But a later rabbinic sage saw matters differently, and transformed this proclamation into a more daring theological assertion. He said: "*When* you are My witnesses, I am God; *but if you are not* My witnesses, *then* (as it were) *I am not God.*"

God is a reality for human life wherever humans attest to God's presence, through the character and commitments of their lives. Covenant theology can guide a person toward such a lifelong testimony. But it can only cultivate a certain sensibility toward God's presence; it cannot prove it.

>>><<<

As we prepare to think about how one may live theologically in the concreteness of everyday life, it will be helpful to restate our basic theological claim. It amounts to this: that God's all-ineffable effectivity informs the vastness of things with the life of its Life; and all we can say about this (thanks to the nomenclature of scripture) is that God is ever YHWH—which means (we are told) that God shall ever be as God shall be. This mode of ever-new omnipresence is confirmed in daily experience, where the multiform pulsations of Divinity so variously impact our lives and minds and hearts. Many are the ways that our thoughtless habituations are smashed and God's living "Shall-Be" is perceived. God is the all-encompassing ground of the vitality that roils in the depths of nature, but also puts tenderness into the animal heart. Both the orchid and the shark are of the breath of God, as are the words of Moses and the demagogue. Without God there is no life; we in the darkness give its all-happening impressions names.

Put your ear to the ground, O son of man, and hear its heartbeat; touch the air and know what you can. Is it not all "I shall be as I shall be"?

The vastness of God's world-being rushes up everywhere. Just how "all these things" are received by us, and fostered for their own good as well as our earthly benefit, is an ongoing challenge for a living theology. Everything depends on human mindfulness, and the realization of the old imperative: "*be-khol dera-khekha da'ehu*" (Know God in all your ways; Prov. 3:6).

What does this mean?

Two interpretations are fundamental. The first puts primary emphasis on the phrase "your *ways*" (*derakhekha*), and thus exhorts one to have a God-mindedness in the entirety of one's life. A person should try to be attentive to the teeming vastness of life *and* acknowledge its ultimate source in God. And insofar as the exhortation also emphasizes the personal aspect of the task, by stressing "*your* ways," one is also bidden to realize that the "way" toward this goal depends on the specifics of each individual's lifeways. In such a manner one might "know" God. For God's ways are part of the fullness of God's universal "Shall-Be," expressed in all reality; and we only know that portion of it which occurs before us at any particular moment, and by the manner we engage it. Just here is the covenant task; for just here is the possibility of living with a God-minded concern for the teeming details of the world. Naturally, human responses are fraught with risk and prone to error. But the theological challenge is to bend this reality toward moral values in the most thoughtful way possible, even as they may be weakened by fear and self-interest.

This (dual) theological manner of living should be understood within the larger framework of the scriptural teaching that God's ways are not human ways: "For my ways [*derakhai*] are not your ways [*darkheikhem*]" (Isa. 54:9). God's ways are always giving life and form to Being, infusing each and every being with its own drive toward existence and cohesion and sustenance—through the four dimensions of mineral, vegetal, animal, and human existence. God directs the inner vitality of these realms; but they may also interact in complex ways. Some forms are organically and physically stronger than others, and affect the growth of elements in their orbit. There are consequently numerous constellations of life, up and down the chain of being, pushing and pressing with their own claims for viability—and they are ultimately *all* God's ways. And we too have a share in God's ways within this domain, since humans are part of this chain of life-forms and produce their own ecological configurations. But because of our intelligence and impulses (also part of God's ways), human acts sometimes get the better of other life-forms and impact the earth in hugely consequential ways. If this is so with respect to our effect on organic life, think how much our actions decisively impact other social beings (for both achievements in medicine and brutality in war are extensions of the divine forces within us). Hence conscious attention to the nature of one's actions and their implications is vital. Moral growth is directly linked to these kinds of human thoughtfulness. In turn, the theological imperative of having a God-mindedness in all one's ways articulates the ideal of raising human consciousness toward a maximal point of theological focus when engaged in the world. For all our behaviors, in one way or another, transform and condition God's ways. *God's ways are thus not human ways in the fullest sense of the term—but they also pass through the human realm and are thereby affected by it.* Religious consciousness is therefore crucial for the sake of God and human beings. "I shall be as I shall be" and "We shall do and we shall hear" meet on earth. The nexus is the proving point of covenant living.

A second interpretation of Proverbs 3:6 provides a different focus. If the first puts emphasis on one's human "ways," the second stresses the adverb *all*: "Know God in *all* your ways." An aspect of this dimension was certainly present in the preceding consideration, but it remains to highlight two issues—both crucial for Jewish theology. The first of these is that no area of life is excluded from covenant theology; the entirety of existence comprises the sites of divine-human engagement. *The junction of heaven and earth may happen everywhere*: the mysterious fullness of divine Being is ever surging and happening in this and that form on earth—*in all the ways our minds and instruments can discern it.* And it is at these points that our religious and moral selves are engaged: our religious selves, insofar as we are conscious of the pulsations of God throughout world-being; and our moral selves as well, insofar as we must respond to each pulsation in the proper or appropriate way (with due deliberation for the phenomena and our human being). How both foci are simultaneously joined in the course of life is of vital concern to a living theology.

But before giving specific examples of this, let us take note of a second consideration that lurks in the adverb *all*. This aspect of "*all* your ways" refers to the full resources of the self. A person may ordinarily bring diverse and scattered modes of mindfulness to the events of life; and thus the work of theology is to cultivate a fuller attunement of the mind and heart to all that is happening in one's life-world so that one can respond more fully to each occurrence in terms of its distinct circumstance and distinctive character. Knowing God in all one's ways would thus include recognizing the different manifestations of human life and the need to attune oneself to the specifics of the moment. One would thus try to bring "all" of one's resources (physical and spiritual) to each occasion, in order to respond to the "all" of each happening with the "all" of one's self. Every moment is, in its way, a kind of

Sinaitic giving and receiving: it is a giving and receiving of love or restraint, in due measure for the occasion; it is a giving and receiving of information or silence, between the parties in the encounter; and it is a giving and receiving of humanity or presence, in words and deeds or just plain silence. Jewish theology begins at Sinai; but Sinai is ever happening through the expressive reality of God's *torah kelulah.* A living theology proves itself in the hearing and the doing of each moment, at all times.

Covenant theology tries to cultivate the self for all the occasions of God's "Shall-Be," such as they are or may be perceived in this world. If we have eyes but do not see, and ears without hearing, would we really be ready "to do" and "to hear" what needs to be heard and done? And would we be ready to see and do the unexpected, or deal with all the futilities that haunt us here in the vastness?

Shema minah. One must take this to mind.

>>><<<

But how does such self-cultivation occur? How can one's eye and ear, or hand and heart, be prepared to receive the refractions of God's "Shall-Be" in this world? To begin an answer, I shall focus on several domains of traditional Jewish religious practice where such a mindfulness is variously cultivated and the challenges of living theologically are engaged. The first of these is *halakha.*

The Practice of Halakha

Halakha fosters and guides Jewish theological living amid the minutiae of the everyday, moment by moment. It is the historical flowering of the Sinai covenant—as initially formulated in the words of the Written Torah, but significantly expanded and transformed by the pulse of ongoing life, generation after generation, as the disciples of Moses investigated what was inscribed and needed interpretation, and as they expanded the original norms through faithful living and ancestral practice. Over time, the breath of the Oral Torah suffused the ancient text and inspired it with new soul and sanctity, extending the path of piety outlined in the initial covenant to the emergent patterns and particulars of everyday life. This path of covenant piety is the *halakha*; and insofar as this piety comprises the values of a God-centered life, *halakha* is living Jewish theology in word and deed.

The ancient sages were aware that they were continuing the hermeneutical revolution of Moses and his disciples. Like them, the rabbinic scholars were determined to receive the totality of the written tradition, and hear and do all that could be determined of its ongoing scope and applicability. In a remarkable sermon, R. Eleazar ben Azariah reinterpreted the phrase preceding the Decalogue, "And the Lord spoke *all these words*" (Exod. 20:1), to refer to all the words of Torah interpretation of the sages, in all their diversity and contradictions—even where some declared a particular matter valid, but others deemed it void, or where some determined a thing pure, while still others found it impure. R. Eleazar rhetorically stressed that the words of scripture were no dead stump but the offshoots of an ever-flowering tree of life. Thus Sinai was deemed a plantation of beneficence and its teachings a regenerating fruit—a bounty of sustenance for those who would cultivate it with care. One should therefore rejoice in the tree of Torah; and if the entangled complexity of its meanings might cause perplexity or despair, or lead one to ask, how can I learn Torah in this circumstance? the teacher's advice is this: "attune your ear" and "acquire a discerning heart, [in order] to listen to the words" of those who interpret passages one way or another—and then decide. There is no other way, and no easy solution. Attentive study must be cultivated with patience. Only in this way might the old words of Sinai be "all these words" of an ever-new Torah and covenant.

Through the process of thinking and living, the shapes of normative action gradually filled out the shapes of scripture in new ways. Biblical cases and principles influenced the various spheres of personal and societal behavior; their scope and limits were determined to allow ideals to be set and practicalities to emerge; priorities and contradictions were resolved to allow actions in one domain to be correlated with those in another; and values were reevaluated in the stark light of justice and righteousness. In some cases, the conflicts of interpretation were between two actions of equal validity, which could not be simultaneously enacted. For such circumstances, hierarchies of practice were determined. What should take precedence: prayer or services for the dead; caring for a life or observing the Sabbath; private mourning or festival joy? In other cases one had to clarify the precise application of scriptural imperatives, whose details were wanting. How does one make the Sabbath holy, or build a tabernacle, or recite the words of Torah? And how does one determine states of bodily purity or proper food, establish judicial evidence, or engage in daily commerce without entrapment and deceit? What kind of marriage procedure would obligate both parties in an ongoing way, and provide protection from abandonment or abuse? Who is a valid witness, and how can the law prevent collusion and deceit? The Written Torah does not always say or spell out the details; but a living covenant theology seeks to work this out—slowly and deliberately, for the sake of what is and will be, in order for these events to be heard and done as sacred action.

Over time there emerged what might be called *the gestures of the generations*, these being the ongoing practices cultivated and inculcated for the varied spheres of life. By imitation and learning, each new generation enters the life-patterns of its ancestors. Hence one does not live in the covenant by oneself or for oneself, but within the framework of past lives and the life-forms built up with considered thoughtfulness over time. The personal character of the act resides in the distinctive tone with which the common gestures are infused; and in this way individual actions reinforce the continuity of the generations and their values. This temporal fund of embodied actions deriving from the past shapes the ongoing halakhic culture in fundamental ways—and not least for the solidarity it effects with prior ages, and the loyalty it induces for the present and future.

THE PATTERNS OF ACTION

The patterns of action and their development across the generations constitute a deepening of one's humanness. Our mortal
selves are archetypally marked by "Adam," a name which denotes
a creature of the earth who lives and struggles with the complexity of choices. Adam's long travail is a wandering into culture and
language and identity, and into the confusions of will and desire. It
is the travail of mortality and morality upon the earth. One never
loses this natural dimension. It is primary and fundamental. Only
gradually does experience accumulate. The shaping of choice and
culture is the labor of generations, and the wisdom of the ancestors
is marked in scripture by such persons as "Abraham and Sarah" and
their progeny. They too are both singular and archetypal, just as
our own mortal naturalness, universal in character, is correspondingly cultivated by untold moments of learning when our natural
ideals are put to the test. In this way there is a spiritual formation
that takes place: there is not just the production of progeny, but
the insight to "walk before God" with "integrity"; there is not just
interest in one's good fortune, but the need to avoid deceit, and
to intervene on behalf of the innocent for the sake of righteousness; and there is not just opportunism and power, but the need
to maintain dignity despite temptation, calumny, and lies. And
then slowly, with time, this accumulated wisdom of the ancestors
is ready to respond to the tasks of an integrated spiritual life—at
first through the pedagogy of individuals like "Moses," our covenant teacher, and all the subsequent sages and faithful followers, who teach the words of their master and shape the old ideals
and purposes through their hearts and lives. But the test of living
in covenant freedom before God's "Shall-Be" is challenging and
difficult. Lapses occur and the hard choices ignored. Thus in the
movement across the generations, there also arises one like "Elijah," who reminds us of the ever-present importance of deciding
for God and not the idols, and of not "hopping on two branches"
like a flighty bird without any resolve. According to rabbinic
legend, it is this same Elijah who spent his time dressing the
wounds of the poor at the gates of Rome, and when asked when

the messiah would come, looked up from this sorrow and said, "Today, if you hear My voice."

These persons are types of the Jewish theological soul: formed of the earth and bound to it, we (like "Adam") are creatures of confused will, beset with death and survival—but we are also the heirs of generations of character and wisdom (the ancestors, like "Abraham" or "Joseph"), who raise us beyond our earthly selves toward ideals of generosity and justice and filial piety; and it is through this cultural shaping that we are also covenant selves (like "Moses" and his disciples), with the spiritual goal of living all of our lives through a sacred tradition of accumulated pieties and moral determinations—as much as possible, and without faltering, whether through duplicity or failed resolve before the complex choices of everyday life. This is done by striving to hear the voice of God's "Shall-Be" wherever it is, even among suffering strangers far from home (like "Elijah" of scripture and legend).

The Jew may be put in mind of this multilayered self each morning near the beginning of the prayer service, in the course of one's passage from natural consciousness to spiritual awareness. The individual is then exhorted to acknowledge before God, "Master of all the worlds," that all one's human supplications depend on divine mercy, and not on one's personal achievements of righteous merit, for

> What [*mah*] are we? What is our life? What is our kindness? What is our righteousness? What is our [capacity for] salvation? What is our strength? What is our might? What shall we say before you, Lord our God, and God of our ancestors? Are not all the mighty like nothing before you, the renowned as if they had not existed, the wise as without knowledge, the perceptive as devoid of understanding? For all their deeds are desolate, and the days of their lives like empty air [*hevel*] before you: "And the preeminence of a human [*adam*] over a beast is non-existent, for it is all futile vanity [*hevel*]" [Eccles. 3:19].

In brutal starkness, the self recites a confession of animality and the reduction of one's human capacity, one's Adamic nature, to wind and vanity. The confessional assertions ("what?!") are then followed by rhetorical queries ("are not?"), and a concluding assertion regarding the futility of human labors as such. In this way, the forms of language inculcate a certain awareness, through rhetoric and repetition, leading to a scriptural crescendo. But at this very point the recitation changes, and abruptly asserts a different status for the praying self: "But we are your people, members of your covenant, descendants of Abraham . . . the seed of Isaac . . . (and) the congregation of Jacob . . . whom you named Israel." Now the mere naturalness of being Adamic creatures is supplemented by the declaration of one's share in a lineage of great ancestors and membership in the covenant. The tone thus changes from query and despair to duty and celebration before God ("Therefore we are obliged to thank you and praise you"), and to a special joyfulness at one's human estate: "So fortunate are we: how [*mah*] good is our portion, how pleasant our lot, and how lovely is our inheritance." One is thus more than a mortal, natural being; one is also the heir of tradition and its teachings, and endowed with a way of being more than just a creature. Through tradition, the Adamic self is able to rise to the status of a Mosaic consciousness, and to serve God through the covenant. This transformation does not deny the "whatness" (or quiddity) of one's animal nature, but converts the plight of existence into ongoing spiritual testimony.

It is thus a core task of covenant theology to live within the naturalness of our natural lives, as creatures of the earth who work and eat and labor and die—like all other living beings; but to try to turn those occasions into markers of praise and thankfulness before God, the Life of all life. Insofar as the self can stand in this conjunction, all moments enact the covenant between God's "I shall be" and the human "We shall do and we shall hear." The routine happenings of life may thus become caesural events of godliness; and the caesural may also somehow be integrated into a coherent spiritual life.

>>><<<

Let us consider this matter further, and reflect on how the human, Adamic self, who eats and hears and smells, may be transfigured

into a covenantal, Mosaic self. A person may be hungry like Adam
and feel things like Adam; but one need not just eat and experience things in a mindless, natural way. Covenant theology fosters a deliberate disjunction between the need or deed and its
fulfillment or enactment. This disjunction inserts the spiritual
dimension of a deliberate or "settled mind" (*yishuv ha-da'at*)
into the life-process; for Jewish covenant living is never merely
natural living, no matter how much it is rooted in naturalness,
but stretches over it a vast skein of religious culture. It is the
religious culture (the accumulated patterns and wisdom of the
ancestors) that determines what are the fixed times for morning
and afternoon and evening prayer; what is the status of dawn
and dusk; when the Sabbath begins, and when it ends; how one
should prepare to eat, and how to give thanks afterward; what
may be eaten and under what conditions; and what is the status
of one type of food accidentally mixed with something forbidden, and at what point is something of sufficient size to qualify
as food, and thus require a blessing. Similar considerations ap-
ply to the calculation of the seasons and the heavenly bodies:
the moon waxes and wanes, but its natural cycle is only meaningful as a cultural fact, for its changes are observed by human
calibrations, and these determine the pattern of the seasons and
the festivals. One does not simply do this or that action; rather,
it is necessary to note what one is doing, and then do it in a
thoughtful and focused manner—from morning to night.

> Scripture says: "These are the festival occasions of the Lord, sacred
> convocations, which you shall proclaim [*tiqre'u otam*] on their occa-
> sions." (Lev. 23:4)

The ancient sages pondered this passage. If the Torah emphasizes "*you* shall proclaim *them*," this surely means that the responsibility for determining the sacred times (festivals and new moons)
is a cultural matter, not something entirely self-evident in the seasons and astral cycles. Based on this interpretation of scripture,
Rabban Gamliel issued a strong decree that even contradicted

the interpretation of his esteemed colleague, R. Joshua, whom he subsequently censored for maintaining his opinion. A later sage, R. Pappa, understood the scriptural proof text a bit differently. According to him, the key word was not *tiqre'u* (*you* shall proclaim) but *otam* (them); for, he taught, scripture is written here with a defective orthography so that one may read *otam* as *atem* (you *yourself*), in the sense that *just you* (the scholars of Torah) are given the right to proclaim sacred days. In this way, an apparently superfluous word with a certain spelling is invested with great legal power, and reinforced for a later generation the authority of the sages to determine the sacred seasons. But this exegetical point was made earlier. For when R. Akiba went to comfort his censored colleague, R. Joshua, he did so by reminding him of his own earlier *derash* of this biblical passage, when he taught that the reason scripture writes *otam* defectively in three places is to instruct us that *even if* "you [*atem*]" err in your calculations or determinations, all authority is in the mouths of the sages—and them alone.

Thus does the word of God speak through human interpretation. Or as we might deduce from scripture: "Moses commanded the Torah *to us*; [hence:] it is a heritage of the congregation of Israel" (Deut. 33:4)—and all that this implies.

THE LANGUAGE OF BLESSINGS

Daily life is filled with events that largely escape routine attention. It is *halakha* that tries to refocus the mind so that one may acknowledge the many occasions of life as they happen. At the nexus of world-being and personhood, the language of blessings is a powerful agent of this transformation.

The early morning recitations, and the blessings for food or unexpected occurrences (of sight or sound), are exemplary. In such cases, a fixed (traditional) formulation is supplemented by a reference to the particular occasion. The first part evokes a cosmic or universal perspective, and states: "Blessed are you, O Lord our God, king of the universe"; the second section is case specific, and adds: "who does *x*." For example, in the early morning recitations, a person regularly gives thanks to God "who gives sight to the blind"; "who clothes the naked"; "who releases the bound"; "who straightens the bent"; "who has provided for all my needs"; "who firms a person's steps"; and so on. Some items of this list are known from traditional sources (the first, third, and fourth praise derive from Psalm 146, which is recited later in the morning service), while others are unique to this recitation. But the key point is that the catalogue contains a detailed recitation of gratitude to the Lord for gifts of daily sustenance: the clothing of the body, the awakening of morning sight, the release from the bonds of sleep, the assumption of upright posture, the wherewithal of living, and the sense of determination and execution. Nothing is taken for granted; every thing is received as a gift flowing from the well of divine giving, and taking shape in the world. For this reason the worshiper addresses the Lord of all Being (YHWH, the all-effectuating "Shall-Be") in personal terms, as "you": the coursing of the (impersonal) vitality of Being passes through the human sphere of life, and as it infuses this sphere there is a touching of heaven and earth in the (personal) life of the individual. The subjective self directs mindfulness to this influx of God's creative force into one's daily life, which is now not a mindless routine of mere naturalness, but seen with a focused spiritual attention. Daily sustenance is experienced as a divine gift; and normal habitude is ruptured. The mind and eyes awaken to thought and sight: the body rises and stands, and walks clothed, unlike an animal, with dignified upright posture and sureness of foot. The earth sustains one's gait and grounds one's gaze—and this is now perceived with a transformed consciousness and confessed in words. The gestures of lying down at night and withdrawing one's sense of self-preservation also have their own distinct formulations. In between, there is the vast world of daily life, with things to see and do with spiritual alertness and in covenant witness to the streaming, in-breaking vastness.

Among the things of the day is food. Here too the natural pattern is interrupted. One does not simply proceed with satisfying the pangs of hunger. An initial preparation of the heart is necessary, undertaken by pausing and directing one's mind to the proper benediction before engaging in the actual act of ingestion. The preparation may include a ritual washing of the hands, if the meal includes bread; but in any case, the act of eating is preceded by a recitation of gratitude to God for the specific gift at hand: "who brings forth food from the earth"; "who creates the fruit of the earth"; "who creates the fruit of the tree"; or more generally, "for all exists through his word." The self is embodied in naturalness, in hunger and physical need; but covenant theology raises the worshiper's consciousness to the spiritual domain, and it is in this realm that one lives out one's natural urges. And if in the course of things one hears an unusual sound, sees an unusual sight, or encounters persons of a distinct or singular character, or again sees a long-lost friend, there is also something to say in order to confirm the moment. One then speaks in thankfulness to God: "whose power and might fill the world"; "who does the work of creation"; and "who has given of his glory to (creatures of) flesh and blood." There is no mere world or matters of fact for covenant theology; there is always the wonder and duty of the concrete moment at hand, where God's illimitable gift of life is given into our hands—to hear and do what is here and now. Theology does not change nature as such, but rather transforms its reception, through spiritual consciousness. Brute facticity remains, while being simultaneously transfigured.

THE TWOFOLD CONSCIOUSNESS

All this is a first level of focusing on the magnitude of God's unfolding, as it is *received in the human realm* and conjoined to halakhic practice. Through the language of blessings, the inner self is guided to a twofold consciousness: of the fullness, vast and sovereign, *and* the particular occasion, specific and personal. The fullness is the illimitable transcendence of Divinity, the Life of all life, ever exceeding human knowledge and grasp; the particular is the experience of God's immanent actuality as the Life of the life we find in the world we know and intuit. As religious persons, the ideal is to try to live at this crossing point and keep both theological dimensions in mind. The vector moves from the universal whole to specific concrescences of existence; and it keeps one centered on the particulars of naturalness, experienced as the gift of God's all-unnamable "Shall-Be." Such a responsive and dutiful "joining" of heaven and earth with spiritual awareness is the core of Jewish religious praxis, of *mitzvah*, understood here fundamentally as *tzavta* (or the "bonding" of human consciousness with Divinity).

But the movement of mind may also go in the other direction, when the primary focus is *directed toward God's plenitude*. If Jewish religious philosophy has (sometimes) had the temerity to suggest that the most one can say about God's ways in this world is an inference of actions based on our human modes of inference and reasoning (the cycles of nature hinting at acts of divine beneficence and care, for example), a similar way of speaking allows us to regard the manifold gifts of world-being as expressions of an omnipresent divine effectivity. On this accounting, the multiple modes of world-appearance are the experiential aspects of absolute truth in all its godly and illimitable otherness, totally beyond the language of action and event. We must thus unsay all that we know at this limit point of mind when we direct our minds through the forms of the world toward its ultimate Ground; and we must even negate the imaginative focus of this meditative state as well as our hearts yearn for God alone, in truth. At the borderland of the imagination we may thus have an intuition of God's Naught; but we cancel this inkling of ultimacy, knowing that it too is a human construct—and bow in silence.

>>><<<

The Sabbath and its observance may cultivate a theological mindfulness of just this sort.

How so?

The Sabbath sanctifies time through sanctioned forms of rest and inaction. On this day certain workaday activities and ordinary busyness are suspended and brought to a halt. In their stead, a whole host of ways of resting the body and mind are cultivated. These are of a special cultural type. For though we have a natural notion of work, and think of it in terms of physical exertion or compulsory performance done in order to sustain one's livelihood, these kinds of labor relate to our Adamic selves: the physical self that is sent forth into the world, and must work the earth to provide sustenance, while losing body strength on one's lifecourse toward death. By contrast, our Mosaic selves are enhanced through the teachings of the Oral Torah, which bring other notions of work and categories of labor to bear. Building on the specified laws of scripture and archetypal acts like the building of the sanctuary, generations of sages sought to define the nature of work and determine permitted Sabbath activities. They also had to fix the temporal onset of the day. Scripture only speaks of "the Sabbath day" as such, but the exact time boundaries had to be established so that the domain of the Sabbath might be set off as a sphere in which unsanctioned labors were off-limits and inaction was sanctified. In so doing, our natural assumptions are stretched: the Sabbath begins by ritual acts already on the day preceding the Sabbath (that is, late Friday afternoon, since the "day" begins at sunset), and concludes the day following, some (fixed) time after the next sunset and the emergence of stars. Thus the temporal sphere of the Sabbath is not a natural day by any account, but a cultural time period that overlaps three natural days; and its "labors" are not natural labors that might be defined by physical effort, but activities delineated by culture and its own inherent logic.

One enters the sphere of inaction through divestment, and this release affects all the elements of the workaday sphere. Business activity and exchange of money are forbidden, and one is urged not just to desist from commerce but to develop more interior spheres of settling the mind from this type of agitation; the carrying of objects is defined as a type of labor, but this is clarified by being restricted to domains outside the home—though the so-called private domain can be extended into more public space through various sanctioned remedies, which variously widen the domain of inclusion. Other Sabbath regulations affect the preparation of foods, and distinguish between hot and cold meals, or the way precooked items might be reheated during the holy day. Similarly cultural are the various occasions of permitted infringement of the strict Sabbath regulations: one cannot perform even light manual labor for a friend if this act violates notions of work established by other means; and one cannot put oneself in a situation that might even tempt a store owner to think that one is a potential buyer. But one must readily and without reserve violate the Sabbath rest to save a life or help someone in danger, even if it is not certain that the cry for help was made in good faith or based on a reasonable assessment of the situation. Slowly, under these multiple conditions, a sense of inaction takes over, and the day does not merely mark the stoppage of work or celebrate the completion of creation, but enforces the value that the earth is a gift of divine creativity, given to humankind in sacred trust. On the Sabbath, the practical benefits of technology are laid aside, and one tries to stand in the cycle of natural time, without manipulation or interference. To the degree possible, one must also attempt to bring the qualities of inaction and rest into the heart and mind. On the Sabbath one tries to let the world be the world and things be things, and not relate to them with an eye to self-interest or anticipated benefit. The Sabbath is thus a period of sacred stasis, a duration of sanctity through the cultivation of inaction in body and spirit (the deeper divestment known traditionally as *shevut*).

Entrance into the forms of Sabbath rest thus entails a shift of consciousness, from the particular details of human life to the cosmic vastness of Divinity. If religious consciousness during the workweek is geared to see the specifics of God's vitality as welling up in earthly forms, observance of the Sabbath trains the mind to move from the habitude of action to the ultimate borders of an imaginable immensity, where one can only put oneself in mind of a reality altogether exceeding normal activities and objects. This reality, as we may imagine it, is a realm of conjunctive interactions, where the actuality of all possibilities embraces in the loving heart of God. For if there is an ultimate domain where "this" and "not this" are conjoined, then it occurs in such an absolute stasis of divine "Being"; and if worshipers are to "sanctify" themselves through Sabbath rest, as the liturgy enjoins, then one path toward this goal is to cultivate a cosmic consciousness—a mindfulness that extends beyond the deeds and details of our earthly lives and their inherent multiplicities, toward the fullest harmony imaginable. This is a sphere so integral that we can only conceive of it in terms of some supernal balance or repose. In our minds we dream of this as the Sabbath that fills God's heart: an absolute and perfect wholeness.

This mode of spiritual intentionality and attachment to God throughout the Sabbath day is not for itself alone. It must also serve lived life. One enters the Sabbath rest in order to cultivate a mindfulness of inaction that can gradually suffuse one's entire consciousness (a kind of supernal soul added to our nature); and one may therefore hope to return to the workweek with this divine gift in one's heart. For though the rite of Separation (*havdalah*) at the conclusion of the Sabbath returns the worshiper to the concrete world of distinctions ("between the holy and the profane, between light and dark, between the seventh day and the six days of labor, and between Israel and the nations"), this ritual may also be viewed as a kind of Sanctification (*kiddush*) blessing for the ensuing week. Considered in this spirit, the self can take something of the unitary repose of the Sabbath into the divisions that cleave our lives in the everyday. The heartbeat of repose may thus suffuse the mind and limbs of one's being, and generate an inner balance poised on quietude and a settled spirit.

>>><<<

One could hardly imagine that these modes and conceptions of inaction simply happen on their own; rather, they emerge slowly, through the wisdom of tradition, as it develops forms of life that remove the self from its mere naturalness in order to cultivate a life of sustained God-mindedness in the everyday. The "heritage" of the Sabbath, as it is designated, may thus become for the worshiper nothing less than the spiritual act of giving "the world and all that is in it" back to God, at all times. As one grows in this consciousness, one may gradually achieve the ideal of "action in inaction," whereby it may be possible to hear and do all that needs to be heard and done on earth with a heart wholly attached to God—"the Lord of Peace," "whose peace is his" alone.

This is dying within life for love of God. It is a divestment of will for God's sake—and the wonder of the world.

>>><<<

The dialectics of a twofold consciousness may thus catalyze spiritual life in the everyday. The earthly pole of *artziyut* (or concrete worldliness) is filled by the challenges and topics of daily existence; and it provides the conditions by which consciousness rises to more transcendent spheres. Celebration of the holidays and festivals further sharpens this dynamic—the special holy days like Rosh Hashanah and Yom Kippur, by virtue of their basis in the concrete factuality of existence: birth, death, and a sense of sin or forgiveness; and the various seasonal festivals like Passover and Tabernacles, by virtue of their connection to historical moments of fundamental human importance: freedom from servitude and the fragility of world-wandering, respectively. The fecund image for this dynamic process may again be Jacob's ladder, the envisioned staircase *mutzav artzah*, set on the earth, but running upward to heaven, *ve-rosho magi'a ha-shamaymah*. Like some sacred nexus it portrays the holy conjunction of divine immanence and transcendence, with human consciousness, in the guise of angelic figures, ascending or descending upon it—vital symbols of the expansion or diminishment of spiritual awareness. Surely by virtue of the vertical hierarchy, a privileged position is accorded the peak. And yet, for all the allure of the heights, and the ideal elevations of the sacred seasons, one may never gainsay the physical realm itself—its brute mortality, its fallible nature, and its mundane deposits of hope or despair. Religious life must be reborn in this realm (from the chains of physical and mental bondage) before there is ever a true rebirth of the soul and ascendant consciousness (spiritual liberation as a transformed sensibility or heightened awareness). Only the self concretely aware of being mortal and world-bound and God-dependent can begin the journey of spiritual quest. And though, to be sure, such an awareness may even occur in an enslaved self (however inchoate and flickering), and thereby prefigure its ultimate liberation, that self must first be devoted to the tasks of worldly facticity and their cultivation. Gradually, the rungs of awareness are ascended—an expansion of consciousness within the self and beyond, toward the great circumscribing vastness. It is at these peaks of sensibility that the self is a reborn creature of God, attuned to the silences of eternity and the infinite harmonics of freedom and necessity—at once so elusive and so impinging. Now the soul is *also* a pilgrim of the cosmic solitudes, turning on God's axis to face all being with love's regard, weeping God's sorrow for the aching body of worldliness—the dry furrows of the earth, the wounds of the sorrowing neighbor.

Now too is God's word spoken anew, silent imprints on the tablets of the human heart.

The divine pulse of giving and care is the eternal truth of Sinai: confirmed daily in our ongoing acts of world-reception, interpretation, and love; and celebrated annually on the festival of Shavuot (the Feast of Weeks) by the community of the faithful, for all to heed and remember and fix firmly in mind. Primordial lights shining through the shapes of existence; primordial vibrations in its sounds: just this is *zeman matan torateinu*, the ever-sacred "Time of the Giving of our Torah"—just now, just here, just always.

The Life of Prayer

There is another way that Jewish tradition attempts to cultivate modes of God-mindedness in everyday life, and that is through

prayer (*tefilah*) and its modes of expression. Within the ritual-
ized structures of Jewish living, prayer partakes of the *halakha*
and is guided by its forms. But it is not merely a mode of *halakha*.
In its diverse aspects, *tefilah* has its own theological dimensions
and character.

WITHIN THE VASTNESS

The phenomenon of prayer responds to the vastness of sounds
and sights which surround us in the natural world. It begins with
the happenings of earthly existence, and the way it opens up as
day and night, tree and river, or sun and birdsong; and it includes a
sense of rebirth in the morning and dying at nightfall; it is affected
by the feel of the earth, soft with seed or tender with shoots; and
it responds to dew and sunlight, and the winds that scatter seeds
or chill the heart. All this happens with the opening of one's eyes
and ears, and the sensibilities of skin and touch; it is the concrete
vastness that presses upon us and reveals the creation moment after moment. But prayer also begins with emptiness and lack, when
existence leaves one hungry and unfulfilled; where there is not sufficient grain for food or cloth to warm the body; and where there is
the blight of disease and insane human hatred. It also begins with
the gaping terrors of the heart, lonely and inconsolable through the
failures of friendship and care, or the unhealed memories of catas-
trophe and loss that bleed in a wounded soul.

Prayer takes these moments and gives them voice. This voice
may be an outcry of thanksgiving or sorrow; and it can express
lack or hope. Such are its many modes. The humanness of the
voice is due to the humanness of the experience; and although
tradition may give formal expression to these topics of human
life, it does not exclude spontaneous prayer or the revitalization
of traditional wording through new intentions or understanding.
Tradition tries to open a verbal space in the unfolding vastness
of things; but with time and repetition the original formulations
may not always ring true, and then they are in need of revival
through the pathos and truth of one's actual life on earth.

The reality of prayer is marked by two fundamental considerations. The first is the specificity of one's humanness in the world. This produces the particularity of one's seeing and hearing and doing, and the singularity of one's hunger and longing and death. The scriptural watchword here is the verse "All the limbs of my being [*kol atzmotai*] shall say, O Lord, who is like you?!" (Ps. 35:10).

This phrase is subject to interpretation.

One possibility understands the speaker to say that each and every part of oneself shall express itself before the incomparable mystery of God's effectivity. Such expressions are through words and physicality—through words that intone the depths of physicality, and through limbs that give gestures to the silence of the mouth. The words respond to the gifts given the body through God's infusion of worldly elements with beneficent vitality, as well as to the aching sorrow when these same elements are thwarted due to ruptures in the natural or human realms. The mouth speaks (in prayer) for the sated mouth and its wants; it speaks for the hand that is given by another or left untouched; it speaks for the eye that can see clearly or the mind's eye that distorts what occurs; it speaks for the blood that supports life in the heart or fetus, and the diseases that may rot the self or weaken its blood flow; it speaks for the joys of human birth or marriage together with their dissolution through tribulation or divorce. And in more silent ways each limb may express the goods of life: in all the ways arms can support a fellow human being—unless they fall slack, not simply through ill will but out of confusion or lack of resolve; in all the ways that hands can give gifts to persons or benefit the earth—unless they become tight-fisted, not solely out of anger or spite but out disregard and self-interest; and in all the ways that one's feet can seek out a stranger to provide care or support—unless they flee the opportunity, not merely out of fear but out of sheer disregard or even anxiety before the face of the impenetrable and unknown of God.

A second interpretation of the biblical phrase takes it as expressing hope in one's ability to respond fully to the wonders of divine presence: to answer the vitality of God's "I shall be" with the fullness of one's consciousness and ability. On this view, the watchword articulates the yearning that all one's limbs and the totality of one's self shall participate in the unfolding divine mystery—that all this shall be in its service, bending the qualities of life toward good and humane ends. For the world becomes a human world through what we see and touch and build and step toward every day; and the world becomes a place of divine indwelling as we attest to the many shapes of God's glory that are realized in all the happenings of the world. Where we do not respond to these forms of glory as hints of God's heartbeat in the pulse of existence, things just are as they are, and the world's deeper dimensions are concealed. Failure to participate in the disclosures of the world is a failure of covenant nerve.

>>><<<

These considerations suggest another matter affecting the life of prayer. If the first underscores the individuality of joy and pain, the second stresses the communal dimension of life and solidarity with all existence. God's world does not affect the single self alone. The life of prayer must register—not only through the communal and historical voice of traditional prayers, but also by the new intentions one may give these old words—the multifaceted dimensions of reality of which humans are a part.

Participation in the world may therefore be regenerated by prayer. We can testify that this earth is the only sphere of God's effectivity we encounter; and while we acknowledge the benefits that have come our way, or the lacks that drain our hearts, we can also confirm our human partnership on this earth and the need to share its gifts. We recite the (psalmist's) words that "you [God] open your hand" (Ps. 104:28), but know that there are human takers and robbers, as well as givers and receivers. Scripture refers to God's "hand" to mark the outreach of divine beneficence, and the human ways that these gifts may reach all creation. God gives the gift of life to the many powers of the world; and it is human beings who, through their lives, may bend them for the goods of nature and social existence, or pervert their vigor through folly and greed. Whether as the recipients and good agents of things, or sufferers deprived of well-being, one may affirm through prayers of thanksgiving or petition, *amen ve-amen*, yes and truly: God is the Life of life—for each and all. We elaborate our prayers with words, because we live with words; but when we speak in prayer, all that we truly say in the depths is *amen ve-amen*: I affirm the gift and presence of the world, and the divine life beating within it.

One may not ask for more; but one can hear and do more.

>>><<<

Through the occasions of prayer, the self is grounded in the concreteness of life; and through the language of prayer one attests to its impact. If the *halakha* guides one to a deeper consciousness of the phenomenon of acting, and the gestures of the generations, prayer may cultivate a new awareness of the powers of speech and how the words used may foster spiritual growth.

Let us consider this.

There are two kinds of silence. One of these is natural silence, and is characterized by the absence of noise. It is a modulation, a diminishment, a negative valence. The other kind of silence is spiritual, and is characterized by potentiality and anticipation. We sense this every time we watch a conductor or an ensemble gesture slightly just prior to the production of sound; and we also sense it during moments of self-collection and focus, before something of significance is said to another person. With respect to music, anticipatory silence helps prepare the self to hear sound sounding; for it focuses attention on the transition from silence to sound. With respect to deliberate speech, silence conveys the ethical potential of words; for it sharpens the transition from inwardness to worldly expression. Prayer may also stand at this juncture of silence and speech. It may do so when one begins to articulate thanks or hope, or prepares to recite a blessing, and thereby affirm a theological dimension in the world. For immediately prior to the onset of prayer or blessing, the self may focus both mind and heart on the content of the words and their reference. This is a spiritually pregnant silence, and gives birth to words framed by that silence and infused by it in every aspiration. Entering into articulation in this way is entering into a world brought to expression through language. The sounds of speech are meaningful only through the silences that precede them or carry them forward. Otherwise, there would only be din and noise.

But we must go further. Prayers are not always new every moment; they are not always the immediate expression of a life-occasion. In the course of tradition, there accumulate the *words of the ancestors*, which arose in response to life-moments past and were reformulated for the ages. How may one enter these older speech forms (which now comprise the liturgy) in ways that cultivate spiritual growth and God-mindedness?

The fourfold method of *PaRDeS* considered earlier may again guide the ensuing reflections—for each level or type of textual meaning organizes the soul's stance toward the world and to God in a different way. They each cultivate a distinct mode of theological thoughtfulness, and thereby open our lives to forms of godliness in ever-new ways. Once more hermeneutics, life, and theology may intersect.

Ta shema. Come and hear.

THE SENSE OF PRAYER

Peshat. When one attempts to engage the plain sense of a prayer, one may consciously move from the vast silence before all speech to the silence before the particular expression at hand, which articulates specific joys and sorrows for members of the covenant community. Hence a person may not simply enter the words of a prayer as such, but the olden words of tradition as well—words that have been framed and recited by generations past, and that have even shaped one's deepest sensibility. The silence before a specific speech event is thus the potential that the language of tradition may offer us here and now as we (latecomers) receive it and recite it anew (in the present). Indeed, as one moves from silence to speech, one also prepares to encounter the religious spirit of the ancestors and enter the *language of the generations*—reviving these efforts through the particular ways their words are intoned and revived in one's heart.

Slowly the recitation moves through the ancient prayer, responding to each turn of phrase and theological predication. It is altogether the record of a living theology. But it is of the past. Not every word or teaching may express one's own theology, now or ever; but, for all that, the words and teachings of the recitation belong to us—inheritors of the Mosaic community and formed by its language and values. At the least, then, one may dutifully recite the words as best as possible, acknowledging their pastness and their influence on our culture and values.

But this recitation may also claim us in the present moment. For we too have memories and seek meaning, as does the speaker of the older prayer; we too may fear for food and sustenance, stumble and fear the evildoer; and we also know that the dead do not praise God, and hope to heaven that our words do not rattle in the void. Like the first speakers of the prayer, we are also creatures of flesh and blood, born of woman and destined for death. The words were formed in the past, but they may yet resonate with our own pathos and pain, and give it unexpected expression or focus.

In this spirit, let us listen closely to the following words of Scripture.

> How many are your works [of creation], O Lord;
>> You have made them all with wisdom;
>> the earth is filled with your creations.

. . . .

> All of them look to you
>> to give them their food at its time.
> When you give it to them, they gather it up;
>> when you open your hand, they are well-sated.
> But when you hide your face, they are terrified;
>> or take away their breath, they die and return to dust.

Just send forth your breath, and [others] are created,
and you renew the face of the earth.

May the glory of the Lord endure forever;
May the Lord rejoice in his works.
He looks at the earth and it trembles;
He but touches the mountains and they smoke.
I shall sing to the Lord all my life;
and shall recite hymns to my God while alive.
May my prayer be pleasing [to him];
I shall rejoice in the Lord.
May sinners disappear from the earth,
and the wicked be no more.
Bless the Lord, O my soul.
Hallelujah.

(Ps. 104:24, 27–35)

The *peshat* of this ancient prayer reveals the voice of a human
being with needs and values. It is expressed in the language of
generations past; but the words and images retain a living force
for later-born speakers, who also recite them *as creatures of the
earth*—and this is because the prayer rings true at the most concrete levels of life-experience. The first speaker, like me or you,
opens his eyes in exclamatory praise before the wonders and
bounty that fill the world, which, in their diversity of life-forms,
are the tangible exponents of deepest divine wisdom. God is thus
experienced as a generative force, whose powers produce the
myriad life-forms that fill the earth. The speaker confesses to it,
as do all creatures, who express their "natural piety" through their
inherent dependence on God's gifts for physical sustenance—be
these provided by natural growth or cultivation, by hunting and
happenstance, or by carnivorous rapine among the higher and
lower species. Everywhere and at all times: "*All* of them look
to you, to give them their food at its time." This is an ultimate
and absolute dependence. Should God's favor be hidden or
withdrawn, leaving plants blasted and people wasted, there is
creature panic; and should the life-force be withdrawn (through

age or disease or battle), there is death. There is no mere nature. Rather, says the speaker, it is truly the ever-present power of God's effectivity that nurtures the earth; and its withdrawal brings wrack and ruin. In the words of the prayer: it is God's face and God's breath that sustain life. This is the exclamatory assertion of the first (just-cited) part.

The factuality of existence asserted, the speaker now expresses the hope that God will keep favor with this creation. Humans huddle in need; and even the solid earth and mountains tremble before God's might. The psalmist therefore beseeches God's care and promises to testify to God's goodness forever. But he expresses another hope as well, beyond the need for sustenance and the breath of life: the desire that evildoers be eradicated and the wicked cease. This too is part of the mortal dream for divine beneficence; for evil is a wound of life that is felt with all the pain of hunger. Giving voice to this, the speaker returns at the end to something he can better control—and that is the state of his soul. The prayer thus ends with an exultant call to one's inner self to bless the Lord. The multiple petitions yield to an inner imperative: the speaker's natural self and voice address a deeper dimension of personal being, and bid it ascend in divine praise as a consummate spiritual act.

At the *peshat* level, we are brought face to face with existence as both bounty and horror: as a place of food and life and good, but also as a realm of hunger and death and evil. God's face is the crucial image here: were it to be concealed or withdrawn, there would be abject terror and distress. God's presence is the object of all creatures, and "all" look to God for their need. Thus the hiding of this presence is the withholding of benefit or care. The starkness of the figure is compelling. It is compelling first of all because of the personified force it condenses: God makes things, opens "his" hand, sends back "his" breath, and hides "his" face. The gifts of life are personal and felt in entirely personal terms. But the language of the text also begs a deeper theological consciousness. For when God "takes away" the breath of life, creatures die, and when God's face is concealed there is anxiety;

but when God's breath is sent back, there is renewed creation, and when God is again manifest "the face of the earth" is itself renewed. In this way a more profound truth is expressed: that the bounty of life upon the earth is somehow God's face, shining through the physicality of nature; and, when creatures are born, their own breath is somehow the very breath of God. These literary figures thus convey the sense of a pulsing and active divine providence, in and through "the nature of things." The concealment of God is therefore all the more terrifying. At the level of *peshat*, one can only endure this mysterious divine action, which exemplifies God's absolute sovereignty over the sources of life; one can only beseech heaven for the renewal of care, and direct one's heart to God in song. But there is no escaping this ultimate dependency, or the despair experienced with the eclipse of God.

The *peshat* sense of prayer may thus cultivate a reattunement of the self toward the gifts and gaps of the world; toward the poignancies of life and death; and toward the dominion of God over all reality. How the human creature responds to the fullness of divine presence, and its concealment or withdrawal, defines the character of his or her soul.

Derash. At this level of interpretation, consciousness shifts from continuous units of a text composed in the past to particular phrases bearing meaning in the present. Reading is now an active engagement with a composition in order to appropriate it for one's ongoing life. With respect to prayer, by means of *derash*, one enters the words and dwells within them for spiritual and moral regeneration.

Let us probe this further, using the selection from Psalm 104 just cited.

If we said earlier that readers of a prayer from the perspective of *peshat* are always creatures of flesh and blood, the readers of prayer through the methods of *derash* are also *creatures of tradition and moral reflection*—seeking to be guided by that tradition to ever-new planes of consciousness. Without losing any of the concrete ground specified by the prayer for God's care, the reader now seeks to be oriented toward it in a new way. The issue of divine concealment may serve as a fulcrum in this process; for the self tries to confront the apparent imperious nature of the phrase "when you hide your face." The prayer does not indicate why this happens; but the heart is troubled and tries to convert this silence to reflection and some understanding. Although the self avers that all Being is empowered by God, through the forms of wisdom that give all beings their viability, it also knows that the forces of life strive with one another in their struggle for existence—the human being included. The praying self may thus reflect on its own responsibilities as a conduit of these divine forces, and the effect of its actions on God's presence. Thus: the sea with all its life-forms may surge beyond control and blindly drown all manner of life, but human self-regard may lead one to abandon a neighbor in one's flight to safety—and then the divine face of care is concealed; the seed-bearing earth may throb with life-forms and nutrients, but if persons disregard its proper cultivation, through misuse of the environment or its protective shields, the crops will wither and people starve—and then the face of heaven is hidden from view; plants or tissues may teem with creativity and healing elements, but if some of them are harvested as deadly toxins in order to enslave the needy and enrich the traffickers, and one stands idly by during this outrage— then too God withdraws beneficence and creatures die. And if a person puts a stumbling block before the blind (through some ruse or another), or spills oil in the ocean, or makes it difficult for the poor to receive medicine—who has withdrawn the spirit of life and turned the face of the earth into darkest gloom?

Thinking of such matters through the words of the psalm, the reader may form a determination to serve God with one's life and transmute the energies of existence into beneficial forms. Addressed by the words of tradition, the person now swears to live his whole life long with this commitment (understanding the parallelism "with my life," *be-ḥayyai*, and "as long as I live," *be-odi*, to mark something enduring and recurring). This not only means rethinking one's actions toward the natural world, and acting as a just steward. It also means not just hoping for the end of evildoers, but changing one's attitude toward them. On this point ancient exegesis offers a stunning gift, helping one revise the vengeful words of the petition and thereby raise one's soul to a new plane of awareness. For we are told that Beruriah once told her husband, R. Meir, not to read the words "may sinners [*ḥatta'im*] disappear from the earth" literally, and thereby promote a desire for retribution, but to read it midrashically, as (if) saying "may sins [*ḥaṭa'im*] disappear from the earth." The phonetic change is slight, but the moral consequences are enormous. It is now the sin and not the sinner that must be removed; and this can happen, she taught, through a merciful concern for the evildoer who may, in response to creature love, repent of past deeds and depart from sins and evil. It is thus with the face of kindness that the breath of life may be restored to the earth. From this perspective, God's renewal of the earth happens through the outreaching love for one's neighbor.

It may be this insight, achieved in the act of prayer, that can enable the soul to be reborn in blessing, and to realize that such a transformed consciousness is God's blessing for the earth. The concluding exultation, "Bless the Lord, O my soul," would then be a recognition of the spiritual path required.

The process of prayer may thus provide a means for spiritual and moral growth, as the self lives at the interface of tradition and personal reflection. The mode of *derash* would then be not only a form of interpretation, but a way of putting one's mind to rights.

Remez. There is an additional way that prayer may guide the mind toward God-consciousness. This one considers the dialectics of silence and speech somewhat differently from those specified earlier. The issue to be discussed here is not the emergence of sound from silence, or even the grounding of sound in silence. It is rather the very allusiveness of sound as a system of signifiers. The word *remez*, it will be recalled, means hint or sign or allusion.

When we reflect on prayer from this perspective, we perceive two ellipses, moving in opposite directions. The first ellipse focuses on the fragility of speech, whereby words are pointers to something thinkable in reality. The word *tree* is not itself what one sees rising up from the earth with branches, or feels as rough or smooth wood, or whose resin one smells and feels as sticky tar. It is none of that, but only "like" it. The word is only a hint or pointer toward it; it is only a conventional sound signifying this tangible reality. The very same botanic phenomenon might also be marked by such words as *arbor* or *boim* or *etz*. Hence the word is not the thing itself, but an expression of it; and were we to fracture the word (reciting "arb" or "et") we would hardly affect the object, though this might significantly impair our own ability to communicate and understand one another.

If this is true of ordinary speech, whose focus is the common world and ordinary frames of reference, how much more is it true of theological speech, which attempts to designate God with names and epithets? Humans have at hand a bundle of everyday words and terms. But which one would turn the trick and name God and divine activity? If all the world were ink and all our speech quills, and if we were ever able to denote all that we and the entirety of humankind has ever thought and felt about divine reality, could we ever truly express or indicate God? And if all the world were sound and all our words could articulate the totality of these sounds, in some majestic polyphonic concordance, could we ever articulate or intone God? The arcs of speech are thus always curving toward the mystery of expression and the gap between words and their references—and all the more so as one tries to express the ineffable reality of God in human language. As the curve of speech bends toward the transcendent, this truth becomes ever more unsayable.

But there is another ellipse, which moves in the opposite direction. It crosses back to the world of human life. It is here that words serve more conventional purposes of denotation, in order to facilitate communication and common action. Shared language allows persons to direct their hearts in love and moral purpose, to give advice and support, and to create new ideas and images that may lift one's spirits beyond the everyday, even toward its mysteries. And this too is a role for religious language. It is not merely grounded in the conventions of common worldliness, but its positivity also lies in the ways that such language serves theological ends. Emergent from our human finitude, theological speech expresses concrete joys and wants; in this respect it often mirrors or reflects the poignancy of human nature. But there is nevertheless a real danger that the words we use in these contexts (when we so necessarily emphasize mortal matters, or speak of God in human terms) might stultify one's spiritual growth. Nevertheless, this curve of the ellipse prefers this risk over the opposite danger, which would be an allegorical depletion of the concrete vivacity of human speech. In this latter instance, one may surely substitute the abstract notion of divine beneficence for the specific image of God's hand, or the idea of providence for the figure of an eye; but then one is no longer reciting prayer as living theology, but as a series of philosophical propositions and thoughts. In so doing, we risk losing the flesh-and-blood ground of our religious lives, and the capacity of speech to point us toward the throbbing heart of divine mystery.

Religious persons may thus seek to pray with both ellipses in mind, or even strive toward a consciousness of their intersection. In such a way, the process of prayer keeps one alert to the fragility of speech and its necessities in all areas of life; but it can also simultaneously help one remember the role of language as signs between our eyes of the sacred mysteries of existence, which we call to mind through names and terms and epithets. To forget this is to wander in delusion and small-mindedness.

>>><<<

How may an interpretation of Psalm 104 further these reflections? How might its language help us think further about the double ellipse of religious speech?

The exegetical modality of *remez* allows persons to consider themselves as *creatures of intellect and discernment*, in addition to being creatures of life and death and of tradition. More specifically, through such discernment one may reflect on the use of speech and the nature of theological signification. And if we do remain focused on such matters in the context of prayer, this does not mean that we are performing an arid intellectual exercise; rather, such reflection provides a type of intentionality or spiritual practice (operating above and below the level of verbalization or expression, and not as its substitute) that may enhance our religious lives. With this caveat in mind, let us return to the concrete language of Psalm 104. The ellipse of sayability invokes God as world maker, who opens "his" hands, has the breath of life, and can hide "his" face. We feel the concrete specificity of this language as we recite it; and we may also recoil at its bold personified starkness. Surely we acknowledge the bounty of life and the complex wisdom in the world, enlivened with numerous creative patterns, at every molecular and organic level of existence. They are all expressive of God's *torah kelulah*, and one would surely be crude and thoughtless to disavow the positivity of their forms and the world-reality to which they point. We perceive and feel them all around us, and we are impacted by them in diverse ways. But just what are we talking about, or what do we think is being said, when they are used in religious discourse? Do we not inestimably cheapen the sense of God's *torah kelulah* through such all-too-human designations and descriptions? Might it not be more spiritually prudent to take a modest and negative approach to our conceptions of divine reality? And is this tack not in keeping with one's sense that God's way is truly one of profound concealment, utterly beyond human capacities of cognition—a hiddenness that is not (in this instance) a withdrawal of favor from humans, but a truth of God's transcendence? All of which suggests that while the world is there for our discernment, and does not resist our inferences, one should respond to it with great theological humility. One must stand before that which we sense as God's "Shall-Be" with terror and awe, mindful that we only see with human eyes and hear with human ears, and that God's own truth (the whole truth, such as it is) is wholly hidden from view. Job came to understand this and confessed himself to be but dust and ashes. This is also the hermeneutical challenge of our psalm passage. The deep hiddenness of divine truth must be sealed in our hearts as we try to articulate the mystery in human terms—steering our souls between the Scylla of silence and the Charybdis of abstract platitudes.

And if the psalm might guide the reflective spirit yet further, might it not also suggest a way to stand before God's hiddenness, within the world that rises so fully, and in often terrifying ways, to our human consciousness? I would find that standpoint in the opening exultation about the wonders of creation, effectuated by God: "How many are your works, O Lord; / *You have made them all with wisdom.*" We live within the darkness of unknowing; but we are also confronted by myriads of creatures, each with their inherent wisdom, generated out of the stock of possibilities and achieved by trial and error. It is to this multiform wisdom that we must bend our minds, attaching ourselves to the wisdom of nature that appears and recurs moment by moment, and, in this way, to be attached to God at all times, insofar as we sense that the wisdom of existence (in all its manifestations) is an attribute of God (so to speak). Along the path of existence, some forms are absorbed into others or destroyed, while still others prevail and achieve different degrees of viability. The divine attribute of wisdom permeates existence and nature, and its fate lies within the mysteries of its own incalculable vagaries and possibilities. Human beings may connect themselves to this wisdom, and guide it, and give it moral and other purpose. This involves naming its features or renaming them, even assessing its capacities and reevaluating our judgments; and it will also involve serving this multiform wisdom with a soul ever raised to higher purposes of spiritual and moral thoughtfulness.

Our prayer in the interpretative mode of *remez* provides the occasion to think about these matters, and affirms our need to bring blessing to God's many works of wisdom by transcending our mortal self-centeredness. "Bless the Lord, O my soul" is the final word. It is the aim of the religious spirit and the goal of covenant theology.

Sod. The *sod*, of course, is the ultimate mystery. It would therefore seem presumptuous to think of it as some philosophical or theosophical secret, hidden in some esoteric realm of reality. Or it at least seems presumptuous to most moderns, who find their theological challenges on earth and not in some concealed chamber on high. If this is so, perhaps all one should do here is rethink the balance between silence and speech. The happening of speech and human thoughtfulness about it was considered in the other levels of interpretation, and in the preceding paragraphs the complex ellipses of articulation and silence were adumbrated. The emphasis here is on silence itself—not on what was earlier called a natural silence, or even a more spiritual silence. Rather, the silence now being adumbrated is that of the high priest who enters the Holy of Holies on the Day of Atonement; it is the silence of the white spaces between the words or vocables of scripture; it is the silence of Job who realized that he "spoke without knowledge"; and it is also the silence of the psalmist who said, "To you silence [*dummiyah*] is praise" (Ps. 65:2). All this is utter silence. It is a radical spiritual caesura, without echo or earthly sound. It pervades consciousness, and is not the prelude to speech in any sense.

Thinking about these matters, we return to Psalm 104.

At the level of *sod* our concern is for the self as a *creature attuned to the unfathomable*, and the capacity or willingness to stand in the silence of God's mystery. The challenge here is to endure the terror of concealment. This is not a silence of why or wherefore; it is simply silence. Nor is it a silence of waiting or expectation; it is simply being silent within the concealment, in the uttermost spiritual stillness.

This is *shetiqah*: an absolute silence and speechlessness within the Void, beyond words. But it is also an ascendant silence, rising toward God's Absolute Transcendence. Caesura is its name.

Perhaps the mode of *sod* can point the heart in this direction.

The Process of Study

There is another form of spiritual cultivation pertinent to covenant theology: the act of Torah study (*talmud torah*). There are several notable aspects to such study, which may shape theological consciousness in distinctive ways.

The theological seeker comes into the world with the Written and Oral Torahs already in existence as cultural facts and records of revelation. These conjoint artifacts attest to the achievements of Moses and his disciples. Repeatedly, the "Shall-Be" of God has been received by the human heart and shaped into modes of spiritual disclosure: in the most formative times the divine reality and pulse of life found expression in the multiform Written Torah (the *torah she-bikhtav*); and in subsequent times, these expressions themselves became the basis for ongoing expansions of the emergent Oral Torah (the *torah she-be'al peh*). In turn, in the most marvelous ways, the latter also remained responsive to changing life-conditions and values, as manifested in God's ongoing and multiform world-expression (the *torah kelulah*). There is therefore no simple return to first things; tradition has forged a chain of achievements that link the generations and set the contours of cultural thinking and expression. The vaunted way into this fund of intellectual labor and spiritual value is through study. In Jewish life, study becomes a form of piety and mode of worship through the submission of the self to the *gift of the generations*. This is accomplished first and foremost through the study of Torah in its various modes, "for its own sake" (*lishmah*). At this level, the mind must be purified of self-interest in order to respond to the voices of the past—as an event in its own right. Spiritually, this involves a devoted attachment to all the words and formulations of the Torah as testimonies of divine revelation or theological direction, and a readiness to let that religious record transform one's nature and spirit. The piety of study cultivates in the theological self-in-the-making a readiness to receive. This is of the essence. Earlier generations attested to their place in the covenant by the avowal "We shall do and we shall hear," and this is the virtue that must be inculcated by the descendants. And then one may also join the chain of generations. Through recitation and assimilation of the words of the past, the oral tradition becomes alive in one's mouth.

INTERIOR DISCOURSE

Not everything that has been transmitted by tradition and lived by prior generations may still strike the self as real or true. Thus the initial task is to direct one's mind and heart to this sacred corpus "for its own sake." The capacity to listen with attention and humility is a spiritual beginning, and the first gift of Torah study.

The process of learning is like a pilgrimage of ascent, a gradual growth in religious consciousness. It is like going from station to station on a journey, as in the wilderness of old, when the nation moved from one place to another: "from Matanah to Naḥaliel, and from Naḥaliel to Bamoth" (Num. 21:19). To what may this be compared? R. Joshua ben Levi taught:

> Whoever is occupied with the study of Torah [*talmud torah*] will ascend; as [scripture] says: "And from Matanah to Naḥaliel, and from Naḥaliel to Bamoth."

This midrashic trope conveys a progressive development from receiving the Torah (a "gift" from God, or *matanah*) to inheriting a divine dimension (a *naḥalah*, or "inheritance," of God), and from this to a personal ascension (in spiritual and actual wisdom, for *bamoth* signifies "heights"). Generations later, Raba son of R. Joseph b. R. Ḥama gave a fuller elaboration of this passage, and connected it to the first toponym in the nomadic sequence, *midbar*, or "desert." In so doing, he gave a deeper spiritual reading of the passage, linking the virtue of humility to the gift of learning, and the latter to other transformations—both spiritual and communal. He taught:

> If a person allows himself to be treated as a desert [*midbar*] upon which everyone treads, the Torah will be given to him as a gift

[*matanah*]; and insofar as it is given to him as a gift, he will become
the inheritance of God, as it says, "from Matanah to Naḥaliel"; and
with the inheritance of God he rises in greatness, since it says, "from
Naḥalah to Bamoth."

Becoming a *midbar* for the reception of Torah is thus an ongoing task of self-cultivation; one must carve out an inner space
of empty openness, and then one may learn. Such acts of divestment are acts of spiritual poverty in the most profound sense.
They constitute a beginning and an end of Torah study.

PUBLIC DIALOGUE

If the first aspect of study cultivates the self in its aloneness, as
a private spiritual self, the second does so in fellowship. Here
the self studies in partnership (*ḥevruta*), and altogether different
features of theological consciousness are involved; for through
Torah study with a partner one moves from interior discourse to
public dialogue. The Torah (in all its parts) is a shared revelation,
belonging to a community of receivers. Hence it will be heard
differently by different persons. In partnership one actually re-
capitulates the differences of opinion of the tradition itself, both
formally and in fact. One person asks and another responds; this
person raises an objection and that one resolves the matter. And
then the topic may be rethought and turned completely around.
Soon a voice from this text raises a pertinent query and the part-
ners respond, and another voice from another text expresses an
objection, and the discourse goes on until the issue is put to rest.
This is living Torah, keeping God's "I shall be" alive in new generations and places. But it only sustains itself through respect
for difference. Controversy is the inevitable bounty of the living
reception of Torah. "The voice of the Lord is in strength," said
the psalmist; and the sages added knowingly, "in the strength
[or capacity] of each person to receive it." And thus common
text study cultivates a different kind of waiting and receiving.
It is the readiness to hear and respond to another viewpoint on
the great mystery of God's instruction and reality. This attitude

serves the ideal of hearing another opinion and reciting it as a valid truth; and it becomes the ideal of living spiritually as an open-ended quest, one that ever entwines the self in the web of interpretation. "*We* shall do and *we* shall hear" is the watchword of the common spiritual enterprise. Sinai remains a living moment when the covenant is shared with another person; for the oral tradition is in more than one mouth.

The sages compressed these matters into four ideals, each one cultivating a different virtue of shared study: there is the ideal of "sharpening" one's partner's intellect so that, in the course of study, this other is enhanced and developed as a student of Torah; there is also the ideal of "gentility" toward one's study partner so that, in the course of study, that person's discourse is heard in its human form, as the words of an individual, not an abstract argument of logic to be confronted; in addition, there is the ideal of "attentive listening" to one's partner's discourse so that it is affirmed in its human character; and finally, there is the ideal of "enhancing" the position of one's partner, who has gathered with oneself for collective study. In all cases, these virtues are presented as reciprocal acts (*zeh et zeh*), "one (person) with the other," not as unilateral or isolated deeds; and in all cases, where such enactments occur, we are even told that God supports the event of learning and guides it to fruition. Something of the sacredness of speech is espoused here, but also its great fragility and divine character. For God, the source of life, participates in such holy moments.

COMMUNITY STEWARDSHIP

There is a third aspect of study that shapes the theological self; it moves beyond singularity and partnership and directs the individual to the community. Now the great ideal of Torah study "for its own sake" is complemented by the goal of learning "for the sake of doing." With this shift, study serves the covenant in the here and now.

Insofar as our focus is on the cultivation of a theological consciousness through study, the issue is not one of mere practicality and application. This has its proper time and place. The exterior world is always there; but it is the interior world of theological thinking that I am concerned with here, as the matrix out of which one lives and acts. And thus the ideal of Torah study "for the sake of doing" will direct attention to the many ways that halakhic action can serve human dignity and enhance its sanctification. One studies with an eye to seeing how this aspect of Torah helps me speak to another person properly and appropriately—in attunement to that person's capacity to hear and understand; and to perceiving how another feature of Torah helps me to use my hands in the right way, so that giving is a gift and not an imposition, and receiving is a thankfulness and not a taking—in attunement to what is required of my hands in any particular circumstance; and to considering how an element of Torah helps me see if there is a stumbling block before someone's blindness, and to remove it in an effective and appropriate way—in attunement with what constitutes a danger to the other person and his or her feelings; and finally, to assessing how teachings of the Torah may serve the recognition of difference and boundaries—all in attunement with knowledge of my neighbor and what seems to be the right intervention for the moment.

There is thus no end to the covenant; it is constantly reshaped to meet new circumstances. The laws and rules and maxims provide structures and make provisions, but they must always be enacted with moral alertness. Each moment gives God's "I shall be," and beyond the traditional ways of doing and hearing, one must be ready to do and hear all this in a personally distinct way. There is thus a complex symmetry between the diverse selves that covenant theology fosters. The speaking and the hearing create a certain balance between persons, which keeps changing in modality and tone; the giving and receiving also establish correlations between oneself and another; as do the ways one may look at or act in the world. By the nature and character of one's covenant response, a person can sanctify hands and mouth and feet—both one's own and those of other persons as well. One must also try to cultivate this mindfulness in the course of Torah study, in order to be cognizant of the various ways one may do and hear justly in this world; and to cultivate one's mind and heart for the readiness to do and hear appropriately. There is thus high theological seriousness to the words of Torah which stress that the teachings are not something unworldly or far-off, "but exceptionally close to you—in your mouth and heart *to do them*" (Deut. 29:11–14). This is covenant theology in real life. Insofar as we can know it, God's "I shall be" confronts us in this realm of our existence. One accepts this covenant in the doing and the hearing, in the very moments of the doing and hearing.

Radical Kindness

In the spaces of communal life, the solitary self is among people, symbolized by the neighbor or nearby one. That "other" is always a possible form of attention for me and capable of breaking down the isolation of self-regard. One simply has to have the capacity to notice and to respond. One of the chief purposes of "Torah," as we have observed, is to help guide the person through life by formulating norms and practices. These norms are abstractions of value and situation that shape the world into spheres of attention; the practices are prescribed actions that are designed to concretize acceptable or prohibited behavior. Torah grows through study, reflection, and revision. One lives with one eye on the textual sources and the other on life; and as these are integrated, they form one's inner eye of evaluation and judgment as one perceives worldly situations with eyes wide open. The practice of the *halakha* is a form of *avodah*, or ritual service. Blessings and prayer are included in this structure. The first is a response to situations, including encountering persons; the second is primarily an expression of gratitude or petition to God, but it includes a preparation of sensibility for engaging the world. In olden antiquity, *avodah* denoted service in the Temple; but subsequent to its destruction the term connotes all religious-ethical action. Sacred space is widened, and extended as a sphere of possibilities, to the world as a whole; priestly service is correspondingly enlarged, and now extended to each person. Gifts to persons become a mode of gifts to God—and that includes proper speech, physical acts, and simple presence and creature care. In a most ancient rabbinic saying, Simeon the Righteous taught, "The world depends [literally, stands] on three things: on Torah, on *avodah*, and on *gemilut ḥasadim.*" The first two are characterized by *nomos*. They are principles of social order and normativity; without them the basis of human existence falls. What, however, is the third thing mentioned?

Gemilut ḥasadim is something radically different. It denotes gratuitous kindness (*ḥesed*); unrequited care; and supererogatory acts. For the sages, such deeds were typified by clothing the poor; providing a dowry for indigent women; and burying the dead. The common core is that these actions express pure giving—works that cannot be repaid. In a characteristic manner, such and other eleemosynary behaviors were gradually grouped under categories of charity, and were thereby integrated with social duties and *nomos* in the fullest sense. But they are not. They are anomic, and reflect an anarchic spirituality. One notices a person in radical need, and gives. Such behaviors therefore serve as paradigms for gratuitous care, in response to the claim that another person makes on the self. *Ḥesed* cuts deeper than *nomos*. It cannot be formalized or routinized; it is the deepest source of human beneficence. Indeed, *ḥesed* is the inner core of *nomos*; for without the reality of *ḥesed*, *nomos* would lose its soul. *Ḥesed* is the awareness of otherness, and one's connection to it; hence it is the heart of care. Without *ḥesed* we would have no world, only rules for protection; we would only have limits and limitations, not excess or self-sacrifice. Thus the world ultimately stands on *ḥesed*. Scripture states this clearly: "The world is built by *ḥesed*."

We observed earlier that study of Torah for its own sake is a pure act, a detaching of oneself from the horizons of concrete application; and that the ideal of the Sabbath is to enter a full and complete rest, a total detachment of oneself (in body and soul) from worldly benefits and activity. Ideally, such Torah study cultivates the self for responding to the world with a disregard for self-interest; and such Sabbath rest cultivates the self for an inwardness of repose and spiritual balance. What is the core of *gemilut ḥesed* and its ultimate beneficence, as a form of spiritual self-fashioning? Does it also cultivate a mode of detachment? Initially, one may think not, since giving and care are involved. But just the opposite is the case.

Ḥesed responds to a lack and wound in the world, and gives toward its repair and healing. The nature of the gift must therefore correspond to the need, as much as possible. This is the primary divestment. One must give up things and preconditions. Correlatively, one must give up expectations and the desire for acknowledgment. This deeper divestment purifies the inner self. The world and its persons make a claim, and the self tries to respond through a redistribution of the gifts of heaven. For *ḥesed*, this is a theological imperative. It is an agency that does not await confirmation of any kind; there is no requital for acts of *ḥesed*. It thus transcends justice, which depends on balance and restitution. Justice tries to act with right proportion. *Ḥesed* does not. *Ḥesed* is founded on disregard: both of the self and of the particular person in need. It is a pure giving, in excess. The world depends on it.

Ḥesed also relates to a lack and wound in the self, when this is inflicted by another person. The gift to be given here is forgiveness, as much as possible. Scripture commands, "Do not take revenge, and do not bear a grudge"; and the sages famously explicated these negative injunctions in terms of acts of recrimination, in the first instance, or by holding on to resentment, in the second case. Both actions extend the wound and repay it in one kind or another. *Ḥesed* tries to snap or modify the cycle in a radical and sudden manner. In some circumstances, however, the personal or national wound is truly grave and has the character of an impassable evil, seemingly beyond healing, which would be its betrayal; and then the task of *ḥesed* must be more modest—to remember the guilt but to try and work for some kind of reconciliation or reconnection, as well. In such ways, *ḥesed* is ever an attempt at new beginnings or renewal; or, at the least, it is an attempt by the self to perceive something human in an other one who may have denied the humanity of one's self or others. Thus the works of *ḥesed* may aid in some divestment of the absolute totalization of memory. In this way, too, it may also be a training in spiritual character. *Ḥesed* is thus an attempt to keep the principles of kindness alive. The world depends on it.

Ultimately, the phenomenon of *ḥesed* is the practice of death. *Ḥesed* is an attempt to give to others, successively divesting oneself— of one's possessions, of one's ego, and of one's expectations. It is a concern to give purely in all respects. Such giving is for itself; but it also cultivates a more profound relinquishment. Job understood this at the beginning of his trial, when he responded to the disasters and challenges of his life with the words: "Naked I came into the world; and naked I shall depart it. Blessed is the name of the Lord." But Job had to learn this lesson of emptiness and poverty again, after the speechlessness of sorrow gave rise to angry claims and demands. His arguments seethe with self-centered logic and are formulated from a human standpoint. Then, unhinged by God's voice, and a series of fantastic and illogical questions requiring impossible cosmic knowledge, Job changed. His growth in wisdom was the capacity to "relent," knowing that he is but "dust and ashes." Eventually, the world of things came back to him in unexpected ways; but he was not the same person as before. He now had detachment in his heart. This is a spiritual dying in the midst of life—a true preparation for mortal death.

>>><<<

Thus it was taught:

The words of Torah are only [truly] fulfilled by one who nullifies himself [makes himself as naught, *ayin*]. As it is written: "Wisdom is achieved through *ayin*." (Job 28:20)

"From whence [*me-ayin*] does Wisdom come?" asks the sage in scripture. And R. Yoḥanan responds out of the depths of his spiritual consciousness, through a bold revision of the text: the wisdom of Torah is achieved by oneself becoming as naught. The original query has thus become spiritual counsel—an ideal of radical self-transformation.

Becoming *ayin* is an ultimate act of divestment. It is the practice of pure doing. In life, such selflessness culminates in *ḥesed*. It is the renewal of creation through the revelation of love.

>>><<<

God passes through all things with the pulse of God's heart; and insofar as that pulse of life also passes through human beings, the human is an image of God. Many and mysterious are the forms of this image (human and nonhuman), and so diverse are they in their realizations and kinds of fulfillment. For the pulse may live in strength or wither; it may back into molecular channels or struggle in one organic effort or another; it may harvest toxins and consume itself or act with will and consume others. In a unique manner, these forms come to us and are expressed through us; and insofar as we live with awareness of our participation in the reception and transformation of all these images, one may strive toward their enhancement and integration into larger wholes. The fine attunements of relationships with one's neighbor—by strengthening the hand or treating it gently; by setting firm the foot or providing it with a crutch; by speaking the truth or not willfully dissembling in any way—all build up the divine image in the world, the living divine image that appears to each person through the other. All this is acting with God in mind and heart, when walking along the way and when lying down, with all one's strength; and in its purity, this is also the love of God that is revealed to us as an imperative for our lives. Such care for God, through the forms and images of the world, and most especially in their human manifestations, is the sacred labor of redemption.

4

Forms of Thought
and Living Theology

Scripture as the Ground of Life and Thought

I asserted earlier that Jewish theology begins at Sinai, both as a paradigmatic event and as an ongoing spiritual reality. Speaking theologically, the "Sinai event" is the center point of scripture, and thus at the center of Jewish religious life in all respects. It is both the magnetic pole of a scripturally grounded religious culture, and the axis of its most far-flung innovations. In ever-widening arcs, the historical base of Sinai extended currents of action and value outward to encircle new spheres of thought and worldly existence. Jewish theology has repeatedly attempted to think about this phenomenon and to take a stand with respect to the multiple dimensions of scripture entailed therein. It is therefore incumbent upon us to do so as well. Without this consideration, Jews may do theology, but not a Jewish theology with any historical or cultural claim.

The initial discussion of the various dimensions of scripture served as a prologue to a consideration of Jewish reading practices, and considered ways that a multifaceted hermeneutics of scripture (constructed on the model of *PaRDeS*) could help restore it to a central position in the mental and spiritual universe of modern Jews.

Specifically, by rethinking the act of reading scripture as a spiritual practice, I tried to demonstrate how it was possible to correlate the ways one reads a text with ways of reading the world, both ethically and experientially; and especially how these various reading processes could contribute to corresponding ways of thinking about God. That is, modes of reading cultivate modalities of hermeneutical consciousness, and these are in turn correlated with modes of worldly perception and theological awareness (or intuition). Such a dynamic process of reflection and interpretation thus signals ways that scripture might again provide an authoritative matrix for contemporary religious thought and life—both at the level of content and that of structure as well. I noted at the outset (of chapter 1) that such a hermeneutical goal has been a salient concern of classic Jewish theology over the ages—involving different modes of accommodating scripture to regnant patterns of thought and value in the larger milieu. This ideal is our own, as well, though the solutions offered here inevitably depart significantly from prior exemplars. This is as it must be. Each generation must produce the exegetical practices appropriate to its historical and intellectual situation, and befitting its own sense of integrity: *dor dor ve-dorshav*. I have suggested that the cognitive and cultural complexities of the modern situation support an approach more aligned to providing a series of multivalent attunements between scriptural hermeneutics and life, than one that seeks to correlate two fixed and coherent orbits of thought (such as scripture and natural philosophy).

Because of the fundamental importance of scripture for Jewish life and thought, and our concern to rescue it from the splintering effects of historicism or the deadening pallor of irrelevance, I now return to that initial discussion and develop it as a theological subject in its own right—not merely as a prologue to its hermeneutical application.

THE PRIMORDIAL MODALITY

The most primary (and most primordial) modality of scripture was designated as the *torah kelulah*; it is also the most universal

and transcendent of the three principal types (the other two
being the *torah she-bekhtav*, or Written Torah, and the *torah she-
be'al peh*, or Oral Torah). As portrayed earlier, the *torah kelulah*
denotes absolute reality, and comprises the totality of existence
and world-being. It is the total fund and formation of divine
truth in our world, and is thus, as such, altogether independent of its revelation through our meager human consciousness.
Hence the *torah kelulah* is the inherent datum and ground of
all world-happening. This Torah is, so to speak, the fullness of
divine effectivity as such, insofar as that effects the being and
becoming of the world in all respects; or, put differently, it is
divine suchness in all its this-worldly fullness, insofar as this
expresses God's all-effecting vitality. Moreover, this Torah be-
speaks God's absolute gift and giving of world-reality, and is
thus a way of designating the all-happening, infinite "Shall-Be"
of Divinity in human and cultural terms. Expressive of God's
sacred effectivity, the *torah kelulah* is therefore as eternal as all
eternity and as mundane as all worldliness; it is both the source
of all possibilities actualized by God, and the actuality of all
possible possibilities enfolded in the depths of Being. So imagined, the *torah kelulah* is a world-expression of absolute divine
freedom and power, and hence the divine Ground of all human
freedom and potentiality. Understood thus, the *torah kelulah* is a
transpersonal reality. It is, so to say, the all-loving throbbing of
God's heart in the here and everywhere—a throbbing that has
the character of an absolute transitivity, inhering in the myriad
movements of energy that charge and sustain every form of existence. And that transitivity is also God's voice, which speaks
through all the expressions of world-being. God's voice (or creative *dibbur*) is thus the stamen in the flower, and its bending
toward light; it is the simple cell dividing and seeking new patterns, and the insistence of cells to hold their own with singular
identity and signature; it is the return of fish upstream and the
mysterious trek of mammals to their olden breeding grounds;
and it is the red claw of hungry violence as well as the protective
impulse that impels parents to shelter their young with their

body. This *dibbur* is the chatter of birds we decode in the rush and the silence of seedlings in the earth; and it resounds in the multiform crystals metamorphosing in veins of rock, expressing hidden aggregates and secret constellations. God's voice speaks through humans as well—both in their physical being, as mammals seeking food and warmth, and in all their acts of creative expression, giving us thereby a world to inhabit and think about. It is also my voice here and now, describing these matters and what they mean to me.

The *torah kelulah* is thus an ultimate divine instruction, conveying in the most primary and evolved ways the infinity of world-expressions; and insofar as this Torah is given to all persons who receive it and accept it in their own ways, as they build culture and meaning and relationships, through endless interpretation and revision—the *torah kelulah* speaks in all the languages of humankind. Moreover, inasmuch as each voice of this primordial Torah (in nature and among people) is heard in the human domain as something direct and immediate, it also has a personal aspect. This duality (of the transpersonal and personal) is a fundamental fact of religious consciousness, too easily forgotten or trivialized. God's primordial and all-saying Torah is thus both the transpersonal truth of "Let there Be," and its personal presence, heard as "I Am." The divine "Let there Be" is the vital impulse in all existent Being: it is the sacred gift of freedom, grounded in God's goodness, allowing all things to be and to happen. And when this sacred gift bursts upon our consciousness, through the multiple elements and events of life, it speaks to us with the particular claim of its inherent nature, saying, "I shall be as I shall be." God's "Shall Be" is God's "Shall-Be." Who would dare make an image of it?

The *torah kelulah* is truly a *torah min ha-shamayim*: a Torah from heaven. It is given by God, and God alone. It is a holy hieroglyph— a divine scripture encoding patterns and forms of every sort. It is God's seal of truth stamped into our universe. And we ever interpret it through the resources of our lives, languages, and traditions.

THE SCRIPTURAL MODALITY

The *torah she-bikhtav* reveals a different, more particularized expression of God's primordial and universal Torah. It is a hermeneutical distillate of this heavenly Torah for a specific time and place on earth, as mediated by the intellectual and spiritual capacity of a great teacher and his heirs. The *torah she-bikhtav* is thus the historical Torah of Moses and his followers, beginning with the formation of the Israelite people after Sinai, and continuing throughout the period of national settlement in the homeland, the exile, and the initial period of the return. This Torah is therefore not a comprehensive instruction but a specific shaping of the *torah kelulah* through the heart and mind of one called Moses (and his disciples), and formulated in the style and idiom of the times. At Sinai, Moses bent his being toward God's great voice and heard therein the enfolded possibilities of life and action. He stood firm in this welter and wonder, and slowly gathered the impulses of the *torah kelulah* in his heart, combining his own wisdom and experience with his recollection of the exodus and a sense of national destiny. In this way he gave God's voice (the Shall Be of possibilities and actualities) his own personal resonance, and shaped it into values and tasks for life in the world: now in the form of certain theological and social imperatives; now as certain legal conditionals; now as moral examples; and now as exhortations to virtue. These are distinctively marked by the sign of the times; and this is a primary stratum for their initial comprehension.

These numerous expressions were "all the words" (*kol ha-devarim*) specified at Sinai, and later elaborated and supplemented over the course of the generations, but also variously revised and explicated as circumstances required. For again and again new realities occurred for which there did not seem to be any precedence in Moses's scripture; and these unfolding occurrences were something like the ever-happening voice of God's *torah kelulah* saying, "Here I am, also here." And then the matrix of God's truth as found in scripture was changed by teachers in some way or another, and new values or concerns found their human voice and expression. For if God's teachings were primarily expressed in fixed formulations about how one should deal with creatures bearing the pulse of life, or in ceremonies regulating how one should thank heaven for all the animals and plants throbbing anew each season, they were also heard in the outcry of the destitute and disenfranchised, and in the people who spoke on their behalf, and in the rulings of judges who sought to be impartial and fair, as well as in the voice of others who tried to quell cheating and lies. These voices were gathered by those who cared for God, and inscribed with care—and thus the written scripture (the *torah she-bikhtav*) slowly became the historical and cultural record of attempts to channel the impartial pulse of life toward justice and societal regulations, again and again, in the true spirit of Moses; and if certain formulations remained problematic, or opened up unsuspected inequities, then new generations, whose moral and spiritual fiber was itself shaped by Mosaic teachings, strove to redress the matter or stem the disruptive possibilities. Repeatedly, we can observe the concern to channel "mere life" and "harmful rules" toward an ever more responsive human holiness, for God's sake. What resulted is the covenant of Sinai in its ongoing social realizations and its ever-new ideological or moral rectifications.

The *torah she-bikhtav* is thus a scriptural record of the spiritual history of the covenant in its initial unfolding, as formulated by the likes of Moses and those who spoke in his voice (and spirit) in the early history of ancient Israel; and as this was passed down through the generations, others spoke in a similar voice and with a similar concern, and challenged and guided the people to obey the teachings of the covenant in all their ways—through prophetic exhortation and teaching, and through historical notes and narratives, and through exegetical elaborations or innovations. Following in the footsteps of their great masters, later teachers gathered all this material and wrote it down for posterity, to heed and to learn. The likes of Jeremiah and Ezra and many nameless others renew the voice and charge of Moses. Formulated and collected, stylized and sifted—this collected wisdom is sacred scripture (*sifrei qodesh*); it is a tangible witness never to be abrogated or forgotten. In its fullness, this scripture continues the spiritual history of the covenant, and the ongoing impact of God's heavenly Torah on the life of the Israelite nation and its teachers.

THE TRADITIONAL MODALITY

The *torah she-be'al peh* is a further modality of scripture, and an extension of the spiritual vitalities inherent in the Written Torah as it strove (through its interpreters) to be a teaching of maximal sanctity and sanctification. There is thus, on the one hand, a further personalization and particularization of the voice of Torah instruction through the exegetical mouths of the disciples of the wise (the sages) and their rabbinic heirs; but there is also a more noticeable counterthrust toward the universal character of the *torah kelulah* as the multifaceted nature of life constantly reveals new topics and spheres of application for the tradition, and thus for the unending modification or adjustment of the written scripture. Older formulations that revealed inequities to a subsequent moral viewpoint were redressed through interpretation; and verbiage of a problematic sort was allowed to sink into the scriptural sediment, that it might not obstruct one's moral vision. Vigilance was vital, together with the courage to keep the tradition answerable to its highest values—in and through its own terms.

Just this is the vibrant paradox of Jewish covenant theology. For such reformative and new developments do not take place off-handedly, without constraint or in free form. Rather, the Oral Torah begins with the received language and textual conditions of the Written Torah (and the larger written scripture), and continuously rereads its formulations through the prism of its own forms of rationality and interpretative tradition. These are the (rabbinic) "measures" or logical "ratios" of meaning (the various *middot* of Jewish hermeneutical practice and tradition), which creatively mediate between the vast *torah kelulah*, pulsing everywhere, and the various formulations of tradition built up by the *torah she-be'al peh*. The modes of thinking with the exegetical techniques of the culture thus provide ways of incorporating new matters into the tradition while maintaining a distinctive cultural voice and tenor. Hence there is an authoritative opening and expansion of scripture toward the conditions of the wider world, even as it seeks to maintain the special character of its language and values. God's living voice (experienced as caesural implosions on human consciousness) could thus press upon the heart of strictly Jewish life in its universal and absolute way (through the *torah kelulah*), and be refracted through the cultural voices of the Written and Oral Torahs—as mediated by Moses and the rabbinic sages from all times and places. As befits its new concerns and voices, the Oral Torah also developed its own forms of expression, and its own ways of giving allegiance to the spiritual history of the covenant, even where it was modified or reformulated in accord with what was believed to be strains of God's ongoing voice (inherent in the Written Torah and galvanized by the heavenly one).

>>><<<

Jewish theology was formed within this complex and dynamic combination of Written Torah (scripture) and Oral Torah, and a living Jewish theology will ever try to maintain this complexity and dynamism. The strict halakhist will tend to see the external world largely through the prism of the Oral Torah, and attempt to structure that world in accordance with its hierarchy of cultural forms and values; whereas the strictly natural self will tend only to see the world with a natural eye, be that for its beauty or structure or use, and will naturally draw conclusions about its forms and values on that basis. But one should resist this dichotomy. For the Jew is Adam, and is, as such, a natural being, affected always and everywhere by God's *torah kelulah* (the universal Torah); and the Jew is also the descendant of Moses and his heirs, and is, as such, also a cultural being, affected through choice by God's *torah she-bikhtav* and *torah she-be'al peh* (the two very particular Torahs of Sinai and the Study Hall). Thus, as we ourselves variously retrace our way through this great inheritance, interpreting Torah in its many modalities, and seeing how its language has shaped spiritual arguments and visions, we may, in turn, receive this multiform Torah anew, and thus think about God and our own spiritual destiny through its modes of interpretation and expression. With the *torah kelulah* in our hearts, as creatures of flesh and blood, we come to the cultural Torahs of Judaism and respond to their many teachings and truths; and likewise, with the *torah she-bikhtav* in our minds and the *torah she-be'al peh* in our mouths, we may stand ever open to God's universal (and primordial) Torah, inscribed in all the forms of the world and expressed in the great fullness of living reality. "Both these and those are the words of the living God."

Standing firm before scripture in all its modes is *emunah*. It is responding to the Torah of God as a *torat ḥayyim*, a "Torah of life" from the Source of life. *Emunah* is thus our ongoing "faithfulness" or fidelity to the wondrous truth of God's transcendent effectivity, inhering in the soul of all world-being.

Emunah *and Theological Integrity*

Emunah is at the core of the spiritual life. It has two dimensions: the first takes shape within the *torah kelulah*, and seeks to ascend (in mind and spirit) to its source in God, and to abide in this truth in the course of life; the second takes shape within the infinite unfolding of this Torah, and its two cultural instantiations (the *torah she-bikhtav* and the *torah she-be'al peh*), and seeks to remain steadfast (in body and soul) before the myriad qualities of life that invite response, each in its own way. The two dimensions constitute two types of faithfulness to God. It is a task of theology to formulate their dual nature, as well as their ideal integration.

GOD: SAYABLE AND UNSAYABLE

The seekers of God must ever unsay the natural world of language and thought, in an effort to raise their spiritual consciousness beyond the terms and texture of ordinary mindfulness. One unsays all manner of reliance and trust and faith in the things of existence (human or otherwise, tangible and insensible), on the way to a mindfulness that strives to transcend the immanent phenomenality of things, and raise one's mind toward the ultimate transcendent vitality that constitutes and informs all Being. In this process, consciousness moves from the ever-flitting attractions of everyday occurrences to an intuitive nesting in a kind of God-mindedness, both expansive and infinite—an ineffable objectless awareness. This divestment and transformation of mind requires much attentive practice, and a desire to achieve a level of spiritual focus not encumbered by the normal idolatries of thought and finitude. But it would be folly and idolatry of a far graver sort to think that this level of mindfulness was actually a perception or experience of God. Such a notion must itself be undone repeatedly, until one comes to the borderland of all Aught, so to speak, at the uttermost brink of consciousness. It is here, where one may have the trace of awareness of pure consciousness, that one senses the ultimate Naught of pure Being—an absolute realm of reality born of God. Holding this trace of consciousness in mind is a kind of cleaving of thought to a most unthinkable ultimacy, ever unfolding in God's well of Being. This is a state of mind known to some medieval kabbalists as *maḥshavah deveiqah*; it is a kind of "fixing of consciousness" on an ineffable God-fulness flooding the absolute Ground of Being. *Emunah* at this ideal level is an act of ultimate faithfulness to God Alone, the true and ultimate reality of all Being.

But *emunah* has a counterthrust. At the cognitive borderland of Aught and Naught there is also the distinct awareness that every existent thing is a delimitation of God's All-Being, a contraction of the flow of divine vitality into myriads of life-forms and modes of effectivity. Realizing this, one now regains the entirety of terms and textures and formations of this world, and experiences them as so many divine modalities. Indeed, everything is now perceived as fraught with modes of Divinity, such that our world is disclosed as a wondrous divine cavalcade that we receive and effect in innumerable ways. Receiving all things in faithfulness to their particular mode and actuality is the second, earthbound level of *emunah*. It is a direct consequence of the first, cosmic level. For that state was achieved through a spiritual practice of relinquishing one's cognitive hold on things; and now the fullness of the world order is appropriated with a corresponding humility and purified receptivity. Faithfulness at this level is thus the resolve to remain steadfast as receivers of God's gifts. A living *emunah* of this type is a faithfulness to the infinite reality of the *torah kelulah*. But it does not mean that this Torah cannot be responded to, or that it should not be transformed or humanized. That, of course, is just what happens (through Moses) with the *torah she-bikhtav*, and repeatedly (through study) with the *torah she-be'al peh*. It only means that we must acknowledge the ultimate primacy of the *torah kelulah* in matters of *emunah*, and that cultural delimitations of it must ever remain responsive to its absolute reality—lest our *emunah* be idolatrously transferred to these elements, and they no longer channel faithfulness to God's ultimate truth.

Standing in faithfulness to the specific infusions of divine modalities in our experience, *together with* a consciousness of their ultimate effacement (or grounding) in God's Naught, may be the higher fusion of the two levels of *emunah* just depicted. It is a focused simultaneity, whereby one keeps a mindfulness on both the ineffable divine Source of all Being *and* the particular modalities whereby it populates our world and experience. Living devotionally in this way, one may enact the exhortation of the sages, who counseled persons in prayer of the necessity to "set one's eyes below [on the earth] and one's heart above [in heaven]." The self in *emunah* conjoins both poles.

>>><<<

This ideal of a double consciousness is the subject of reflection by medieval masters, and they project its difficulties into biblical antiquity through deft turns of exegesis. At an earlier point we adduced R. Azriel's use of the philosophical terms *yesh* and *ayin* to convey the cognitive realities of Aught and Naught, and their relationship to Divinity. A contemporaneous teaching from the Book of Zohar utilizes the same terminology in order to explore the notion of spiritual dichotomies and their deeper theological truth.

> Rabbi Abba said: What did the Israelites mean by saying: "Is [*ha-yesh*] the Lord (YHWH) among us, or not [*ayin*]?" (Exodus 17:7). Could it be that in their folly they were not aware that He was among them? Did they not see the Shekhinah (divine Presence) before them and the clouds of Glory above them roundabout? Did they not, by the sea, behold the resplendent majesty of their King? And have we not learned (in the tradition) that a serving maid at the Red Sea was vouchsafed a greater vision than (the prophet) Ezekiel? Could they truly have been so foolish as to say this?!
>
> The explanation is as Rabbi Simeon has said: that the Israelites wished to determine whether the Divine manifestation which they had been given was of the Ancient One, the All-hidden and Transcendent, who, utterly beyond comprehension, is designated *ayin* (Nothing), or whether it was of the "Small Countenance," the Immanent, which is designated YHWH. Therefore instead of the word *lo* (not) we have here the word *ayin* (nothing).
>
> One may ask, why then were the Israelites chastised? The reason is that they made a distinction between these two aspects in God, and "tried the Lord" (ibid.), saying to themselves, We shall pray one way, if it is the One, and in another way, if it is the Other. (Zohar 2.64b)

The world-effecting *yesh* is the omnipresent Aught of YHWH's discernible "Shall-Be"; the ever-unknowable modality of this one reality is the *ayin* or Naught of Divinity. To pose the question as the Israelites putatively do (namely, is YHWH *yesh* or *ayin*?) is to fall into a false dichotomy and bifurcated religious consciousness. True *emunah* is a standing firm within the incomprehensible divine mystery (*ayin*), in humble receptiveness before the ever-happening world of sense and thought (*yesh*).

God's immanence is only a trace of transcendence—it is not transcendence itself; but it is integrated with and part of the incognizable and unimaginable Naught, for aught we know.

Living with steadfast *emunah* in the world means, theologically, to stand steadfastly within the world as an expression of God's ever-happening effectivity. This is, as we suggested, a vital aspect of the *torah kelulah*, and it transforms existence into an omnipresent or ever-occurring "Sinai" bidding us to hear and do what is required or possible in the given moment. Our faithfulness is tested by the character of our responses, and by our capacity to sustain the full brunt of what occurs at any time, without sliding into simplicities or reducing the complexities. A remarkable rabbinic text gives voice to the multiform nature of reality we contend with on a daily basis, and does so by a bold rereading of the Torah's statement that "God spoke all [*kol*] these words" at Sinai (Exod. 20:1). In its primary sense, noted earlier, "all these words" refers to the ensuing words of the Decalogue (the core of the *torah she-bikhtav*). But we also observed that R. Eleazar ben Azariah once dynamically reinterpreted this phrase in terms of the variety of interpretations and meanings unfolding in the *torah she-be'al peh*. In the present instance, the phrase gives expression to the *torah kelulah*. What are "all" the expressions of God understood to indicate? An anonymous teacher comments as follows in the *Midrash Tanḥuma*:

> "All [*kol*] at one time: He kills and restores to life, at one time; He smites and heals, at one time; He answers the woman in labor, and those who go on the sea and in the desert, those who are imprisoned and released—they being simultaneously in the east, west, north and south; 'He forms light and creates darkness, He makes peace and creates evil' [Isaiah 48:7]—all these things at one time."

The text continues with several other features of this type, such as the formation of humans from dust and their return to dust or the interrelations of sea and dry land. These were added to supplement the initial list. But the original point is clear and powerful in its own right: God is the voice effectuating all world-expressions and world-values (day and night; peace and evil), and all the mysteries and paradoxes of human experience (death and life; weal and woe)—all simultaneously, all at the same time. The fact that this teaching is presented within the specific context of Sinai, so concerned with the establishment of human justice and holiness, conveys the realization that God's truth (designated as "all these words" or "things") is something that both precedes and coexists with the national covenant (where "all these words" marks both the Written Torah of Sinai and the Oral Torah of the Study Hall, as just noted). To stand firmly before the multiform expressions of God's *torah kelulah* requires a spiritual steadfastness before the incomprehensible fullness and diversity of God's "Shall-Be."

Significantly, this teaching concerning the *torah kelulah* is not given to the natural self as such; it is given to the natural self who is *also* a covenant self, the heir of Moses and the sages. And that means that one experiences this vast and unfathomable reality within the specific framework of the Written and Oral Torahs, and their guidance for living in affirmation and responsiveness to the diversity of worldly happenings. Another old midrash gives striking expression to this in the theological terms we are now exploring. I refer to the words of a sage who once commented on the words of scripture concerning a "righteous nation who preserves faithfulness [*shomer emunim*]" (Isa. 26:2). What does it mean to act in this way? In an unexpected turn, the teacher remarks that such behavior refers to those "who say [*she-omerim*] 'amen' [*amen*]." This is no mere teaching, but a revelation of high spiritual purpose. The covenant self that would stand firm in the course of life, faithful to God and the Torah, says *amen*: "Truly"; "Surely." He says this to the words of prayer, which express teachings about God; and he expresses this in the full course of life. Faithfulness is an avowal of steadfastness. It is a correlate to the response "We shall do and we shall hear" at Sinai. It takes up David's exclamation, "Blessed is his glorious Name forever; his glory fills the whole world. Amen and Amen" (Ps. 72:19), and turns it into a covenant byword. Here on earth, in all things and in all ways, the person who is steadfast with God, who lives a life of faithfulness (*emunim*), expresses in every word and deed: amen.

Much spiritual training is necessary to cultivate such a person—one who can stand firm with ready resolve before God's "Shall-Be." For though, sometimes, the task seems clear, and a person's "amen" is easily mustered, at many other moments matters are confusing, and the proper disposition is unclear. It is then that one can only hope to be a disciple of Moses, who said to the Pharaoh in a moment of challenge and consternation: "We shall not know with what we shall worship the Lord [YHWH] our God *until we arrive there*" (Exod. 10:26).

There seems no greater courage than this expression of "amen." It is the task of covenant theology to prepare a person to live with such unknowing, and to live in anticipation of events with a cultivated thoughtfulness and spiritual resolve.

>>><<<

What is this preparation for readiness?

The cultivation of readiness involves the spiritual preparation of the self to be properly attuned to reality and the tasks and moments of our life-world. *Readiness* is a settling of one's spirit through training and thoughtful reflection so that the fullness of what one has learned and experienced may serve as resources to guide oneself and make one prepared for the more confusing happenings in the midst of life. All this involves a withdrawal of sorts, as part of the preparation—be this an act of physical distantiation, in order to create the proper space for something to unfold in its own proper way, or be this a spiritual act of concentration or inward focus, so that one may properly attend to the event that is to happen or the tasks that one may undertake. Surely there is no hard and fast separation between these two acts (the bodily and the mental), and they may in fact be complexly interrelated. Who would suppose that Moses's charge to the people to "be ready" and "prepared" (*nekhonim*) for the divine advent on Sinai (Exod. 19:11) was only a physical separation from ordinary acts, and did not also include a spiritual sanctification as well (vv. 14–15)? For the preparations required them to be ready and true for what was about to take place. Similarly, Moses himself was told to "be ready" and "prepared" (*nakhon*) for the moment of his personal ascent up the mountain (Exod. 34:2), when he would ascend to God and again attend to the voice out of heaven and a disclosure of the divine mystery (vv. 3–7). This certainly does not refer to the physical preparations themselves, which precede this command, but is an exhortation to spiritual exercises and alertness to the moment to come, as the medieval masters rightly perceived.

The cultivation of readiness begins in the heart, as the locus of inner balance; and it seeks to establish a "prepared" and "resolute heart" (*lev nakhon*), so that one's outward actions emerge from this center toward the world and whatever befalls the self (Ps. 112:7). Such soul work proceeds with humility and repeated failure; for the heart is also dominated by diverse and unfocused instincts or forces. It longs for a healing beyond oneself; it longs for God to heal the fractured self and help guide it; and it longs for the creator of life to "create a new heart" within, and thus "renew a *ruaḥ nakhon*" for one's ongoing life (Ps. 51:12)—for the true work of self-cultivation can only proceed with an honest awareness of one's fractured spiritual state. But just what is this *ruaḥ nakhon* that is here so ardently requested? What is its nature and character?

A *ruaḥ nakhon* is a "right" and "ready spirit"; it is the inner quality that helps prepare the self for a proper attunement to the pulse of the world—so that one can breathe rightly and truly in its presence; and it is a steadiness of comportment and inner balance—so that one has the strength and resolve to stand firm before whatever is heard or happens. The prayer for a "ready spirit" expresses the inner desire of the self to be a fit and proper vessel for the indwelling of God in the world, and the reception of

God's "I am" in a ready and right manner. The readiness of spirit is a state of self-collection, as well as an ingathering of one's resources for life and its tasks. It is an inner state that readies the entire body and will. And it is just this condition that the soul prays for in these words: "May the favor of the Lord, our God, be upon us; let the work of our hands be readily fit [*konenah*]; [O God!] Make fit [*konenehu*] the work of our hands!" (Ps. 90:17). This is the true and proper prayer of covenant theology: to be properly fit for the tasks to come.

To live in this way is to cultivate *naḥat ruaḥ*, a settled and balanced comportment of one's spirit and breath. With respect to God, in the fullest sense, this involves a "quietude of spirit" of the most profound sort; and with respect to humankind, whom we meet in the fullest round of life, this involves a "pleasantness of being." But in fact, the two types (metaphysical and moral) conjoin: for the right *naḥat*, or pleasantness of manner accorded persons, in all respects, is also a quiet calmness of spirit that allows their presence to appear as it appears; and the deep quietude of heart that the self sets before God's heart, pulsing into the veins of life, in all aspects, is also the humble joy that is felt before the manifold images of God's all-forming presence—and in that of human beings most of all. Both with respect to God and persons, the proper response is ever and only: "amen." This is *naḥat ruaḥ*. It is a life of *emunah* in the most perfected manner.

Covenant theology aims at this steadfastness of spirit. But other forces intervene. We miss the mark with *timhon leivav*—with a confused and irresolute heart. And the human spirit is ever unsettled by the sense of futility.

Futility and the Sense of Hevel

Emunah and futility are locked in battle. Our souls try to hear God's "I am," here and everywhere; but our minds whisper, "It is all vanity [*hevel*] and a striving after wind."

Koheleth, the Preacher, speaks in this way. He throws down the gauntlet of futility: "What [*mah*] benefit is there for a person [*adam*] in all that he achieves under the sun?" (Eccles. 1:2) For things go round and round like the wind, listing here and blowing there, in a most wearisome way; and habit leads to lassitude and to a sense of futility. Nothing seems new, but then nothing of the past is remembered either; and if there are achievements, well then they are often destroyed by chance or lost to happenstance; and in any case, in the end there is death, and nothing is reaped but dust. Humans seem to have just enough knowledge to further their curiosity, adds the Preacher; but such knowledge is more a torment than a boon, for all the real clarity it provides; and pleasure or prudence seems to add up to little in the end as well, and thus there is hardly much good reason to care for the earth or act with thoughtfulness. Looked at from the perspective of ends and benefits, nothing really seems to justify one pattern of living over another; and looked at from the angle of utility and consequence, the self is thrown into perplexity and futility—and sometimes into amoral disregard altogether.

All these are the statements of the natural self, which assesses experience and collects results and tries to determine which actions would seem to be of the most personal benefit. And as we listen to Koheleth there is much that rings true. Who could deny these observations? They also tug at our hearts. There is a howling emptiness all around, which mocks our limited attempts to make order and interpret the world. Things come and go with no apparent sense, and the true interconnections between things elude and mock our vain pretensions at wisdom. But: does our sense of meaninglessness and antivalue undermine the values themselves or their purpose and meaning? Does the fact that one observes "all the oppression" on the earth (Eccles. 4:1) negate the command "do not oppress the stranger" (Exod. 22:7; compare Lev. 19:33); and if one sees all "the extortion of justice and right," with "one high official . . . protected by a higher one" (Eccles. 5:7), does that subvert the command to "establish judges and overseers in all your gates . . . who will judge the people with a righteous justice," and "not tilt verdicts" or "take bribes" (Deut. 16:18–19); and if one notes that "former things" are "forgotten," as are the ways the wise (Eccles. 1:11, 2:15), does this cancel the command to "remember olden times" (Deut. 32:7), and that "you were a slave in the land of Egypt" (and therefore should treat the stranger and poor with kindness; Deut. 24:17–18, 21–22)? Does the fact that a person dies like an animal (Eccles. 3:19) negate the command to "choose life" (Deut. 30:19); and does the fact that "all things are wearisome" (Eccles. 1:8) mean that there may not be real meaning on "this day"—if one hears the voice that calls (compare Ps. 95:7)?

The covenant self takes all this accumulated natural experience as it is, without denial, but avers, "in the end," when all is said and done, and all the assessments of experience are weighed up and down, that one should "fear God and observe his commandments" (Eccles. 12:13). For in the end, the covenant self does not make calculations and determinations based on the sum of experience and its personal utility or benefits. The covenant self stands in trembling awe before the might of Divinity *and* sets about to do the tasks that transform this awesome sensibility into life-enhancing actions in this world. Part of that divine might is the pulsing will of all life for more and enhanced life, for life in different ways and expressions; and the commands of God that are heard in all this (caesural moments great and small) become the norms by which we establish justice and care on earth so that human and organic life may flourish. All this conduces to an attitude of firm and steadfast attentiveness, oriented to the here and now. For if the natural self speaks of what things indicate, and does so by projecting future patterns and their meaning for *adam*, the covenant self is addressed by imperatives in the present, which speak personally and directly, quite apart from their value to the individual self alone.

The covenant self tries to be ready to respond, and this readiness makes no calculations or assessments of utility as a precondition for action. Trying to stand firm in this way, before God's awesome world-Being and its challenges, is *emunah*. This is a living covenant theology. It is a theology that tries to be steadfast and faithful to the world at hand, as much as possible, and to the ways that God's effectivity happens here and now. Without ever denying one's natural self, the self of covenant theology tries to be ready to hear and do whatever the moment demands—with a heart and mind cultivated by a tradition of value and a life of thoughtfulness. This is a spiritual posture that tries to answer *amen* wholeheartedly, true to the highest truths of the situation insofar as we can know them.

Such a posture is noble, and heroic, and determined.

Covenant theology is thus a heroic theology. It strives to transform the amoral vastness into a site of sacred value—so that the mute may find expression, and bonds of meaning be established. Trembling and travail are endured; and resoluteness is the spiritual imperative.

>>><<<

Why was the Torah given in the desert—in a place where darkness and the demonic predominate, where emptiness and terror prevail? The Zohar gives this response, counseling a deliberate mode of spiritual resistance and overcoming:

> The words of Torah dwell [*mityashvin*] only there [in the desert], for there is no light except that which emerges from darkness. When that (Other) Side is suppressed, the Holy One, blessed be he, ascends above and is glorified in his Glory. And there is no worship of God (namely, the Holy One) except within darkness, and there is no good except within evil. When a person enters an evil way and abandons it, then the Holy One, Blessed be he, ascends in his Glory. Accordingly, the perfection of all is (the encounter of) good and evil together, and (then) ascend to the good. For there is no good except that which emerges from evil, . . . and this is perfected worship of God. (Zohar 2.84a)

The spiritual life walks this perilous path—through the howl of evil and emptiness in the world, consciously confronting its terrors and tasks, striving for integrity without denials or any evasions.

Be-khol Atar ve-Atar: *Central Places*

The spaces of the world widen and contract precipitously; they are often precarious realities, fraught with despair and fear and the specters of evil. For Jewish theological consciousness, just this is the sense of fracture and fatefulness of our human condition since Adam's banishment from Eden, fated to work the harsh earth because of greed and desire; it is the further dislocation of our habitat since Cain's exile further east of Eden, due to anger and jealousy; and it is the breakdown of common labor and construction since the tower of Babel, because of hubris and overreaching. Spatial dislocation thus symbolizes all our exiles and alienations in the world, both historical and mental. It is the deepest of archetypes carried in our hearts and souls, and attests to a primordial anxiety over the nature of our human condition. But this negative valence has its ballast. The recurrent dream of harmony and ingathering in a place of blessing is its counterpoint, the longing of the soul since Abraham. It too is archetypal and primordial. It is older than Sinai, and older than Moses as well, who inherited the ancestral promises of the patriarchs, kept alive from generation to generation as a reiterated divine hope. It is the deep yearning for Eden amid the fractures of life.

Hopes for restoration in a safe haven are resolutely borne through the times and spaces of the world. Temporality is ordered with respect to its fulfillment, and spatiality is outlined in terms of the shelters and places that prefigure its realization. For Jewish theology, three spaces are particularly central and condition religious consciousness in distinctive ways. Separately and together they cultivate the values of community and its continuity.

HOME, SYNAGOGUE, AND HOMELAND

Home is fundamental. It is the womb space of daily rebirth, the special place of gestation and growth. Home is also a realm of familiarity and shelter. Here generations are ordered and cared for; here they are instructed in the past and prepared for the future;

and here too they are sheltered against the dangers or disruptions of the outside world. Home is a sphere of intimacy, threaded by family bonds. It has its own character. The narrative of the family is of a particular kind: it is shaped by distinct memories and hopes; the hierarchy of the family is also particular in nature: it is ordered by specific parents with specific names and histories; and the culture of the family is of a particular character, guided by specific forms of honor and respect, nurture and regard. But the family is not utterly de novo. Rooted in past generations and tradition, it grows through practices cultivated by the ancestors, and flourishes by means of values honed over time. The specific and the particular are thus also communal and historical. We know this primordially from the shared name of the family— which indicates common origin and descent; but we also know this through the cultural and physical gifts of many others who do not bear our name. We are bound to them as well and rooted in their lives. Families join and expand; homes are linked and blended; generations are joined one to the other.

One might therefore imagine that the reality of "home" is a natural creation, and that homes are material growths, emergent somehow from the soil of one's native land. But this is not so. A home is not a spontaneous outgrowth. Rather, it is built and fortified; safeguarded and preserved; furbished with care and concern. A home is infused with memory, not instinct; and it is composed of different rooms for different persons and purposes. Each threshold is mysterious, and one crosses its lintel with anticipation, aware of the private or public areas to be entered. The boundary with outer space is the most crucial of all, for it marks the fundamental transition from the external, public realms of the world to the sacred place of home, with its shared rituals and recitations. The line separating the world from the home is liminal, and in a Jewish home it is marked by scripture and its teachings. "You shall write them on the doorposts of your house and upon your gates." These words, encased in a *mezuzah*, mark off the common space with the intentions of sanctity. "And you shall speak of them when you lie down and rise up"—because the home is a place of primary instruction, ever cultivated and reinforced. These words also accompany one "on the way" outside, so that the inside is carried within the heart, guiding one's mouth and hands and legs, directing one's mind, or sustaining one's spirit and will. And fundamentally, these words guide one at table, inculcating special reverence for the bounty of the earth, and thereby transforming this piece of furniture into an altar and the shared event of eating into an act of communion. According to tradition, the four legs of the table represent the four elements of the world, and thereby raise one's heart and mind to the heavenly chariot that sustains all life. Thankfulness is the core of such eating, transforming the physical body into a reflective soul. Just to eat is to graze; but to give blessing is to live in divine acknowledgment. The home cultivates this value. It is therefore a preparation for thoughtful living and its realization; and it is also a cultivation of generosity and responsibility. The family shares food and words, it opens its door to the neighbor, and it teaches paternity and maternity—and child care. None of this is natural, for all our naturalness. Home is thus the primary ground of self-transcendence. When family members so live with God in mind, the mere house, or *bayit*, becomes a *bayit ne'eman*, a home of faithfulness, firmly and faithfully grounded in the mystery of things. The home is first community.

>>><<<

Synagogue is foundational. It is second community, transcending the family unit. A synagogue is a *beit knesset*, a house of gathering; it is a place for the spirit and the people, a community of families—even a metafamily. It is a home of homes. For Jewish theology, the synagogue is the eternal Sinai in communal space— for it is the place where the primary words of the covenant are recited and interpreted before the people. It is also the spiritual Temple in physical space—for it is the place where the words of liturgy proclaim hope and celebration, and where its acts inspire devotion and sacrifice. If the temporality of home and family is diachronic, and its instructions are geared to the age of the receiver, the time of the synagogue congregation (a family of families) is synchronic, and its instructions and rites are over-arching and collective in nature. The synagogue is also the space of tradition, ideally permeated by teachings of God's reality and realized presence, and infused by the values of sanctity and sanctification. Speech here is distinct: Scripture is declaimed by cantillated chants, and prayers are uttered in communal recitation, punctuated by the conjoint avowal of "amen." The tone of liturgy is at once sotto voce, recited singly in a special rhythm, utterly different from ordinary speech; but it is also shared song, chanted in unison and loud celebration. Whether the one or the other, the words of liturgy are infused with special reverence and melody and longing. Like the teachings and memories of the home, those of the house of worship are binding and distinctive. Life and language on the inside are different.

Entering the synagogue, the worshiper declares, "By your great kindness I enter your house, I bow down in your holy shrine in reverential awe." For the synagogue is a place of divine dwelling, built *be-khol atar ve-atar*, "in every place" and everywhere, as a fence against communal dispersion and wandering. It is an asylum in exile, both physical and spiritual, a veritable *miqdash me'at*, or Sanctuary in miniature, as the prophet Ezekiel long ago declared. Crossing into the synagogue is thus a recurrent pilgrimage from the wayward paths of the world to a sacred site, repeatedly, over the arc of time that constitutes a natural day. The lines of physical movement thus link the home to the synagogue, the workplace to the synagogue, and the social space to the synagogue—where all the faces of the world are replaced by the special presence of those gathered for worship and learning. Hence the time of the synagogue also conjoins and transcends our singular rhythms. It is a temporality shared with the community of the faithful of all places and times; it is marked by the godly patterns of the sacred seasons; and it rises beyond the merely diurnal sequences of life to a time where ordinary speech is suspended and one's language serves holy purposes.

In the times of exile, the synagogue is wholeness and preparation; it is a community in anticipation of peace and fellowship, and a place where gifts are bestowed and received. In the synagogue the community lives with deepest density, suffused by the memory of the dead, the absent members of this living communion. Those of the past are recalled daily and annually, according to ancient custom; and the entire community assents with "amen" to their recollection in the context of exalting God's numinous transcendence—so "beyond all blessing and song," or any "praise and consolation" that is "utterable in this world" by humankind. The presence of the gathering past and present thus extends time into immemorial recesses, and space to the *beit al-min*, the "house of eternity," or cemetery, situated at the outskirts of communal space—the home of those in the extended "bond of life." Just as the synagogue is not a natural dwelling but built and cultivated as a sacred space for divine presence, the cemetery is also not a natural site marked by flowering plants and trees. It is rather a realm of cultural memory overset with slabs bearing names and inscriptions—standing and leaning like angelic wings that give God's shelter to the restless and sorrowful souls of the living.

The temporal vectors of the synagogue also extend toward the future. Like the home of the family, the gathering place of the community has a messianic horizon, by virtue of the human care and divinely oriented speech it engenders. However, as an enclave of separate units, the "house of gathering" is pitched toward this future in a distinctive way. For the synagogue is not so much an enclosure of the familiar and "the same" (as in a family) as it is one that embraces "the other" who is different (from me). Moreover, as a structure built *be-khol atar*, the members of a synagogue must bear in mind that their spiritual enclave both includes and excludes, not solely by virtue of language and memory, but by dint of its traditions of membership and acceptance. A house of gathering for Jews must therefore always be preparatory for and proleptic of a more inclusive congregation. The God who fills heaven and earth, as a vast sphere of indwelling, can hardly be bounded by a specific "house" (Isa. 66:1)—and if at all, only in the here and now, while the tasks of care and speech are cultivated. In the end, God's place will be a "house of prayer for all peoples" (Isa. 56:8). This is the ultimate horizon of spiritual labor projected by prophetic tradition. At such a time of ingathering, there will be no inside and no outsider.

>>><<<

Homeland is the space of third community; it is the ideal and real gathering place of the people Israel—a world-spanning community of communities. From the first, homeland is the place of promise, a heartland of hope to be settled and sanctified. So it was for Abraham, and all who repeat his model. It is thus space transformed, a point of orientation among the regions of the world. As a true center, homeland defines the peripheries as exile and diaspora; it designates spatial movement as near or far; and it delineates the goal as an ascension from a lower physical and spiritual state. Cognitively, homeland is both utopian and restorative; and for this reason all other dwellings are booths in a wasteland, merely temporary places on the path to true settlement. Theologically interiorized, homeland and heartland comprise a magnetic pole, charging the mind with longing and memory. Exile thus becomes the space of weeping and diminishment, of vows and rites of remembrance. By contrast, any and every restoration of the people is an ingathering of the remnant and a harvest of song (Ps. 126). In exile one is always a homeless pilgrim, in body and soul, ever a wanderer "east of Eden." But in the homeland one becomes a dweller, well rooted in the earth. In exile there is waiting, hopeful expectation, and prophetic promise. Viewed in its light, the settlement seems like fulfillment and a grounding in earthly nativity.

But homeland (like home) is never natural; it is always cultural. One doesn't grow out of the soil, but rather cultivates values upon it. Homeland is therefore something to be achieved, again and again, as the collective settlement for a community of communities. It thus bears the challenge of integrating and protecting human differences in a shared space. As it was said: "Zion shall be redeemed through justice, and its returners by righteousness" (Isa. 1:27). The heartland is this ideal social space, the moral core of the homeland for which generations yearn. In this place, the physical safety of the people must be safeguarded, and their spiritual virtues built up. Such are the tasks and concerns of a concrete theology. Of old, when historical conditions imposed a disjunction between an ever-real (ideal) heartland within, and an unrealized homeland in the (brute) outer world, the homeland was itself imagined as a pure heartland; and this vision guided and consoled the people in the wastes of exile. For all its conditioned character, such a conjunction of the two values (of homeland and heartland) must not be sundered—even under changed circumstances, when now the heartland also beats in a political body and the tasks of life confront impure choices. To be like all the nations is thus not an unqualified value. The moral heartland must give guidance and orientation.

The entire people Israel bear responsibility for heartland and homeland, *be-khol atar ve-atar*—in all their dwelling places, whether this task is perceived as a theological imperative or in wholly worldly terms; and whether it takes place in the national homeland or somewhere else. Shared memory, suffering, and hope demand as much.

Primordially, all Israel are descendants of Ever (Eber), ancestor of Abraham; each is an Ivri—a Hebrew. They thus share a common bond. To what may this be compared? Perhaps to the "tablets" of the covenant, "written on their two sides [*evreyhem*]" (Exod. 32:15). According to a midrashic teaching, these two sides were not necessarily on the same plane, side by side (five to a half), but were composed front and back (ten together, both fore and aft)—presumably taking the next phrase of the passage ("*mi-zeh umi-zeh* were they written"; ibid.) as indicating their composition "on one side and the other." Thus, accordingly, said R. Hisdai, the great miracle of the tablets is that though the chiseling on the one side bore through to the other, and the same letter incisions were perceived differently from each side, both halves comprised the unified teaching of the Ten Command-ments. Hence, despite the inverse facing of the two sides, and the functional difference in the reading of the same character shapes, the two tablets proclaimed one complete truth. They are there-fore one whole from different perspectives. Just so, we may aver, the people Israel are one and united, conjoined and correlated one to the other. This has been so since the formative covenant alliance at Sinai, and through the manifold extensions of tradi-tion. Not singly, but as parts of a whole, do the members consti-tute the covenant people. Divergent and convergent at once, the two sides of the tablets represent the mystic bond of the com-munity and the complex unity of its differences. In dialogue and coresponsibility, the people Israel, from here and there (*mi-zeh umi-zeh*), complete one another and conjointly face the chal-lenges of their collective heritage and existence.

> Houses of life and habitations of death;
> blood pulse of family and tears;
> fortitude, unity, and fragmentation:
> God-longing, People-binding:
> The Mystery of Israel.

> Eyes like fathomless caverns—for the sorrow and witness;
> mouths proclaiming: Shall Be—in testimony and task;
> and
> ears and hands
> still
> Hearing and Doing.

SPATIAL ORIENTATIONS

The foregoing spatial settings (home, synagogue, and homeland) with their primariness are themselves grounded in even more primordial spatial orientations, linguistically preserved in the axial prepositions and adverbs of direction. These terms encode world-attitudes and world-dispositions that cut deeper than cul-ture and its constructions (both physical and conceptual), and are ultimately preverbal in nature. In this sense, they reflect something of our most basic human being within the physical habitat of our earthbound lives. Becoming aware of these elements is therefore crucial for a more responsible self-awareness. Indeed, through a deeper understanding of our basic axes in space, we may even catch a glimpse of the root structures of certain ethical attitudes and cultural institutions. The guiding intuition of the ensuing phenomenological reflections is that primordial orientations in space condition primary human relations and social associations (home, community, and homeland most especially).

We must therefore begin with our feet on the earth, and the physical situation of our lives. The basic spatial prepositions or adverbs encoding these settings are best seen in terms of dynamic polarities. The issues of values and ethics emerge from this primary ground.

The first of these polarities is *in-out*. What do they fundamentally express of our human being in space? Principally, the word *in* conveys the sense of being situated inside a boundary or frame, and thus denotes such conditions as incorporation, protection, safety, and belonging; it also has the character of being physically or conceptually closed off and private, and is thus primarily a place of nativity (containing and sustaining blood natives or persons adopted through relationship and friendship) and intimacy. Because of these qualities, there is a different sense of ethos and ethnos for those within the bounds and those outside them. To be *in* is to have asylum and care, to expect love and care, and somehow to be "in place" and "at the goal." Only in dangerous situations is this "insideness" considered an incarceration, protecting those outside from harm—and then this inversion is itself conceptually inverted so that one conceives oneself to be safe and not "in harm's way."

Correspondingly, there is the word *out* and its meanings. As with all binaries, each term of a pair always lurks within the sense field of the other, the two being dialectically correlated. But if we try to think of the valence of being *out* on its own, we call to mind the fundamental reality of being apart from or beyond something, and thus variously excluded, beyond the pale and somewhere "out in the open." To be in this situation is to be physically and emotionally barred, and kept separate or distinct, and even a nonnative or foreigner. The stranger is figuratively and literally always "at the gate," outside, such that hospitality or inclusion is a "taking in" and an act of reception. The "other" is thus ontically "outside," and not one who inherently shares the in-group culture or values. And by inversion, a person on the "outs" is "closed out" of participation. One feels this dimensionality with all one's being, the pariah most absolutely.

Culture is grounded in notions of those who are *in* and *out*, physically and otherwise. But there are also ideals that try to reconceive the boundaries and project new inclusions. For the older biblical law and its ongoing Jewish interpretation, the formulation "You shall have one law for the stranger and the native alike" (Num. 9:14, 15:15) is the projected estate for the real and ideal polity. Where it does not merely attempt to regulate the stranger's life, but also provide a fundamental enfranchisement, such a rule assumes a messianic import. Indeed, it injects a prophetic challenge into the heart of human relations, so that the boundaries of nature may be crossed and slowly permeated by values—step by step, heartbeat by heartbeat. By this process, the stranger is nativized as one's neighbor.

Home, synagogue, and homeland may have closed or open doors, and sealed or porous boundaries. Reflecting on the terms *in* and *out* keeps us alert to the deep and disguised roots of our social relations. It may also put us in mind of even more primary boundaries and their ethical negotiation. The injunction in Deuteronomy 24:10–11 helps frame the issue. In that ancient rule, we are told: "When you make a loan to your compatriot, you may not enter his house to take the pledge; you must remain outside, and the person to whom you made the loan will bring the loan out to you." This is a straightforward statement with ethical force. Exchanges in the outside world do not permit one to enter the private space of another to retrieve a given object. The boundary between *out* and *in* must not be freely crossed, but must be treated with respect. But is this all? Certainly, this legal directive allows for a deeper, more paradigmatic reading, where the ethics of an economic rule entail basic interpersonal values. At this hermeneutical level, the law reveals something fundamental about the sacred boundaries between individuals. For there are all forms of exchange, and these create various types of material and spiritual obligation; and there are also many ways that the gifts of friendship and education transfer life-processes from one person to the other, and these similarly create their own loops of relationship. Considered thus, the biblical rule may also direct attention to the core value of privacy, and what constitutes the inwardness or personal space of another. These are not human boundaries to be crossed with impunity. One must rather learn to wait on the outside, allowing a cycle of giving and receiving to unfold in its own way. One's presence (in mind, memory, or actuality) for another already conditions that other one's response. In its time the exchange will occur; and then the first giver may become a receiver as well.

The dyad *in-out* is thus crucial in the transformation of space into spheres of value.

A second primary binary, also expressive of our primordial and prereflective emplacement in the world, is *near-far*. What different spatial relations are expressed thereby? For starters, the word *near* conveys the quality of being proximate to something in the world, this something being variously distinct and separate from it (by choice or imposition). *Nearness* is thus not an absolute term, but a relative value: one is more or less *near* an object or person in space, and only distinctively so (so near one could be no nearer) because one has progressed in degrees of nearness. Thus the word *near* captures a type of progressive relationship in space, and it does so via a certain autocenteredness, insofar as being *near* something is perceived in relation to oneself (the axis of orientation). From such a self-centered perspective, one deems oneself relationally *near* something insofar as one is just here and not there (*here* and *there* being more static allomorphs of the polarity *near* and *far*). This is a neutral depiction. However, as a spatial value, *near* may be positive or negative, and charged by desire or repulsion. It depends whether what is proximate is deemed somehow good for the self or not. Presumably, the sense of being *near* an object of worth (like home or community) originates in primordial situations of parental care or protection, or in primary situations of benefit or help. *Near* can also be a mixed blessing. One can be too *near* as well. And in times of longing or delusion, *near* may even be a mirage—a fata morgana that is not necessarily a personal error, but a distortion that may extend to a group at large.

On the other side, the word *far* correspondingly expresses extension and distance from the self, and thus a place "far different" or "beyond" what is just here and now. For something to be *far* means that it is "away" and "off" and "atopic"—not this place; or it means that it is "well away" from realization and thus an ideal or distant reality. When something is *"far* off" or *"far* away," one can strive for it and move from where one now is, hereby and near at hand, to some place out there, not-yet and still *far*-to-go. The sense of something being far off or far away may incite inducement or even despair, depending on the values in the here and near, both spatially and interpersonally. The *far* may thus be something humanly intimate and longed for, with its distance marking the register of its high value and the character of its attainability; or the term may be of a more practical nature, and express something to be achieved through strategies of addition or substitution.

Culture is also structured around these primary spatial elements of *near* and *far*, and to the extent that the *near* connotes the homegrown or native, and the *far* the outlander or exile, the terms convey a spatial divide and a conceptual contrast. Thus the prophetic word proclaiming "Peace, peace for the near and far" (Isa. 57:19) is initially an announcement of common healing and national well-being, an overcoming of the far-flung exiles by conjoining them to others more near to home. It is a word of national comfort in the present with an eye to the future. But the biblical call may ring deeper through ongoing interpretation, for if the prophetic announcement is also understood in view of a more universal horizon, the spatial dimension of the terms is transformed and one then may envision the word of *shalom*, or peaceful harmony, as the bond integrating the outlying and in-dwelling of all nations. In this way, a fundamental spatial division and relation achieves a more universal character and interhuman correlation—so that the ideal of harmony would then transcend a specific place and include people in a common world-space. On this more messianic alternative, the prophet's word would mean that "peace" will relate those near and afar, whatever the character of their nearness and distance.

How one embodies the valences of *near* and *far* thus has value consequences; the spatial senses of one's physical being condition sensibilities toward persons and places. Before we are ever ethical and theological beings, we are encoded human animals on the earth.

The third spatial binary is *with-before*. It too conveys a primordial aspect of our humanity on the earth. Starting with the term *with*, we come to reflect on the moments of primary togetherness in space, when one has some commonality with another thing or person, and does not experience one's being-there in space in any sense of aloneness or singleness. The deep dimension conveyed by the word *with* is the sense of being "alongside" something, in a relationship of "togetherness" and with degrees of commonality (of intention, purpose, or result). Hence the quality of being *with* something in space conveys the sensation of its combination or association with oneself; and if this quality is rather *with* someone, there is then the sense of fellowship, shared pathos, and even sympathy. With respect to our lives with persons, moreover, being *with* them (in a spatial dimension) also means being in a common world or sharing a common origin and destiny. Fundamentally, when one is *with* something or someone, these have a certain eminence—they are regarded, taken into account, and given recognition; for one cannot be *with* something or someone in a mindless or inattentive manner in any meaningful way. A "Mitmensch" and "neighbor" is a cocreature—both *with* me and nigh. And insofar as the term *with* is charged with spatial density, this includes a consciousness of the presence and claim of other realities in and for one's life.

Correlatively, the word *before* conveys something "frontal" (rather than being alongside), where the self and the other thing or person address the same geometric plane (rather than sharing a common plane or perspective *with* another). The confronting elements are thus in some manner face to face, in a primary encounter of presence—this being something quite different from the shoulder-to-shoulder character of standing "with" another, face by face, not looking at the "other" but sharing a common outlook. Being *before* something or someone is thus to regard this entity as otherwise than oneself, and to recognize that the two (oneself and the other) do not share the same place in space or angle of vision. Nevertheless, and despite this difference, one is drawn into a common spatial sphere with the other person or thing. This is not merely evident by their joint circumscription in one shared milieu, but by the fact that in a vital confrontation one is variously transfixed by the other reality, held in place by its appearance, and charged by its aura. One is therefore called up short *before* this reality, addressed by its visage or value, and confronted by its numinous or fascinating character. The Gorgon's head transfixes, as does the Burning Bush; a friend coming into view transfixes a self, as one's enemy may do; and the pain of another person may transfix the self, as well as the specter of death and an open grave.

Cultures trade on the virtues of fellowship *with* and the duties *before* another being. They imply a necessary and primary regard for what is alongside or before oneself in the lived world—persons most especially. If the first term embodies fellowship and togetherness, the second one conveys difference and otherness. The word *with* implies shared pathos or purpose; whereas the word *before* implies distinction and relatedness. Whether the frontal aspect is from the perspective of honor or duty, or a matter of respect or care; and whether this vis-à-vis is one of height or depth, or of proximity or distance, when something is *before* oneself it has a claim or presence (both morally and consciously). Hence it is other-in-relation, difference-in-connection, there-and-here together. The shared sphere is thus a place of meeting and obligation. Cultures may first speak of these matters in ways that specify those within and without a core group (be it family, people, or nation); but this division may be overcome. This is notably achieved by the following biblical injunctions, which may serve as ideal types for such matters.

The first overcoming must be that of self-regard, when a person is shut up within internal space, and must look outward to what lies before oneself. Such an act is an overcoming of a state of being within-oneself for the sake of seeing what is before-oneself. It is enjoined through the following legal paradigm: "If you see your fellow's ass or ox fallen upon the road—do not ignore it, [but] you must surely help him raise it" (Deut. 22:4). Here the operative conditions are one's relationship to the burden of one's fellow or compatriot, and the natural tendency to "disappear" from its presence, or to disregard it in actuality. This law addresses the fact that though people can share a common world, this realm is only a virtual space when people look past or through what lies before them; and it is only when one attends to the happenings of another person's life and is morally transfixed by the event that they share a real space—one before-the other, one now in-relation-to the other. In this way we realize that moral space is humanly constructed: it is a realized or transfigured space, rising up out of the primariness of human settlement, threat, or sustenance—but ever grounded in these spatial realities.

The second overcoming of insularity extends further, and is encapsulated in the following injunction: "If you see the ass of your enemy lying under its burden, and would refrain from aiding him—you must surely raise it up with him" (Exod. 23:5). Now the conditions entail the self (addressed by the law) and the events happening to one's enemy, who appears in one's line of sight and sphere of action. The natural tendency may be to foreclose the significance of this shared space, and neutralize it (thereby making it virtual); but this is countered by a deeper bond. The self and one's enemy are fellow creatures, and this bond cuts deeper than historical enmity and disregard. A person is therefore enjoined to act in terms of human values, the shared labor of subsisting on this earth. Now a larger realm of the earth stands before and around the self. One is taught to see deeper, to acknowledge the happenings in space, and thus to turn this zone, the ground of our social being, into an ethical sphere, and give our eyesight a moral horizon.

>>><<<

So it is that our earthbound natures are primordially spatial, and expressed through fundamental physical orientations (embodied in certain linguistic terms and binaries). In various ways, these modalities condition the nature of our human being and its moral possibilities. For if we are first and foremost creatures of the world, and infused by the realities that emerge from the spatial character of our plane of action, we are also creatures with ideals and values, and may draw ethical implications from these conditions, thereby giving significance and purpose to our deeds. To have such thoughts, and see the world in terms of values, is not only to be physically situated beings, but to live in the spirit and with a sense of responsibility for the world we have received and will transmit (thoughtfully or not). Standing tall within our naturalness, we attend to the world lying in the outreaches of space, and all that comes before us in every here and now. Our height gives us vision and perspective all our days, until we lie low in the earth, to replenish it through our bodies. But our souls ascend, memorials of values achieved through spiritual travail.

Toward a Theology of Ḥiyyuv

Within the covenant there are duties and commitments; life and values impose assorted claims of obligation (or *ḥiyyuv*) on the self. This occurs on many levels. At a primary level, a sense of *ḥiyyuv* is conditioned upon an awakening to the actuality of experience, to what is given us to hear and do. Slowly or with sudden shock the mind may be opened to the facticity of things, to the fact that there is something (compelling out there) and not nothing (but habit and dull routine). This sharpening of consciousness within the everyday gives the sense that only certain things impose a claim or obligation, and that choice begins with a decision of the self to cross over to the external world from the private, autonomous enclosure of one's being. But this is a limited and flawed perspective. It hardly accounts for the truth of what it means to engage the phenomenal world in the most primary way. It may be a first step toward that awareness; but it is not that awareness itself.

What is our primordial condition, to be recovered through reflection? Perhaps this: already with the opening of eyes, the hearing of ears, and the tactility of the body—already from such inadvertent moments the world imposes itself on us. It is always already there for me, just as I become there for it. There is no gap to be crossed (between the cognizing ego and the world): there is miraculously an immediate, primordial thereness of reality. Already from the first, and with every act of sensation, the world is "there" as a field of phenomenality, as a world of claims imposing themselves with an *ever-present* and evident presence. These claims put one under a primary obligation: one can respond or not respond; heal or destroy; attend or neglect; consume or build up. We have that choice. But we do not choose the world and its thereness at each moment. This does not mean that one can know all that can be known at the given time, or see all that needs to be seen; nor does it suggest that what the self may now perceive or have in mind may not be better perceived or brought to mind from another time or place, or even by another person. But this does not change matters. It does not alter the reality that imposes itself on the self with each and every act of perception, and does not diminish the need to respond. Already from the very outset of every moment, and repeatedly, one is put under the claim of the world—ever and always, the world asserts:

Here; Now (the primordial "yes" of Being), and the self has an obligation to respond, to hear or to do. I am not given my subjectivity by the objective field of the world; nor is the world given objectivity from the vantage of my subjectivity. Rather, the world and I coinstantiate each other; I am subject to it and become real with the reality of my experiences, even as the "world" is formed and becomes real through my perceptions of it. At every moment the self is under a *ḥiyyuv*. The tablets of the world are inscribed with evidence; and one can receive them in freedom or not, as one wills and chooses.

With this, human beings takes their place in the larger order of existence.

>>><<<

What is that order? It is "the world and all that fills it"; and it includes God, "whose Glory fills the world." What fills the world is God's Glory, in all its infinite world-being.

There are cells, and molecules, and proteins; and there are structures and orbits and organisms, insofar as there is life. Necessity and freedom are their attributes, in different orders of realization. They all variously conjoin or disjoin, select or grope, or play host or guest, depending on who or what they are. Already molecular impulses have an inner *ḥiyyuv*, which strives for the ongoing coherence and sustenance of their reality; and they are coupled by degrees of freedom, this being their capacity to seek out or select creative possibilities for ongoing existence, within the circuit of all that imposes claims on them. Other, more complex organisms do this in different ways. But they too are driven by their own inner necessity for coherence and survival, and by diverse capacities to elect new situations within a wider orbit of things. Plants are under the *ḥiyyuv* of sun and water and other nutrients, and can respond by bending toward the light, if possible, or extending roots to claim moisture from the earth; and they may variously benefit from larvae or bees or larger shading branches—or not. Their capacity for freedom is impulsive and reactive; but they are not altogether "mindless," as we can see from the ways these organisms create or find new solutions, through insistence or luck, but in any case through an inherent drive to be and become. And quite different from all these genera are the spheres of necessity and freedom of cold- or warm-blooded creatures. They too are in a field of realities that impose themselves, and they can in different degrees seek new solutions. The realities imposed from within and without, in terms of internal hunger or external danger, put them variously under claims to themselves and their environments; and the capacity and desire to solve or acquit these obligations is the measure of the survival of the different species. The tense alertness of some creatures, darting this way and that for food and safety, quickly picking up a shadow or a scent for some perceived benefit or danger, shows how complexly necessity and freedom interpenetrate. And to the extent that these creatures can also group together in schools and flocks and bands (not to mention the colonies of ants or the hives of bees), they deal with the *ḥiyyuv* of existence in ways that both expand and contract their freedoms. Such is life.

Human beings are a class apart. A vast field of claims (both within and without) imposes itself, to be sure, and the claims can be variously grounded in nature, psychology, or history. But a human being is hardly or necessarily a mere field of blind forces grounded in nature, or the sum of successes and failures in the struggle to survive. Rather, persons can willfully transform impulses into creative energy; they can bend inclinations toward spiritual values; and they dramatically juxtapose urges to values and initiate the internal dialogue of conscience. Under these conditions, persons can fall in line with physical needs, or sublimate or suspend them—refusing to eat in moral protest or giving food to the needy, against their purely natural being and in response to higher duties; similarly, persons can sacrifice food to higher powers, in the belief that a present lack will be rewarded by greater goods in the future, thus foregoing immediate benefits for long-term goals. Humans thus have the singular capacity to live thoughtfully and deliberately—in a responsible freedom. Indeed, a great realm of freedom marks their finitude, and they can even substitute one *ḥiyyuv* for another or establish different hierarchies of duty and obligation. This is also a notable feature of human culture, as is the capacity to turn a *ḥiyyuv* into a freedom, and vice versa. Hence it is often the remarkable fact that humans may even "see" the broad spectrum of worldly phenomena not as events of nature and society, but as topics of value or responsibility or concern. When this transformation happens, the inchoate freedom of doing or hearing is understood in terms of obedience or transgression. As one grows in thoughtfulness, one may put all this under a constant scrutiny and self-monitoring. But we must never lose sight of the primariness and otherness of *ḥiyyuv*, which lies all around us in the full sweep of our living environment and leaps up before our eyes and ears like an epiphany. And then we may also sense the world-reality of God, disposing everywhere.

The vast creative surge of world-being derives from divine effectivity, in the well of becoming, and it is always interfused with *ḥiyyuv* and freedom. This is the double helix of life, wherever and as it ever happens. It is the cosmic *eros*—God's all-happening love, ever giving through the necessities of each form and the freedom of each necessity; ever giving despite the dead ends of selective aspects of *ḥiyyuv*, of moments poorly chosen in search of life; and ever giving even though some creatures ravage others, not only for sustenance but out of perverse or insane pleasure. This ever-giving love (despite its misuses throughout organic being) is God's Good; and it is not withdrawn. This Good lies at the heart of reality, and is inscribed in the great depths of creation. It is beyond good and evil.

The fact is that humans can and do withdraw their freedom, suspend love and care, and even pervert the pulsing possibilities of life. But we are, for all that, a wondrous mode of expression of God's Good, with the distinct and special capacity for conceiving of this truth of our lives. And thus, insofar as we, as creatures of a certain type, are (in our way) in God's image, we can be self-reflective and thoughtful extensions of this ongoing giving. This is an obligation of love, born of God's love, and we may choose to keep its current flowing, even where and when it is callously distorted or falls futilely to the ground. This is the hard task of doing and hearing. But the signs of God's giving are all around us, in the natural and human worlds alike; and these can give us courage, fortitude, and a model for imitation.

>>><<<

Scripture also provides a sign, through the gift of tradition—as in the following exegetical revelation:

> "To walk in all His ways" (Deuteronomy 11:22)
> These are the ways of the Omnipresent;
> as it is said: "The Lord (YHWH), the Lord, God, merciful and gracious, long-suffering and abundant in kindness and truth; keeping mercy to the thousandth generation, forgiving iniquity and transgression and sin . . ."
> (Exodus 34:6);
> and it is said: "Whoever shall call upon the name of the Lord shall be delivered" (Joel 3:5).
> But how can a person call on the name of the Omnipresent?
> Rather: as the Omnipresent is called merciful and gracious, you too must be merciful and gracious, and give freely to all;
> [and]: as the Holy One, Blessed be He, is called righteous, as it is said: "The Lord is righteous in all His ways" (Psalm 145:8),
> you too must be righteous;
> [and]: as the Omnipresent is called kindly, as it is said: "And kindly in all His ways" (ibid., v. 17), you too must be kindly.

This teaching transforms scripture several times over. It begins by citing Deuteronomy 11:22, in which Moses enjoins the worshiper to walk in God's ways. The unsuspecting listener may readily suppose that this means to obey the divine commandments mentioned in the first part of the verse; but the teacher is not inclined in this direction. For if Moses had already stressed obedience, why would he issue a redundancy and stress following the Law? The passage must therefore teach something else, and via this perception the teacher jolts the audience with the verse detailing the divine attributes of mercy in Exodus 34:6–7. Hence, it seems, one is now told not to obey the covenant prescriptions but to follow God's ways of mercy. But this point is deferred. Instead, a verse from the prophet Joel is cited, indicating the saving power of calling upon God's Name. One may wonder why this passage is adduced. Quite certainly the teacher knows that the recitation of the attributes of mercy was preceded by the notation that when God descended to Moses, that man "called" or "invoked" the "Name of the Lord"—and then God passed by and "called" out God's own Name and recited God's ways of mercy. Hence one may initially assume that the teacher adduces this passage to indicate that if one were to call upon God, the master of mercies, he would be saved from judgment or sorrow. But not only would this intent subvert the initial teaching that a person should follow God's ways of kindness; it is itself blatantly subverted (by the teacher himself) as a theological impossibility. How indeed could a creature of flesh and blood invoke God's sacred Name? Such an act of invocation or petition is unthinkable in any way. And then the teacher returns to his initial theme, and spells out the ideal of *imitatio dei* explicitly—doing so through another scriptural use of the attribute formulary (found in Psalm 145:8, 17), but with certain exhortations added, such as the fact that being merciful and gracious is not only an attitude of feeling and compassion, but one that includes concrete beneficence and gifts.

But all this merely defers and deepens the puzzlement concerning the citation of Joel 3:5 and its rejection. Why didn't the teacher move directly from the recitation of the attributes at the outset to the explicit application at the end? What new theological issue does he set in motion? Perhaps this:

To truly walk in God's ways invites a conversion of consciousness. If God is merciful and munificent, the ceaseless Giver of life, then to imitate these traits would require the total cancellation of any desire to receive mercy or petition its benefits. It rather obliges one to become a giver in every sense, and to do so freely and graciously. This is the true imitation of God's ways—such as we may experience them (or infer them) in the natural world all around us. One must not call upon God's aid and mercy, but must oneself be merciful and kind. Petitionary prayer is transformed into acts of bestowal. Mercy is in the gracious hearing and kindly doing; it is not an abstract virtue. A living theology is ever an embodied theology, one that is enacted every day in the everyday. It is a living God-mindedness in "all one's ways."

This is covenant theology as we have come to understand it. It is a heroic transvaluation of values within the framework of scripture and tradition. It is an ever-present human attunement to God's "Shall-Be," and with it the obligation to respond. Doing and hearing are the tasks of gracious love.

>>><<<

The ever-imminent presence of the world, whose appearances are, ultimately, God's gracious giving, always and everywhere, is most strongly symbolized by the opening of eyes. With this event, there is before us a full sweep of marvelous worldliness, a vast and imposing presence. To be sure, one is always in and of the world; and it, in its own way, is also in and of oneself. For the self and the world are profoundly intertwined. What I see outwardly, fills me inwardly; and what I am inwardly has much to do with what the world is for me as a human being. Thus, at one and the same time: the world is both its own thick (natural) graininess upon my body and a spiritual reality in my mind. It is a "thatness"—both for me and for itself, every day within the everyday. This is the sphere of my tasks and loves, and I am attached to it. But God's giving has a deeper claim, and a sense of it may come upon me with theophanic force—when I open my eyes. Such an occurrence also happens in the everyday; but not in its routine everydayness. It happens when the features of the everyday are seen in some great unexpected depth, and that depth is revealed to consciousness as a primordial dimension pulsing with God and godliness. Now the world is no mere geography, no mere inscription of the earth to be read and construed as best we can. For now we may sense the world as a spectrum of openings, filled with life and color and light: the goodness of God, just here. With this awareness, the self has not lost the world; it has found God.

The masters of spiritual insight saw a hint of this in scripture, when it says that Tamar "dwelt in Petaḥ Einayim, which is on the way to Timnah" (Gen. 38:14).

> Rabbi Abba said: This passage proves that the (the meanings of) Torah are both concealed and revealed. For indeed, I have perused the entire Torah and not found any place called Petaḥ Einayim. Rather, this (reference) is (something) entirely concealed—a supernal mystery . . . What then is (the meaning of) Petaḥ Einayim?—It (the word Petaḥ) is as (scripture) says, "And he (Abraham) sat at the *petaḥ* (opening) of the tent" (Genesis 18:1); and like "And the Lord passed over the *petaḥ*" (Exodus 12:23); and also "Open (*pitḥu*) for me gates of righteousness and I shall enter them and praise the Lord" (Psalm 118:19). (And the word) Einayim, (should be understood in this context to mean) that all (human) eyes (*einayin*) look to this opening (*pitḥa*). (And as regards) "Which is on the way to Timna," (one may ask) What is 'to Timna' (*timnata*)?—It is like that which is written, "And he shall see the image (*temunat*) of the Lord" (Numbers 12:8). (Zohar 3.71b–72a)

The masters interpret out of the truth of their experience and the language of scripture, revealing a hidden truth concealed in the everyday. Such is the case for Rabbi Abba, who takes an old midrashic teaching (preserved in the name of Rabbi) that already found a way to turn a mere geographical reference into a theological event, and gives it a new and remarkable interpretation. The earlier instance of exegesis was also puzzled by the unknown toponym Petaḥ Einayim, and proposed that the passage means that Tamar raised her eyes to the opening (*petaḥ*) on which all eyes (*einayim*) are dependent (God), and prayed for her deliverance. The older teaching thus transformed the toponym into a specific moment of petitionary prayer. Rabbi Abba proceeds otherwise. For him, the passage discloses a more profound spiritual truth for whoever would attend, namely that the Divine becomes manifest in those places where the human heart perceives an opening for transcendence in the everyday—be that in the depths of human sorrow and abandonment (as in the case of Tamar), or in situations of hospitality or justice (as in the other cases). One may already be "in" that opening, needing merely to come to a consciousness of it; or one may have to effect it more actively, as by heeding the call of justice to "open up" its possibilities, wherever they may be. There is no one "way to the Presence": it is everywhere along the way, just there where one is sitting or dwelling, when one opens the eyes. And then one may perceive God's gracious giving as a shining of Divinity in the world, and be moved to act likewise. This is theological consciousness in the fullest sense, a waiting in readiness for the appearances of God—calling to one's inner self.

> I am asleep, but my heart is awake.
> Behold, my Beloved knocks!
> "Open for Me" [*pitḥi li*].

"In the cranny of the rock, in the hiddenness"

In the pulsing of things, there is a sense of emergence that streams forth into the open eye; and it flows into the heart and soul. Everywhere, it seems, there is a coming forth of Godly presence—a vast and voluminous advent of color, and texture, and sound, and rhythm. Everywhere and in all things there is the proclamation: "I have come to My Garden, My sister, My bride." This is a primordial sensibility, prior to the emergence of figure from ground, and its claims of direction or decision. Indeed, because of that opening, we may be given over to something more primary at the very foundation of our mortal consciousness. It is a sense of divine inherence in an inhering vastness that presses all around; it is a sense of God's providential love, ever giving within ever-pulsing life.

The self stands here at the edge of consciousness: neither submerged in some "pure presence" nor held captive by "worldly things." It stands at the boundary, between the formless not-yet and the informing this-is. Here, somehow, we are given a sense of the vast divine Unfolding and our share in its happening. This is a miraculous conjunction; it is the trace of a primary attunement—perhaps the most primary of all. But it is only a trace. There is no direct seeing of ultimate things from within "the crevice of the rock," which is the condition of our mortal consciousness; there is only a sensed glimpse of a faint turning into infinitude. At the very moment one comes to language and awareness, there is already a receding of God into unknown and unsayable depths. Only our lives can bear witness to what has been sensed.

In the holy Unfolding there is song and speech: it is sung by the heavens and spoken by the earth, day after day, in ceaseless expressions of light and sound and birth and decay. Each saying informs every other: the dying plants fertilize the ground, the breath of children revive the earth, and there is love and sorrow and brute violence. This is the chorus of existence from one end of the world to the other, spanning the vast horizons, and hurtling along the great spaces. And we hear and imagine and think in metaphors—perhaps making the world more human through our images of life, shining our speech upon it, like a sun. And we shape the songs that come from God into instructions and tasks all our mortal lives—and this shaping is also a song to God (from God). It is our wisdom and hope, and the joy of our hearts, guiding our steps along the dark abysses. For in the hiddenness there is mortal error and the passions that pulse in our blood. Overwhelmed, we pray for protection and integrity—and hope in the power of goodwill, that it might fill our words and purify our hearts. In the end, this wish must become our duty and song. For goodwill is the way of ways: it is the rock of salvation.

Sof ve-Ein Sof: *Finitude and Infinity*

Two types of finitude eminently characterize humankind: one is of the spirit, the other of the flesh.

The finitude of the spirit pertains to our bounded understandings and interpretations. It is a limitation fundamentally conditioned by the fact that we are embedded in the world we seek to understand and by the language which gives it sense. Of the two, our natality is worldly but our language is spiritual. Insofar as we rise to self-understanding and meaning, language is the font of our outreaching and its fissure; and insofar as we achieve any cognition or awareness, just this is the primary truth that pervades our consciousness.

Our hermeneutical finitude is ever with us. It bears upon us first and foremost in the practice of our everyday lives as we seek to live and act with hopes of achieving degrees of utility—both in the narrow pragmatic sense of disposing its details or recognizing patterns, and also in the grander sense of applying scientific reason to its elements or giving them empirical applications (in crude and wondrous ways). Both these kinds of disposition, whether putting the world to work for oneself or harnessing its powers technologically, are ultimately conditioned by the reflexes of our human nature and conceived in its image. Forgetting this is hubris and an untimely wreckage. Our interpretative finitude also bears upon us through the agency of the imagination as we seek to revise our understanding of things by means of creative insights and conceptions—both in the narrow sense of intuitive solutions to the knots of reality, and also in the grander sense of the striking perceptions of the world opened to consciousness by innovative forms of the artistic imagination. Here too our senses of the *imago mundi*, be it conventional or surreal, realist or otherwise, are always rough reflections in the mirror of human nature and its capacities for understanding. There is no way through the looking glass.

Finally, our particular spiritual finitude is with us in our modes of meditative awareness as we attend to the receding or ascending qualities of being that impose themselves on our minds—both in the narrow sense of the smaller mysteries of nature, inherent in the details, and also in the grander sense of our consciousness of the vast Mystery of Being, which shatters every pretension to a transcendent human comprehension. Encompassed by language, our spiritual breakthroughs mark the borders of wonder at the edges of thought.

Such modes of hermeneutical finitude are sharpened by the great diversity of persons and cultures, whose multitude of solutions occur both nearby and mediated by received tradition, or in the sometimes far-flung and utterly different interpretations found among the "others." This diversity calls us up short, and reveals both the short-sighted and self-serving nature of our own meager perspectives, along with the omnipresent obstructions in our viewpoint. But such a reality is dialectical as well; for it also drives home the rich infinity of possibilities that abound among our cowalkers on the earth—the unfinished dialogues of the sayable with this or that speech partner, who faces us looking in a different direction; the diversity of voices of the debatable from one or another contestant, who weighs the truths of experience with other scales and balances; and also the impenetrable depths of the truly unsayable, darkly refracted in a vast forest of symbols—whose own configurations conceal conundrums of the sacred.

We therefore need one another—so that more of the fullness may be realized in deed and in thought; so that something further of the obscure may be brought to light and awareness; and so that the regency of our viewpoints may be qualified and more broadly shared. Such common labor is our work for the Kingdom of God, and involves the ongoing humanization of the infinite *torah kelulah* through interpretations that are conducive to species enlightenment and the rule of righteousness. Common labor is the moral impetus of the *torah kelulah*, focused on futurity and fulfillment, but ever enacted in the here and now. From a theological perspective, this impetus is also to be conjoined with a spiritual valence that strives to see ever more of emergent world-being in terms of God's all-shaping effectivity. This involves a spiritual revaluation of the everyday—a hearing of the covenant call to attention and attentiveness in and through all things.

But such a sacred labor for the kingdom is forever finite, a striving in human time for human goals. Imagined from the divine side, in the depths of infinitude, there is no kingdom come.

For it ever is, already, proclaiming: What is shall be as it is; effluxes of the *torah kelulah*: infinities within infinities—unfolding everywhere; yes and no—pulsing vastly; and the *emet ve-emunah* of God—steadfastly giving and sustaining, world-new always. To affirm this truth is to receive the kingdom in the quickness of immediate nearness, *bizman qariv*, even here and now.

>>><<<

There is a second, more ultimate human finitude; it is the finitude of the flesh.

Death is the final caesura, carried within our mortal lives until the end. Death is the finitude of all existence, but borne by ourselves most self-consciously. Death is the truth of each breath and silence, of each disruption and break, and the completion of each act of joy and love. Death is the fading of color and its autumn spangle; it is the image of departure in the eye; and it is the anticipation of end upon arrival. Death and life are one. Together they express infinitude.

The caesura opens with both the cry of birth and the rattle of death. It is inevitable and omnipresent. Earthling, do you not know this? Let this truth radiate through your hands and eyes and mouth; let it affect all that you do and say. Carry death as life.

But though loving harder and deeper, we cannot diminish death, past or future, for death cannot be overcome; or though speaking gently and humbly, we cannot erase death, now or ever, for death cannot be denied; and though feeling with compassion and care, we cannot evade death, neither yours nor mine nor others'—not now; not ever.

The finitude of life is part of infinity, as is death. Life and death are one—dual portions of God's truth. This is as it is. "Shall we accept the good from God," the gift of life, "and not the evil"— the harshness of suffering and the reality of death? Job's question opens a caesura. But such rhetoric is only a partial wisdom. More profound is the realization that opens us to the divine Ground, such as we may know it or imagine it humanly through the rhythms of breath and the swirl of things all around:

"The Lord has given and the Lord has taken."
To this we too must affirm, with humble resoluteness,
"Blessed be the Name of the Lord."

Giving and Taking
are primordial,
deeper than history.
They are the diastole and systole at the heart of Being.
O soul!
Receive this truth in holy solitude,
hands outstretched.

Epilogue

The task of theology is lifelong; an ongoing centering within life—
in preparation for death. Theology is a training in receiving and
releasing with alert thankfulness. It is a lifelong attempt to overcome the trance-torpor of mere existence, and become attuned
to "the dearest freshness deep down things" (Hopkins)—surging
from the depths of God's Godhood.

To begin to achieve this task is to work at putting oneself in
ever-new balance, or spiritual correlation, with the givenness of
things—always at first with their tangible facticity, and then also
with the less tangible dimensions of godly reality they put us
into contact with. The notion of *hishtavut* marks this modality
of world-engagement; and as we bring it to consciousness and to
refinement, we live theologically.

Hishtavut is thus not one thing, any more than are our lives or
life itself; but it is always changing in accordance with the tasks
of the self in the world. The following three types of spiritual
correlation are exemplary, and are chosen to reprise under a different sign some of the issues considered earlier.

The first type is that of breath. We live in rhythms of breath;
it is the balance point of vitality itself. But we may breathe differently if we are calm or excited, alone or in communion, silent or in
conversation. Our breathing is ideally adjusted to circumstances,

and attuning ourselves to their rhythms or demands. The character and shape of our ethical lives depend on this; and so too does our ability to perceive what is unfolding in the world all around. Even more fundamental is our capacity to monitor this breathing, and thus become acutely perceptive of its pacing—and ultimately of the mutability and fragility of our lives. Attunement to breath is a training in humility within the vastness of God's god-ing.

The second type of *hishtavut* involves speech. Our words (both their actuality and their silences) must be calibrated to circumstances. Just who is this person before me, and just what can and should be said just now? One must hear well in order to speak properly; and one must speak with the expectation of hearing in turn. Otherwise, speech becomes monologue or self-enclosed rhetoric; otherwise it may become self-centered or self-absorbed—a kind of muteness in the very process of speaking; and otherwise it may also tongue-tie one's speech partner, instead of opening that person's heart in communication. The *hishtavut* of speech thus involves rhythms and pacing, proximity and distance, and a sense of the sayable and unsayable—and all this keeps changing in dialogue as one tries to realize the God-given possibilities of life. According to the counsel of some spiritual masters, true speaking gives the human a soul quality—a revelation of the godliness of giving; whereas the perversion of speech is correspondingly dire—a manifestation of the snake of subversion and evil. The scriptural watchword is both the objective command, "Guard your tongue from evil" (Ps. 34:14), and the more subjective condemnation, "I was dumb with silence, I spoke no good" (Ps. 39:3). The first phrase overarches all human life; the second takes us into the realm of spiritual growth. On the one hand, it is a confession and expression of shame: the self realizes the power of perverse speech ("I spoke *no* good") and falls silent before the wound that ill-speech has caused. But perhaps it reveals something more; namely, that the self judges itself both for remaining silent, and not speaking the good, but also for not speaking good at all ("I spoke no *good*")—allowing this reality to remain moot. The attunements of speech are complex;

it is our sacred trust in the task of transforming the outrunning vastness into a human sphere of value, again and again.

The third type of *hishtavut* to be noted involves action. Indeed, the life-rhythms of *hashva'ah* (or correlation) involve our moral lives—the way we actualize the *torah kelulah* unfolding in life. We may have standards of value, but every moment involves its own balances and tasks—its own way of taking up the covenant challenge, of doing and hearing what is happening in the world. It involves ongoing hermeneutic assessments and evaluations; and is nothing less than bringing God's reality into human life in thoughtful ways. We are reminded of this challenge through the following passage—itself a hermeneutic event, and bespeaking the core of a hermeneutic theology.

> "(If you walk in My statutes, and keep My commandments, and do them,) then I will give you your rains in their season . . ." (Leviticus 26:3–4). Each one will bestow its power upon you. Which are they? They are the restoration that you have made, which is the Holy Name. It is also written: "That they may keep the way of the Lord, to do righteousness and justice" (Genesis 18:19). Since it says, "that they may keep the way of the Lord," why then does it say, "to do (*la-'asot*) righteousness and justice"? The meaning of this (clause) is that one who keeps the ways of Torah, makes (*'oseh*), as it were, Righteousness (*Zedaqah*) and Justice (*Mishpat*). And what is *Zedaqah* and *Mishpat*? It is the Holy One, blessed be He." (Zohar 3.113b)

What are we taught here? From the outset, the teacher disconnects any link between the fulfillment of the commandments and material benefactions. The emphasis is rather on more supernal and thus spiritual gifts. Hence we are told that if a person walks in God's ways, through the performance of the deeds of Torah, there is an unfolding of the powers latent in these actions, deriving from the depths of Divine possibility, into the realm of human life. For the deeds of Torah condense structures of value for earthly life, and their enactment releases their godly force into the world. Indeed, the teaching stresses that it is within the capacity of humans to effect repair and restoration of the fabric of Divine reality, for if the garments of reality are rent by evil and inaction, they may be variously mended by positive actions—and this is symbolized by the sanctification of the Divine Name which human actions effect; and if improper behaviors are a desecration and fracturing of the holy Name on earth, their repair is correspondingly a restoration of the glory of Divinity in the world of human meaning. And to further underscore this point through another passage, the teacher adduces Genesis 18:19 in order to indicate that when persons face life situations in a godly manner (walking in "the way of the Lord"), they attune themselves to the reality at hand, and try to make a balance between the strictures of justice and right in a given situation, and those of righteousness and mercy. This action similarly actualizes the two divine dimensions of Justice and Righteousness in the deepest reality of Divinity, and effects a fusion or synthesis of the two—this being the Divine dimension of Splendor, symbolized by the Name: "Holy One." Thus, according to the teacher, the effectuation of a balance between justice and righteousness is nothing less than an actualization of a modality God's truth in reality; it is a making of God, as it were, by making the world "God-real."

This is covenant theology, brought to mind and kept in mind by hermeneutical practice. Keeping ourselves attuned to the many interpretative possibilities at the core of life, and guided by the standards of scripture, one may effectuate divine reality— bringing God to a human presence through ourselves, just here in the midst of the vastness.

Raza de-razin
stima de-khol stimin.

[Mystery of mysteries; the most concealed truth of all.]

Acknowledgments

Theology is a protean process—for myself especially; but I repeatedly deferred the task of transforming endless brooding into something tangible. This was due to an inner sense of not being ready. A certain urgency has now claimed me: to make my thoughts clear to myself, for honesty's sake in due season; and to provide my family with a spiritual testament of my values and worldview. The initial drafts of this work had this private character; but over time, and with ongoing reflections on the content, the horizon of concern and audience expanded. The result is a more evolved and public document. I therefore wish to inform my sons, dear Eitan and Elisha, of the original intention, and to urge them to read the present version with its first aim in mind: a father's gift of tradition and truthfulness. I am confident that the lights of a lifetime of shared study and conversation will still shine through the garments of this new formulation.

In the various stages of its unfolding, this book benefited from the kindness and concern of many friends. Daniel Marom of the Mandel Foundation (in Jerusalem) was an important catalyst, quickly realizing that a project on the "textual self" was rapidly becoming theological, and doing much to facilitate it though diverse discussion groups, with characteristic generosity of spirit. His ongoing care for this work is a special blessing. The financial support of the foundation, and the active involvement of Seymour Fox, its late director, are gratefully acknowledged. Observations of Susan Handelman and Michael Swirsky, stemming from the discussion groups, gradually had their impact. Over the course of several drafts, I benefited from many thoughtful and joyous exchanges with Kalman Bland; and during the final phase, the comments and reflections of Bernard McGinn and Elliot Wolfson, as well as timely advice from Paul Mendes-Flohr, all proved beneficial. Nearer the end, the detailed reports of Arnold Eisen and Edward K. Kaplan for the University of Chicago Press were of considerable value and stimulation (especially Eisen's insistence on the pertinence of certain topics made me reconsider matters initially set aside). Alan G. Thomas of the Press has been unfailingly courteous, efficient, and involved in the fate of this project; Sandra Hazel, senior manuscript editor, has added sharp and sensitive guidance. The index was skillfully prepared by my students, Sarah Imhoff and Dov Weiss. To each and all—my sincerest and most heartfelt thanks.

During the final months of this work, deep sadness infused my meditations—due to the death of my mother, Bernice Fishbane, and the sudden loss of my daughter-in-law, Leah Levitz Fishbane. My mother's life was and remains a blessing of outflowing love, grace, and studious passion; the core of Leah's life was gentle love for her family and abiding intellectual energy. Their memory fills my heart at this time. But I must dedicate this book to my lifelong love and partner, dearest Mona—again a first reader; again a prod to clarity; again a stay and support; and always the gift of heaven in my life, *a tayere brochele.*

Erev Yom Kippur, 5768
September 2007

Notes

The following notes primarily refer to passages used or cited; they are thus in support of the text only. Unless otherwise noted, all translations are my own. For the Hebrew Bible, I have occasionally consulted the New Jewish Publication Society rendition, and adopted some of its formulations.

PREFACE

P. ix   "prowl aimlessly." See Kafka's formulation in *Parables and Paradoxes* (1935; reprinted with translations, New York: Schocken Books, 1961), 44–45 (the verb used is *umschleichen*).

"the stark consciousness of mortality." See Rosenzweig's *Der Stern der Erlösung*, 2nd ed. (Frankfurt am Main: J. Kauffmann, 1930), 1:7–9, in the introductory section entitled "Vom Tode."

"natality." I adapt this term for present purposes from Hannah Arendt, who employed it in the English translation of her dissertation (dealing with Augustine and his notion of *initium*), and in subsequent writings (where the focus is on the beginning or initiating factors of political action). See her *Love and Saint Augustine* (Chicago: University of Chicago Press, 1996), and especially the discussion of the term and its uses in the appendix by the editors J. Scott and J. Stark, pp. 146–48. Cf. the usage in *The Life of the Mind* (New York: Harcourt, 1977), part 2, "Willing," 109–10, 217.

P. x   "in Jean Wahl's phrase." See in his *Existence Humaine et Transcendence* (Neuchâtel: Éditions de la Baconnière, 1944), 10.

P. xii   "notion of 'speech-thinking.'" Rosenzweig reflected on this mat-
ter in 1925 ("Das neue Denken"); see in *Franz Rosenzweig: Der
Mensch und seine Werke; Gesammelte Schriften. III: Zweistromland:
Kleinere Schriften zu Glauben und Denken*, ed. R. and A.
Mayer (Dordrecht: Martinus Nijhoff, 1984), 139–61; trans. P. Franks
and M. Morgan, *Franz Rosenzweig: Philosophical and Theological
Writings* (Indianapolis: Hackett Publishing Co., 2000), 109–39.
"stimulated by Rosenstock-Huessy." This is acknowledged by
Rosenzweig in the above-noted essay. See Rosenstock-Huessy's
Angewandte Seelenkunde, in *Die Sprache des Menschengleshlechts*
(Heidelberg: Lambert Schneider, 1963–64), 2:739–810.
"Bewährung." See in M. Buber, *Ich und Du* (Leipzig: Inselverlag,
1923), 120. (For a consideration of this term and related uses by
Buber, see my essay "Justification through Living: Martin Buber's
Third Alternative," in *Martin Buber: A Contemporary Perspective*,
ed. P. Mendes-Flohr [Syracuse-Jerusalem: Syracuse University
Press and The Israel Academy of Sciences and the Humanities,
2002], 12–32.)

P. xiii   "love is strong as death." Song of Songs 8:10.
"urge to flight." I have in mind here the wide-ranging phenom-
enology of spiritual flight found in Max Picard, *Die Flucht vor
Gott* (Erlenbach-Zürich: E. Rentsch, 1936); translated as *The
Flight from God* (Chicago: Regnery-Gateway, 1951).
"*kelipah*, or 'shell' mentality." The term *kelipah* is Kabbalistic and
its reality ontological; however, I have been induced to think of
it more epistemologically on the basis of the unexpected comments of P. Florensky, *Iconostasis* (Crestwood, NY: St. Vladimir's
Seminary Press, 1996), 56, where he speaks of a false consciousness and sense of reality (manifest in the face) as an "astral mask"
(his term): "in the Kabbalah it is called the *klipot* (the husk),
while in Theosophy it is termed the 'shell'"; it results in blocked
and thwarted perceptions of existence.

P. xiv   "an exegetical revision." Found in *Leviticus Rabba* 35.7. See in the
edition of M. Margulies, *Vayiqra Rabba* (Jerusalem: Wahrmann
Books, 1962), 2:825–26; the teaching is reported in the name of
R. Ḥanina ben Papa.

CHAPTER ONE

P. 2   "habit." On these dynamics, see F. Ravaisson, *De l'Habitude*
(1838; reprint, Paris: Payot & Rivages, 1997).

P. 2　"Where are you . . .?" The quotation alludes to Genesis 3:9, and is used here under the influence of Martin Buber's rendition of a tradition of Rabbi Shneur Zalman of Liadi's interpretation of it; see his *Darko shel Adam al pi Torat ha-Ḥasidut* (Jerusalem: Mossad Bialik, 1957), chap. 1 (*Ḥeshbon ha-Nefesh*, 7–13); translated as *The Way of Man according to the Teachings of Hasidism* (Secaucus, NJ: Citadel Press, 1966), 9–14. The account is based on a family tradition recorded by H. M. Heilman, *Beis Rabbi* (Berditchev, 1902), 29a. For this interpretation in classical rabbinic literature, see *Midrash Tanḥuma, Tazri'a*, 9.

P. 9　"Protagoras's dictum." See Plato, *Theatetus* 171a.

P. 12　"Schopenhauer." His criticism of Kant occurs in *The World as Will and Idea*, appendix to bk. 1 ("Criticism of the Kantian Philosophy"), where he cites and critiques Kant's formulations in *Prolegomenena to Any Future Metaphysic*, preamble, sec. 1. Kant stresses that "[the source] of metaphysics must throughout be non-empirical . . . [and] must never be taken from either inner or outer experience"; whereas Schopenhauer ripostes that "we have no grounds for shutting ourselves off, in the case of the most important . . . questions, from the richest of all sources of knowledge, inner and outer experience." See in the R. B. Haldane and J. Kemp translation (1883; reprint, New York: Charles Scribner's Sons, 1948), 2:19–20.

"natural piety." For the phrase, see the conclusion of Wordsworth's fragment beginning "My heart leaps up" (bk. 1, line 9); and also in *The Excursion*, bk. 3, line 266. See in *Wordsworth: Poetical Works*, ed. T. Hutchinson and revised by E. de Selincourt (London: Oxford University Press, 1936), 62 and 617, respectively.

"shudder before the . . . mysteries." Referring to Goethe's *Faust*, pt. 2, 1:6272: "The shudder [*Schauden*] is the best part of man" (it being the deep inward feeling of "the terrifying"; *das Ungeheure*).

P. 13　"mental modes." This notion was influenced by the overall discussions of E. Souriau, *Les Différents modes d'existence* (Paris: Presses Universitaires, 1943).

P. 14　"the interpreted world." This alludes to Rilke's phrase ("*in der gedeuteten Welt*") in the *Duino Elegies* (I), where he so hauntingly refers to our human condition, which isolates us from the angels. A related expression is used by Jean Grenier, when considering this main principle of Nietzsche's thought ("Being [*L'Etre*] is always and necessarily Being-interpreted [*L'Etre interprété*]");

see his *Le Problème de la vérité dans la philosophie de Nietzsche* (Paris: Seuil, 1963), 304.

P. 15 "in the most elemental sense." The ensuing phrase still bears the impact of reading E. Becker's account of the elemental nature of the "human organism," in his *Escape from Evil* (New York: Free Press, 1975), 1–2.

"primary rationality." See E. Creighton, "Reason and Feeling," *Philosophical Review* 30 (1921), 469, who says that "what falls in any way within experience partakes of the rational form of the mind."

"minds." K. Britton, *Communication: A Philosophical Study of Language* (New York: Harcourt Brace; London: K. Paul Trench, Trubner, 1939), 204–6, has emphasized that "a world without minds is a world without structure, without relations and qualities, *without facts.*"

P. 16 "discovered in the doing." Cf. Aristotle, *Nicomachean Ethics* 2.4, "It is by the doing of just acts that the just man is produced"; and also Ralph Waldo Emerson, *Nature* (Boston: James Monroe & Co., 1836), 6, "Every man's condition is a solution in hieroglyphic to those inquiries he would put. He acts it as life before he apprehends it as truth."

"compresence." For the term, see S. A. Alexander, "The Basis of Realism," in *Proceedings of the British Academy 1913–14* (Oxford: Humphrey Milford, Oxford University Press), 284–85.

P. 19 "inconceivable chasm . . . amber." From James Agee, *A Death in the Family* (1938; New York: Bantam / Grosset & Dunlap, 1969), 84.

P. 23 "dread . . . fascination." This language alludes of course to the categories of *mysterium tremendum et fascinans*, famously discussed by R. Otto, in *Das Heilige: Über das Irrationale in der Idee des göttlichen und sein Verhältnis zum Rationalen*, 12th ed. (Gotha/Stuttgart: Friedrich Andreas Perthes, 1924), chaps. 4 and 7.

P. 24 "superimposed planes . . . visual memory." See the penetrating remarks of Daniel-Henry Kahnweiler, in his *Juan Gris: His Life and Work* (New York: Henry N. Abrams, Inc., 1969), 75, 110 (trans. D. Cooper, from the French edition of 1946).

P. 25 "shapes of value." Alluding to H. Rickert's pregnant term *Wertform*, in his *Der Gegenstand der Erkenntnis*, 6th ed. (Tübingen: J. C. B. Mohr, 1928).

P. 25 "remarks by Cézanne." From two letters to Émile Bernard in 1904. See in *Paul Cézanne: Correspondence*, ed. J. Rewald (Paris: Bernard Grasset Éditeur, 1937), letters 168–169 (pp. 261–62); and also the rendition in *Letters*, ed. John Rewald (London: Bruno Cassirer, 1941).

P. 26 "comment by Matisse." See *Henri Matisse*, ed. Alfred Barr (New York: Museum of Modern Art, 1931), 29–30.
"The technique of painting . . ." From Gris's lecture "On the Possibilities of Painting," originally published in *Transatlantic Review* 1, no. 6 (1924): 482–88; and 2, no. 1 (1924): 75–79. It is reprinted in Kahnweiler's *Juan Gris*, 195–210; the citations appear on p. 198.

P. 27 "set free." This thought is inspired by the comment of Ernst Bloch, *Essays on the Philosophy of Music* (Cambridge: Cambridge University Press, 1985), 140, where he speaks of the birth of music in its capacity to "surmount" its originally sacred instruments (such as a magic rattle) to become something independent.
"music . . . human spirit." The title of a lecture from which the ensuing quotes are taken; see Aaron Copeland, *Copeland on Music* (New York: W. W. Norton & Company, 1963), 64–65.

P. 28 "sounding forms in motion" (*tönend-bewegte Form*). See Eduard Hanslick, *Vom Musikalisch-Schönen, ein Beitrag zur Revision der Aesthetik der Ton Kunst*, 9th ed. (Leipzig: J. A. Barth, 1896); trans. Gustav Cohen, *The Beautiful in Music*, 7th ed. (London: Novello, 1891).
"Beethoven, in a conversation." *Ludwig von Beethoven: Briefe und Gespräche*, ed. M. Hürlimann (Zürich: Atlantis Verlag, 1944), 146.

P. 29 "Wallace Stevens's poem." The poem appears in *Palm at the End of the Mind* (New York: Vintage Books), 396–97; quotation is from p. 397.

P. 31 "pre-syntactic and pre-logical." The phrase is from E. Levinas, in his *Paul Celan de l'être à l'autre* (Montpellier: Editions Fata Morgana, 2002), 17 ("pré-syntaxique et pré-logique").
"caged tiger." From "Black Cat" (Schwarze Katze); text and translation in *The Selected Poems of Rainer Maria Rilke*, trans. Steven Mitchell (New York: Vintage Books, 1984), 64–65.

P. 32 "sculpture of Apollo." The ensuing lines are from "Archaic Torso of Apollo" (Archaïscher Torso Apollos), in ibid., 60–61.

P. 32   "implacably seized." Cf. the extraordinary remark of Thierry Maulnier, *Introduction à la Poésie Française* (Paris: Gallimard, 1939), 32: "La poème n'existe que là où existe cette prise de possession implacable de l'âme don't le rythme est l'instrument."

P. 35   "God is in *this* . . . place." Gen. 28:16.

P. 36   "R. Azriel of Gerona." The text (based on MS Halberstam 444) was published by Gershom Scholem as "Derekh Ha-Emunah ve-Derekh Ha-Kefirah," in *Sefer Zikkaron le-Asher Gulak ve-Shemuel Klein* (Jerusalem, 1942), and attributed to R. Azriel by him. The selection treated here is found on p. 207 (MS 63b). Confirmation of the attribution may be found in the fact that this topic and the ensuing scriptural citation appear in the pamphlet *Peirush Eser Sefirot*, printed together with the work *Sefer Derekh Emunah*, by R. Meir ibn Gabbai (16th century), who comments on it and refers to its author as R. Azriel, student of R. Isaac the Blind (see the reprint edition, Jerusalem, 1967; pp. 6b, 7a, 16b). R. Azriel apparently received the textual reference via the so-called Circle of Contemplation (Hug Ha-'Iyyun), since in an important source the words *etzot, omen,* and *emunah* occur regarding the emanation, though this is not presented as a scriptural citation; whereas, when R. Azriel's material was passed on to R. Moses of Burgos, the latter gives this material as a citation. For the occurrences, see the text editions in M. Verman, *The Books of Contemplation* (New York: State University of New York Press, 1992), pp. 91, ll. 36–38, and 228, ll. 18–19 (respectively).

       "Naught (or *ayin*)." For a contemporary explanation, cf. the words of R. David b. Abraham Halavan, who defined *ayin* as "having more being (*yesh*) than any other being in the world; but since it is simple, and all other simple things are complex when compared with its simiplicity, it is called 'Nothing' (*ayin*)." See his *Masoret Ha-Berit*, ed. G. Scholem, *Kobetz al Yad*, n.s., 1 (1936), 31.

P. 39   "God-real." (Gottwirklich). See in the introduction to the collected edition of Buber's "Addresses on Judaism," *Reden über das Judentums* (Frankfurt-am-Main: Rütten & Loenig, 1923).

P. 45   "The Lord is One!" Alternatively, "the Lord alone"; cf. R. Samuel b. Meir (Rashbam) and R. Abraham ibn Ezra, ad loc. The latter adduces Zech. 14:9.

CHAPTER TWO

P. 48   "studies" Hebrew, *yehegeh*. Alternatively, "recites," since the He-
         brew verbal stem *hgh* is cognate with Ugaritic *hg* (recite, ex-
         press). Hence here: to recite in study. In Ps. 19:15, a more inward
         recitation is denoted.

P. 49   "On this day." See *Pesiqta de-Rav Kahana*, ed. B. Mandelbaum
         (New York: Jewish Theological Seminary of America, 1962), vol. 1,
         Ba-ḥodesh Ha-shelishi, 12.21, p. 219.

P. 50   "Named Ones . . . moment." Alluding to the ideas about the
         "special" and "momentary gods" (and their names) studied by
         H. Usener, *Götternamen: Versuch einer Lehre von der religiösen Be-
         griffsbildung* (Bonn: F. Cohen, 1896).

P. 51   "Why was the Torah given?" See *Pesiqta de-Rav Kahana*, 1.12.20,
         pp. 218–19.

P. 60   "A Threefold Chord." Eccles. 4:12.

P. 61   "*torah kelulah*." This phrase has a kabbalistic forebear; cf. its usage
         by "Rabbi Isaac the Old," who uses it to designate the preter-
         natural Torah, all-enfolded with the infinities of forms, in all-
         unimaginable ways, within the gradation of *ḥesed* (Grace),
         the right hand of God (see Jewish Theological Seminary MS
         1777.4=EMC 669). By contrast with this type of supernal in-
         wardness, I am using the expression to convey the absolute and
         existential fullness of world-being, ever effectuated by Divinity,
         the Life of all life.

P. 63   "citation-centered existence." With this phrase I allude to
         Thomas Mann's phrase "zitathaftes Leben," which he under-
         stood to refer to the ways persons relive and reactivate exem-
         plary models of existence. See his "Freud und die Zukunft," in
         Gesammelte Werke (Frankfurt am Main: Fischer, 1960), ix, 497.

P. 66   "Rashi utilized a phrase." See his statement of principles at Gen.
         3:8.

P. 67   "breath units." See the strong formulation of this by Franz
         Rosenzweig "Scripture and Word," in *Scripture and Word: Mar-
         tin Buber and Franz Rosenzweig*, trans. L. Rosenwald with
         E. Fox (Bloomington: Indiana University Press, 1994), 43. This
         essay originally appeared in *Die Kreatur* (1925), and has been
         reprinted in *Franz Rosenzweig: Der Mensch und Sein Werk*,
         Band 3, *Zweistromland* (The Hague: Martinus Nijhoff, 1984),
         777–83.

P. 73   "Life of all life." This phrase alludes to the divine epithet *ḥayyei kol ha-ḥayyim ha-olamim* employed by Saadia Gaon in a prayer entitled "Magen u-Meḥayyeh," and published (from a Dropsie College MS) by B. Halper, in *Post-Biblical Hebrew Literature* (Philadelphia: Jewish Publication Society, 1921), 60 ("life of all eternal life"). I have found the phrase *ḥei ha-ḥayyim* (Life of life) as a divine name or epithet in the sermons of R. Menaḥem Naḥum of Chernobyl, *Sefer Me'irat Einayim*, 41c (*Va-yaqhel*).

P. 76   "the voice of Sinai was ceaseless." Cf. Deut. 5:19 (following *Targum Onqelos* and Rashi's elaboration), with its midrashic interpretation.

P. 77   "midrashically infer . . . divine entreaty." See *Genesis Rabba* 68.9, in the edition of Theodor-Albeck (Jerusalem: Wahrmann, 1965), 2:778 (line 6).

P. 78   "Jacob . . . fits the same mold." The *locus classicus* for the patriarchs "establishing" the times of daily prayer is *Babylonian Talmud*, tractate *Berakhot* 26b; the passage from Genesis 28:10 is cited and applied accordingly.

P. 79   "Rabbi Bar Kappara." See *Genesis Rabba* 68.12, in the edition of Theodor-Albeck, 2:785 (line 5)–86 (line 3). "the rabbis interpret." Ibid., 786 (ll. 3–7).

P. 80   "they too (and many more)." Ibid., 786 (line 7)–90 (line 6).

P. 82   "Thinking about similarity." The perception of similarity is a fundamental cognitive feature, conditioned by a preexistent "set"—such that one sees something (indistinct or unknown) as like another. Cf. G. N. A. Vesey, "Seeing and Seeing As," *Proceedings of the Aristotelian Society* 56 (1955–56): 121–23.

P. 85   "misplaced . . . concreteness." Alluding to the famous expression of A. N. Whitehead, in his *Science and the Modern World* (New York: Free Press, 1967), 51.

P. 86   "unsaid." For the usage, see M. Sells, *Mystical Languages of Unsaying* (Chicago: University of Chicago Press, 1994).

P. 88   "'Scripture speaks like human language'" (*dibberah torah kelashon benei adam*). See in *Babylonian Talmud*, tractate *Berakhot* 31b, and tractate *Bava Metzi'a* 31b.

P. 89   "According to Maimonides." All ensuing renditions from Maimonides are from *The Guide of the Perplexed*, trans. Shlomo Pines (Chicago: University of Chicago Press, 1963); citation references appear in the text.

P. 90 "another Spanish sage." Citations from *Rabbeinu Bahye: Be'ur al Ha-Torah*, ed. H. Chavel (Jerusalem: Mossad Ha-Rav Kook, 1983), 1:242–43.

P. 92 "searching for evidential paradigms." The phrase echoes the title of Carlo Ginzburg's stimulating essay, "Clues: Roots of an Evidential Paradigm"; see his book, *Clues, Myths, and the Historical Method* (Baltimore: Johns Hopkins University Press, 1989), 96–125.
"divinatory." Cf. E. Reiner, *Astral Magic in Babylonia* (Philadelphia: American Philosophical Society, 1995), chap. 4 ("Divination").

P. 94 "the appearance of a national record." Cf. Zohar 3.152a, which distinguishes between scripture's external layer of historical narrative and its most internal spiritual core.

P. 97 "estimations of one's heart." See Zohar 1.103b for such a pun on *sha'ar*. Also cf. 2.38a, and the expression "opening the gates of the secrets of wisdom."

P. 98 "The appearances of the eye occur immediately." Cf. Hans Jonas, *The Phenomenon of Life: Toward a Philosophical Biology* (New York: Harper & Row, 1966), 135: "A view comprehends many things . . . in an instant."

P. 99 "the revelations of sound happen successively." Cf. ibid., "hearing . . . [is] wholly governed by succession."

P. 102 "*Amen ve-Amen.*" Cf. Ps. 72:19.

P. 104 "'Scripture never loses its plain sense'" (*ein miqra yotzei midei peshuto*). See *Babylonian Talmud*, tractate *Shabbat* 63a, and *Yevamot* 11b and 24a.

P. 107 "the thick cloud . . . revealed." Alluding to Exodus 24:18 with a twist. And cf. *Midrash Bemidbar Rabba* 12.2, which adduces Psalm 90:1 as cotext.

CHAPTER THREE

P. 108 "concrete immediacy." This sense of concreteness anent theology broadly echoes the philosophical usage of Gabriel Marcel. See his essay "Ébauche d'une philosophie concrète," in *Du Refus A L'Invocation* (Paris: Gallimard, 1940), 81–110. The significant difference between the two uses is that Marcel's reflections maintain the character of a radical personal subjectivity, whereas the present theological enterprise (though rooted in personal reflections) is formulated in terms of a collective phenomenological subject (that is also connected to a specific religious tradition).

P. 110 "A later rabbinic sage." See *Sifrei Deuteronomy*, 346; in the edition of L. Finkelstein (New York: Jewish Theological Seminary of America, 1969), 403–4.

P. 111 "Just here is the covenant task." Referring to this verse ("in all your ways"), Bar Kappara remarked that it was "a small passage upon which all the essentials of the Torah depend"; see in *Babylonian Talmud*, tractate *Berakhot* 63a.

P. 114 "interpretation . . . and . . . faithful living." The reported encounter between Hillel and the people of Betyra with respect to a ritual procedure during Passover is a classic instance of this double process. See *Babylonian Talmud*, tractate *Pesaḥim* 66a.

P. 115 "In . . . sermon." See *Babylonian Talmud*, tractate *Ḥagiga* 3b. Cf. *Tosefta Soṭa* 7.11.

P. 117 "walk before God." Literally, "walk before Me and be pure"; Gen. 17:1.

"to intervene." Alluding to Abraham's behavior in Genesis 18.

"to maintain . . . despite temptation." Alluding to Joseph's behavior in Genesis 39.

"hopping on two branches." Literally, "hop on two branches"; 1 Kings 18:21.

P. 118 "Today, if you hear My voice." The citation is from Psalm 95:7; the legend is in *Babylonian Talmud*, tractate *Sanhedrin* 98b.

"What are we?" See in the prayer book *Avodat Yisrael*, ed. S. Baer (Rödelheim, 1868; corrected ed., Berlin: Schocken, 1937), 44–45 (with notes to rabbinic and medieval sources).

P. 120 "settled mind." Cf. Maimonides' use of the idiom in *Mishneh Torah, Sefer Ha-Mada, Hilkhot Yesodei Ha-Torah* 4.13. (In *Hilkhot De'ot* 2.3 the usage refers to a controlled mind, free of the turmoil of anger.) The phrase is also used to convey spiritual focus and divine connection by R. Yehudah Aryeh Leib of Gur, in *Sefas Emes, Shemini*, 3:56a (1871).

"The ancient sages pondered." For the following, see the collection of teachings in *Babylonian Talmud*, tractate *Rosh Hashanah* 25a.

P. 122 "who gives sight." An ancient list of these blessings (with explanations) is found in *Babylonian Talmud*, tractate *Berachot* 60b.

"upright posture." On this matter, see the compelling phenome-

P. 124 nological analysis of E. Straus, "The Upright Posture," *Psychiatric Quarterly* 26 (1952): 529–61, and specifically pp. 541–43.

P. 124 "specific concrescences." For this terminology, see A. N. Whitehead, *Process and Reality*, rev. ed. by D. Griffin and D. Sherburne (New York: Free Press, 1978), s.v. in the index (pp. 358–59).

"*tzavta.*" This understanding of *mitzvah* recurs widely in Hasidic literature. Cf. *Degel Mahaneh Ephraim, Va-yeshev* (s.v. "*od*"); *Kedushat Levi, Va-yera*; and *Ohev Yisrael, Huqqat.*

"Jewish religious philosophy." For the classic articulation of such inferences, cf. Maimonides' *Guide for the Perplexed*, 1.54.

P. 127 "between the holy and the profane." Baer, ed., *Avodat Yisrael*, 312.

"the self can take something." Cf. the teaching of R. Yehudah Aryeh Leib of Gur (*Sefas Emes*, vol. 2, *Va-yetzei*: 1872).

P. 128 "the world and all that is in it." Ps. 24:1.

"the Lord of Peace" (*Adon Ha-shalom*). This epithet occurs in the Magen Avot prayer, recited during the reader's repetition of the main prayer on Sabbath eve. The epithet "whose peace is his" alone, recurs in rabbinic literature and is based on a midrashic interpretation of King Solomon (Ha-Melekh Shelomoh).

"*artziyut.*" This locution is a Hasidic neologism, used to highlight the concrete physicality of human worldliness as a foundational locus of spiritual life. Cf. the comments of Rabbi Levi Yitzhak of Berditchev, *Kedushat Levi, Va-yetzei, s.v. Va-yeitzei.*

"expansion or diminishment." This notion of the angels on the staircase as symbolic of such modes of consciousness (called *gadlut* and *qatnut*) can be found in a teaching of Rabbi Ephraim Hayyim of Sudlikov, *Degel Mahaneh Ephraim, Va-yeitzei, s.v. va-yeitzei.* In his comment, the rungs of the ladder are the supernal gradations (called *madreigot*).

P. 129 "tablets of the human heart." Cf. Jer. 31:32.

"*zeman matan torateinu.*" A traditional designation, employed in liturgical references to the festival.

P. 135 "it is of the past." This thought concurs with the reflections of Hans-Georg Gadamer anent the pastness of certain poetic images—a double loss: first in terms of their religious immediacy, and then also in terms of their meaningful content. See his "Das Vers und das Ganze," in *Das Stefan-George-Seminar 1978 in Bingen am Rhein*, ed. P. L. Lehmann and R. Wolff (Heidelberg:

Lothar Stiehm Verlag, 1979), 36. However, I would stress the sense of pastness as well—a sense which commits one to the enduring presence of the works of tradition, and thus to their potential retrieval through interpretation.

P. 140 "Beruriah once told her husband." The teaching is found in *Babylonian Talmud*, tractate *Berakhot* 10b.

P. 145 "*shetiqah*." See the meditation of Rabbi Naḥman of Bratzlav, *Liqquṭei Moharan*, pt. 1, 64c, which radically transforms the aggadah in *Babylonian Talmud*, tractate *Menaḥot* 29b. Thanks to my friend Naftali Loewenthal, who reminded me of R. Naḥman's teaching.

P. 146 "'for its own sake.'" A classical rabbinic designation; cf. *Babylonian Talmud*, tractate *Sanhedrin* 99b.

P. 147 "Whoever is occupied." *M. Avot* 6.2.
"'If a person.'" See in *Babylonian Talmud*, tractate *Eruvin* 54a.

P. 148 "'The voice of the Lord is in strength.'" The citation is from Psalm 29:5; the teaching occurs in *Mekhilta de-Rabbi Ishmael*, *Yitro*, 9; see in the edition of H. S. Horovitz and I. A. Rabin (Jerusalem: Bamberger & Wahrman, 1960), 235.

P. 149 "four ideals." See the teachings in *Babylonian Talmud*, tractate *Shabbat* 63a (the first teaching is transmitted in the name of R. Eleazar; the next three in the name of R. Simeon ben Lakish).
"'for the sake of doing.'" Namely, for practical enactment. Cf. principle enunciated in *Babylonian Talmud*, tractate *Bava Batra* 130b.

P. 152 "Simeon the Righteous taught." See in *M. Avot* 1.2.
"For the sages." The ideal behaviors are classically presented in *Babylonian Talmud*, tractate *Soṭah* 14a. Modeled on divine acts, such supererogatory deeds are deemed *imitatio dei*. In *Avot de-Rabbi Natan*, 4 (A version), the issue is *ad hominem*, and the exemplar is Daniel; see in the third edition by S. Schechter (New York: P. Feldheim, 1967), 11a (p. 21).
"categories of charity." Cf. the contemporary traditional classic, *Sefer Ahavat Ḥesed*, by R. Israel Meir Ha-Kohen of Radzin, the revered Ḥafetz Ḥayyim (Jerusalem: Da'at Ve-Tevunah, 1964), pt. 2, chaps. 17–23.
"*Ḥesed* cuts deeper than *nomos*." Cf. the striking teaching of Rav Huna in *Babylonian Talmud*, tractate *Avodah Zarah* 17b, where he states that a person who has acquired Torah learning, but

does not practice *gemilut ḥasadim*, is "without a God"; namely, is as though godless, according to the explication of *Tosafot*, ad loc., s.v. *"kol."*

P. 152   "Scripture states." Ps. 89:3.

P. 153   "'Do not take revenge.'" Lev. 19:18.

"the sages famously explicated." In *Torat Kohanim, Kedoshim,* sec. 7, chap. 4.10; the passage is classically cited by Rashi (ad loc.). The example of revenge depicts a person who was refused the loan of an object, replying, when that neighbor subsequently asks for something, "I shall not lend to you just as you did not lend to me"; whereas the example of bearing a grudge depicts the same person now replying, "Here you are, I am not like you who did not lend to me." One may read the third injunction (to love one's neighbor) as a (superordinate) motive-clause. Rabbi Akiba (here) calls it "An arch-principle of the Torah."

P. 154   "'I came into the world naked.'" Job 1:21.

"'relent.'" Job 42:6.

"Thus it was taught." See in the *Babylonian Talmud*, tractate *Soṭa* 21b.

CHAPTER FOUR

P. 157   *"dor dor ve-dorshav."* Literally, "each generation and its interpreters." See *Babylonian Talmud*, tractate *Avodah Zarah* 5a.

P. 159   "God's seal of truth." Cf. *Babylonian Talmud*, tractate *Shabbat* 55a.

P. 164   "'Both these and those.'" Cited in *Babylonian Talmud*, tractate *Yevamot* 13b.

P. 165   *"maḥshavah deveiqah."* Literally, the "cleaving of thought"—to a divine point of reference. The phrase occurs in R. Azriel of Gerona's *Peirush ha-Aggadah le-Rabbi Azriel*, ed. Tishby (Jerusalem: Magnes Press, 1983), 40 (ll. 4–5). Similar terminology (*maḥshavah deveiqah* and *dibbuq ha-maḥshavah*) occurs in the work of R. Yitzḥaq de-min Akko (in bound pronominal forms); see his *Me'irat Einayim*, critical ed. by A. Goldreich (Jerusalem, 1981), 217 (ll. 11–12, 20, 24).

"Naught." The discussion of "Naught" and "Aught" is intended to allude to earlier discussions of the matter, in connection with R. Azriel's usage of *yesh* and *ayin*. However, I am mindful here of the deep and long-standing influence of Franz Rosenzweig upon my thinking; regarding this matter, cf. his discussion of "Nichts" and "Etwas" in *Der Stern der Erlösung*, 1:28–32.

P. 166   "'Set one's eyes.'" Stated in *Babylonian Talmud*, tractate *Yevamot* 105b. I am reinterpreting the directive; in its original setting the worshiper seems called upon to combine God-consciousness and humility in prayer.

P. 167   "Ancient One." The phrase refers to the epithet "Atiqa," who is designated "most hidden" or "recondite," and thus most utterly transcendent to comprehension. The author identifies this level of divine manifestation with *ayin*, and refers not so much to the ultimate Naught, which is beyond all designation, as to the border point of its supernal actualization in "existence." Correspondingly, the "Small Countenance" refers to the gradation of Tiferet (Splendor), which takes on the tetragrammaton YHWH, being that dimension of divine actualization which becomes present in the world, the immanent Aught ("Shall-Be") of Divinity. The solution to the theological issue draws on (or echoes) Rabbi Simeon's luminous teaching found in the Zohar, *Naso* (3.129a), at the great mystical gathering known as the Idra Rabba.

P. 168   "An anonymous teacher." The teaching is found in *Midrash Tanḥuma, Yitro*, 12.

P. 169   "Another old midrash." See *Babylonian Talmud*, tractate *Sanhedrin* 110b.

P. 172   "'Make fit.'" With Rashi, who understands *konenehu* as *konen oto*, "make it fit."

"This is the true . . . prayer." Cf. Zohar 3.93b, which comments on this passage: "Not everyone is able to set their will and heart to rectify all things . . . ; therefore he prays this prayer."

"fit for the tasks to come." Zohar, ibid.: "If something should occur for a person, and he focuses on it—how meritorious is he."

"*naḥat ruaḥ*." For this ideal, see the beginning of Naḥmanides' "Letter to His Son": "Accustom yourself to speak to all persons with gentleness, at all times." This so-called epistle on humility is frequently found at the end of traditional prayer books. See the printed edition of I. Abrahams, in *Hebrew Ethical Wills* (Philadelphia: Jewish Publication Society, 1926), 1:95. Other versions of the epistle exist.

P. 177   "'You shall write.'" The ensuing citations are from Deuteronomy 6:6–8.

P. 178 "According to tradition." Cf. in R. Baḥye b. Asher's *Shulḥan shel Arba*, in *Kitvei Rabbeinu Baḥye*, ed. H. Chavel (Jerusalem: Mosad Ha-Rav Kook, 1970), 461; and see also the entire composition.

P. 179 "ideally permeated . . . values of sanctity and sanctification." Cf. the striking gloss by R. Moses Isserles to the opening words of R. Joseph Karo's *Shulḥan Aruḥ, Oraḥ Ḥayyim* (*hilkhot hanhagat adam ba-boqer*), 1.1, where he compares the home and synagogue in terms of their styles of comportment and mental attitudes.
"'By your great kindness.'" This phrase occurs in the so-called Mah Tovu paragraph, found at the beginning of the traditional daily prayer book.
"*miqdash me'at*." Ezek. 11:16. In context, this passage refers to God's proclamation of God's reduced presence in the exile. The *Targum Jonathan* classically glosses this in terms of "synagogues" (*batei kenishta*), and Rashi simply cites it as the authoritative meaning. R. Isaiah diTrani integrates the *peshat* and the *derash*, understanding God to say, "I shall dwell in your synagogues . . ."

P. 180 "'beyond all blessing.'" This and the ensuing phrases are part of the Kaddish (Sanctification) prayer recited by mourners; it is part of a paragraph found in all other versions of this recitation.
"'bond of life.'" Hebrew, *tzeror ha-ḥayyim*. The traditional phrase, included in the traditional "Memorial Prayer" for the dead, combines two words from 2 Samuel 17:13.

P. 182 "'its returners.'" I have so translated *ve-shaveyha* to combine the two traditional possibilities: "returnees" from exile (R. David Kimḥi; R. Eliezer of Beaugency) and "penitents" in Zion (Rashi; R. Abraham ibn Ezra).
"According to a midrashic teaching." See in the *Babylonian Talmud*, tractate *Shabbat* 104a.

P. 183 "'habitations of death.'" This alludes to the phrase "Wohnungen des Todes" by Nellie Sachs in her poem "O die Shornsteine," from her collection *In den Wohnungen des Todes* (1946). The translation follows that of Michael Roloff in the bilingual collection *O The Chimneys* (New York: Farrar, Straus and Giroux, 1967), 2–3.

P. 185 "given object." Cf. *Babylonian Talmud*, tractate *Bava Metzi'a* 115a; and Rashi on the biblical passage ("any debt whatever").

A primary concern is with the privacy and potential shame of the debtor; cf. the comment of R. Joseph Bechor Shor to Deut. 24:10, in *Peirushei Rabbi Yosef Bechor Shor al Ha-Torah*, ed. Y. Nevo (Jerusalem: Mossad Ha-Rav Kook, 1994), 361.

P. 187   "'the near and far.'" In a more extended national religious sense, "the near and far" has been interpreted to refer to the righteous and sinners, or the penitents and sinners; cf. the teaching of R. Yoḥanan in *Babylonian Talmud*, tractate *Berachot* 34b. A more universal application is found in *Midrash Shoḥer Ṭov*, ed. S. Buber (Vilna, 1891), at Psalm 120:7.

P. 190   "'your enemy.'" This formulation (vs. fellow or native) was understood by the rabbinic sages to be a deliberate attempt by scripture to counter the evil instinct, urging one to disregard one's enemy. Cf. *Sifrei Deuteronomy*, ed. L. Finkelstein (New York: Jewish Theological Seminary, 1969), section 225 (p. 257).

"'you must surely raise it up.'" This emphatic phrase renders the doubling of the verb (*azov ta'azov*). The sages used this formulation to make an ethical point; namely, the verb is repeated to indicate that one must repeatedly come to the aid of another, helping for as long as it takes to reset the load. See *Babylonian Talmud*, tractate *Bava Metzi'a* 32a; and cf. Rashi on the scriptural passage.

P. 193   "The tablets . . . are inscribed." Alluding to the midrashic play found in *M. Avot* 6.2, where what is "inscribed [*ḥarut*] on the tablets" (Exod. 32:16) is understood as the terms and conditions of spiritual freedom (*ḥerut*).

"'the world . . . fills it.'" Ps. 24:1.

"'whose Glory fills the world.'" Isa. 6:3.

P. 195   "God's Good." See R. Moshe Cordovero, *Tomer Devorah*, chap. 1, in his discussion of the first attribute: "Who is a God like You?"

"We can be . . . extensions." Cf. ibid. (at the end).

P. 196   "'To walk in . . . His ways.'" Finkelstein, ed., *Sifrei Deuteronomy*, section 49, p. 114. In the various versions of this teaching, the divine epithets (Omnipresent One, Holy One) vary somewhat. The phrase "give freely" is literally "give gifts freely."

P. 197   "such as we may experience them." See Maimonides, *The Guide of the Perplexed*, 1.54, discussing Moses's request to know God's ways, and teaching the imitation of God's attributes of mercy. This is a striking philosophical reprise of the old midrashic topic; Cordovero's discussion (see above) is conversant with it, and his use of the terms *pe'ulot* to indicate divine "actions" and *hanhagot* to indicate human (spiritual) "practices" is evidently influenced by the ibn Tibbon translation of *The Guide*.

P. 198   "filled with . . . color." For this modality as a way of denoting the illuminations or refractions of divine revelation in human experience, see H. N. Bialik, *Kol Kitvei Ḥ. N. Bialik* (Tel Aviv: Dvir, 1962), 100 (in the poem "Ha-Bereikhah," 1905; the term is *gavnei gevanim*); and Rabbi A. Y. Kook, *Iggrot Ha-Ra'ayah* (Jerusalem: Mossad Ha-Rav Kook, 1985), 1:48 (in a letter to S. Alexandrov, 1907; the term is *gevanim*).

P. 199   "on the way to Timnah." The teaching is that "the way to" the image or figure of YHWH (symbolizing the supernal gradation of Tiferet, "Splendor"), is through, or by way of, Malkhut, "Kingship," the feminine domain of Shekhinah (consonant with our world here below).

"an old midrashic teaching." See in *Genesis Rabba* (*Va-yeshev*), 85.7 (following the edition of J. Theodor–Ch. Albeck, *Bereschit Rabba* [Jerusalem: Wahrmann Books, 1965], 2:1041; in the *ed. princeps* R(abbi) is R. Ami (also note the double version in *Midrash Ha-Gadol*, ad loc, in the edition of M. Margulies [Jerusalem: Mossad Ha-Rav Kook, 1967], 647).

P. 200   "heeding the call." The text understands *pitḥu* (open) as a human call to the heavenly powers. Cf. Zohar 3.85a.

"'I am asleep.'" Song of Songs 5:2 (*er*, "awake"); in the Jewish spiritual tradition this term has often been used to convey the notion of spiritual arousal or alertness; and in the context of the prior verse, indicating sleep, the passage was understood to indicate a meditative focus, despite one's sensual condition. Cf. R. Joseph ibn Aqnin, *Hitgalut Ha-Sodot ve-Hofa'at Ha-Me'orot: Peirush Shir Ha-Shirim*, ed. A. S. Halkin (Jerusalem: Mekitze Nirdamim, 1964), 262ff. I am using the passage to suggest spiritual yearning and readiness, or even a certain spiritual lassitude at the surface level, conjoined to a deeper soulful readiness.

"'In the cranny of the rock.'" Song of Songs 2:14.

"'I have come to my garden.'" Song of Songs 5:1.

P. 201 "'the crevice of the rock.'" Exod. 34:22.

"song and speech." The ensuing passage reworks the language and imagery of Psalm 19.

P. 202 "conceived in its image." This too is the testimony of modern physicists, who contend that in purporting to know nature, "we" humans "only encounter ourselves." Cf. Werner Heisenberg, *Das Naturbild in der heutigen Physik* (Hamburg: Rowoht, 1957), 17–18. ("Wenn man versucht, von der Situation in der modernen Naturwissenschaft ausgehend, sich zu den in Bewegung geratenen Fundamenten vorzutasten, so hat man den Eindruck . . . dass zum erstenmal im Laufe der Geschichte der Mensch auf dieser Erde nur uns selbst gegenübersteht . . . , dass wir gewissermassen immer nur uns selbst begegnen.")

P. 203 "forest of symbols." The phrase derives from Charles Baudelaire (*forêt de symboles*), from *The Flowers of Evil* ("Correspondences"); see in the bilingual edition *The Flowers of Evil & Paris Spleen*, trans. William H. Crosby (Brockport, NY: BOA Editions, 1991), 28–31.

"covenant call . . . through all things." Cf. in this regard the remarkable interpretation of Isaiah 40:3 given by R. Dov Baer Friedman, the "Great Maggid" of Mezerich, in *Maggid Devarav Le-Ya'aqov*, ed. R. Shatz-Uffenheimer (Jerusalem: Magnes Press, 1976), section 42, pp. 62ff.

P. 204 "*emet ve-emunah*." Literally, "true and certain" or "steadfast." I hereby allude to earlier discussions. The phrase occurs at the beginning of a liturgical response to the concluding third paragraph of the Shema recitation in the daily evening (Ma'ariv) prayer service. See Baer, ed., *Avodat Yisrael*, 166. This unit was declared a liturgical requirement already in rabbinic antiquity; cf. *Babylonian Talmud*, tractate *Berachot* 12a.

"world-new." Alluding to the divine praise "Who renews the act of creation every day," found at the beginning and end of the Yotzer prayer in the daily morning (Shaharit) service. Cf. Baer, ed., *Avodat Yisrael*, 76, 79. The phrase derives from the *Babylonian Talmud*, tractate *Hagiga* 12b.

"immediate nearness." Alluding to the phrase *bizman qariv* in the Kaddish, which refers to the supplication that the Kingdom of God be manifest speedily, in the near future.

P. 204   "'Shall we accept.'" Job 2:10.

P. 205   "'The Lord has given . . . Lord.'" Job 1:22. See the profound meditation on this passage by S. Kierkegaard, in his *Edifying Discourses*, trans. D. and L. Swenson (Minneapolis: Augsburg Publishing House, 1944), 2:7–26 (originally appearing as *Four Edifying Discourses* in 1843).

EPILOGUE

P. 206   "'the dearest freshness.'" From the poem "God's Grandeur"; see in W. H. Gardner, *Gerard Manley Hopkins: A Selection of His Poems and Prose* (Harmondsworth, UK: Penguin Books, 1953), 27.

P. 207   "some spiritual masters." This is a reworking of Zohar 3.46b.

P. 208   "'bestow its power.'" The powers are the supernal divine gradations, or *sefirot*.

"'the Holy Name.'" This would apparently refer to the Divine Name YHWH; in Genesis 18:19 this name is explicitly mentioned.

Index